NEXT

Cover Art: Collage by Kelley Choate

Edited by: Catherine Clinch

HekaRose Publishing Group
January 2014

ISBN: 978-0-9914964-1-9

Peter Dekom provides simple solutions and practical information for anyone trying to effectively communicate in today's modern society. His insights help us understand how technology has created a disconnected and polarized world. Ron Meyer, **President and Chief Operating Officer, Universal Studios.**

Even with detailed tracking and complex metrics, you have to take active control of your own professional future. Just following your own children doesn't always tell you what's NEXT. For those in search of "out of the box" thinking, Peter Dekom's book shatters the myth that the box even exists anymore. Dekom creates an easy-to-follow path that allows content creators and marketers to survive and thrive in the chaos of constant social and technological change. He summarizes and simplifies the seemingly elusive new rules of reaching audiences and consumers in appropriate ways with appropriate messages. Mark Cuban, **television personality, author, entrepreneur, owner of the National Basketball Association's Dallas Mavericks, Landmark Theatres, as well as Magnolia Pictures, and the chairman of the HDTV cable network AXS TV.**

The media and entertainment Industry is undergoing major and rapid changes. We frequently witness new technologies, political, cultural, and sociological trends. Peter Dekom clearly identifies and lucidly articulates these trends. By organizing fragmented phenomena into basic rules, he also presents insightful managerial implications for companies attempting to experiment, cope, and survive under such unstable environmental conditions. Jehoshua Eliashberg, **Sebastian S. Kresge Professor of Marketing and Professor of Operations and Information Management, The Wharton School.**

An insightful examination of this seminal moment in the history of communications and marketing – but it's more than that, too. It's a survival guide for anyone who has to motivate consumers and a welcome relief from the onslaught of information that merely identifies the problem. Peter offers workable solutions for those of us in the trenches. Jim Gallagher, **marketing consultant and former President of Marketing for The Walt Disney Company.**

It has been said the true genius of creativity is the ability to relate that which has previously been unrelated. The great minds through time have shown us this ability: Newton, Gates, Einstein, Bezos, Jobs, Darwin, Zuckerberg etc. ... This same ability is Dekom's real strength. Most of the trends he discusses are already part of our daily lives. But Dekom puts the pieces together and builds a framework of linkage and understanding that is both fresh and insightful. This is the real power of Next. Peter Sealey, **PhD, former Coca Cola Chief Marketing Officer, former President of Marketing and Distribution Columbia Pictures who has also served on the faculty of UC Berkeley Haas School, Stanford Business School and the Claremont Graduate University.**

If you plan to create or market anything in the next decade, you need this book right now. Peter Dekom synthesizes big data and big insights into a roadmap for how to succeed at media and messaging, and shows you how to stay ahead of the next curve. Adam Leipzig, **CEO, Entertainment Media Partners; publisher, CulturalWeekly.com; former president, National Geographic Films.**

Cover Art: Collage by Kelley Choate

N
E
X
T

Reinventing Media, Marketing & Entertainment

by

Peter Dekom

To Kelley Choate, my inspiration and support system…my bride.
&
To Christopher Dekom, my teacher and friend…my son.

With Love and Dedication

Table of Contents

*charts

The Mission

While we are all focused on new technologies and seismic economic shifts – hyper-accelerating moving targets of change – the more important alterations in our universe have been in the minds and expectations of our audience, our constituents, our consumers. The notion of a "generation" as a twenty-year cohort has died. Add these super-speed time accelerants to the commonality of experience that allows us to label people as Baby Boomers, X-gen or Millennials, and we are creating smaller and smaller groups with such shared attitudes and cultural values. The upshot is that we need to approach these many and newly-evolved cohorts differently, communicating and marketing to them as appropriate, learning to flow and change as they flow and change.

Next is all about managing the task of communicating, marketing and entertaining in this complex world of shifting sands and howling winds of transition. It is about understanding how to wade through this quagmire, rise above the clutter and reach out with relevant hooks to those we want to address… measuring our progress along the way. *Next* approaches the mission with detailed discussions of five basic rules:

Rule One: The Medium is the Message (Still) – We begin the journey by simply looking at the platforms where messages, marketing and entertainment are carried – from traditional to the recent explosions of social media. There are key questions we must face: How does where you communicate impact whom you reach? How can we be economically efficient in the choices of that vehicle? And what is change doing to those platforms and their continued viability?

Rule Two: Scaling Up with Appropriate Messages Targeting Appropriate Audiences – As we understand the platform choices, we also have to know how to shape our messages/content to fit that platform and, more importantly, how to fit the audience we are trying to embrace. The "one size fits all" notion has vaporized. We can niche-communicate to our varied demographic strata, but how do we maintain consistency across different constituencies? And if we communicate in one vehicle, how do we layer messages for the varied demographic cohorts we have identified as our target audience? What exactly is the value of a "brand," one of the most overused expressions in marketing today? Is it raw identification we seek or genuineness and consistency? And how are we establishing direct, interactive, contacts with our audience… cutting out all those intervening middlemen trying to slant, siphon and convince along the way? Or do we need those middlemen at some level?

Rule Three: Master Damage Control – Mismanaging consumer/audience expectations is an easily preventable crime. And we do live in a fishbowl world.

Everything from state secrets to personal absurdities find their way to the public eye. Our opinions, perceptions and values are shaped by the voyeuristic exposures of our idols and our leaders. Cadres of "journalists" join larger groups of hackers dedicated to unveiling and bringing down. Misstatements drift through the ether masquerading as truth, and even truth is amplified beyond reason. Companies, politicians, entertainers and just plain folks are hoisted before a judgmental public with financial and reputational ruin hanging in the balance. Not planning to contain and counter the harm, where appropriate, can only exacerbate already-difficult situations, taking bad to much, much worse. *Next* creates a reasoned methodology for dealing with the harm and minimizing or countering the consequences of this horrific social trend.

Rule Four: *Learn How to Scale Up, Segment Your Audience &* Reach *Them* – While it is easy to talk about tailoring content and messages for differing market and demographic segments, it isn't always that easy finding out who they are and what resonates with them. But we live in a world with so many technologies and experimental platforms to get those answers. In this section of *Next,* we develop the basic audience/consumer identification skills and many of the available metrics and measurement tools we need to know in order to assess the effectiveness of our reach.

Rule Five: "If you Can't Beat 'em, Let them Join You!" – *Reach* Beyond Your Own Walls for Answers – This last category is the result of the new "bottom-up" consumer empowerment, a threat to top-down dictatorial marketing but a new door to reaching consumers and turning them into your own lean, mean marketing machines. It allows people to engage consumers in the design process, finds answers to complex questions beyond the four walls of a typical organization, and allows access to expertise that was once reserved only to the biggest and wealthiest. It is the way of the future of our entrepreneurial growth.

When you finish *Next,* you will probably have many more questions as you apply its lessons to your own missions… but at least you will know how and where to look. I believe that *Next* will materially change the way you look at the deluge of messages and entertainment around you and reshape how you yourself communicate.

Foreword

by Richard Cook (Former Chairman, Walt Disney Studios)

The last few decades have generated the greatest number of mind-boggling changes in the shortest time span in recorded history. The Soviet Union has fallen, China is rapidly rising, destined to become the largest economy on earth, and a major recession has shaken the modern, market-driven economy to its roots. But the parallels in technology advances have done even more to change patterns of daily life in almost every corner of the world.

Next is an exploration of the impact of social upheaval, hyper-connectivity in the mobile and Web-driven universe and the enhanced and accelerated rate of change that have forever altered how we communicate with and to each other. With such massive change comes massive complexity, and some rather significant redefinitions of who we are and how to reach each other with entertainment, messages and marketing. *Next* is also a road map through these seminal changes, an explanation of what these changes really are and how to use this new world to your and your organization's advantage. And most importantly, *Next* is a directive of what to embrace and what to avoid in such communications efforts.

With hyper-accelerating change comes a new definition of what constitutes a "generation." If the hallmarks that define a "generation" are commonality of experience and attitudinal approaches to life, then as younger people move through life, does pooling them into 20-year generational cohorts make the slightest sense? While Baby Boomers and X'ers might be the last vestige of this overreaching two-decade grouping, will those born today have enough in common with people even just five years their senior to justify lumping them into the same generational cohort? I think not.

Today, marketing to, communicating with and entertaining mass audiences requires addressing every targeted group with a message that resonates with each and is delivered through a technology that is a likely and compatible vehicle for their individual taste and comfort zone. Shorter generational cohorts mean more generations need to be separately addressed. Consumers often sneer at top-down corporate directives, and many believe that they have a right to be listened to and taken very seriously. Ignore these wishes at your peril. Peter Dekom examines all of these variables with strong suggested practices to deal effectively with them.

Entertainment and human interactivity are basic needs. Babies don't have technological predispositions, but they are socialized into a world that their parents could never have envisioned. What they learn, how they operate and what they see are quite different from the experiences of past generations.

But in this mix remains some stubborn commonality. Motion pictures and television programs still draw huge crowds, in person or though some ubiquitous device. Families can still go to the movies together, and for the right entertainment, it can be a joyful and shared moment. Finding that cross-generational creative meeting-point has pretty much been my mission in life, defining my own journey at the Walt Disney Studios and clearly my continuing travels into the next generation of family entertainment production and distribution architecture that I believe will redefine the future of global entertainment.

Ten savvy entrepreneurs can have the impact of a hundred, perhaps even a thousand, by accessing global resources now readily available through the worldwide Web. While retaining core competencies within a small body of passionate experts, all the pieces of successful organizational operation can be accessed on "the outside" if you know what you are doing. *Next* opens this door and explores exactly how to implement this new and exciting possibility.

Further, the ability to track, react to and with your target audience in real time or near-real time allows messages and content to be shaped, is wondrous opportunity, offering new paths to success for those who deploy these tools accurately and learn to adapt quickly and change directions when appropriate trends suggest a different path. Again, *Next* provides primer for this level of interactivity.

But with this uber-connectivity comes significant dangers…the danger of false rumors, and mistakes can be instantly blown across the ether into every nook and cranny of public consciousness. Damage control has become a necessary skill-set, but the methods of dealing with this rather significant risk have changed just as much as the rest of modern human communications. *Next* addresses this treacherous field, examining past mistakes and suggesting appropriate methods for clearing the air and moving on.

I've known Peter Dekom for three decades and worked closely with him over the past three years. His constant curiosity, a need to know, has driven him in this quest to explain these massive paradigm shifts in the way we market, communicate and entertain. He is a painstaking trend analyst, capable of taking numbers and vectors from many different fields, consolidating their aggregate impact, and projecting new paths and with new methodologies to maximize success. For those who feel overwhelmed with the aggregation of change to those who are attempting to increase their efficiency in dealing with such changes, *Next* is a concise and clear explanation of both of these big changes and the specifics necessary to prosper in this brave new interconnected world.

Richard "Dick" Cook built his rather stellar reputation as a marketing, distribution and creative executive over his 38-year career at The Walt Disney Studios. Rising to chairman of that entity, Mr. Cook was instrumental in the branding and marketing of Walt Disney Pictures, Touchstone Pictures, Pixar Animation and the selection, creative supervision and exploitation of films like the Pirates of the Caribbean *franchise,* National Treasure, Toy Story, Alice in Wonderland, *and* Secretariat, *to name just a very few.*

Acknowledgements

There are so many people who have contributed to this book, so forgive me if I have missed a few brave souls along the way. The inspiration for this work, and the source of constant links and supporting references, is my son, Christopher Dekom, an Investment Officer with the United States Department of Energy, a trend-spotter extraordinaire. Likewise, my beautiful and MBA-infused wife, Kelley Choate, combed periodicals and texts, supplying valuable additions to the body of the book and creating the underlying artistic direction for the cover. My long-time assistant, Adrienne Crayton-Sarpy, cleaned up my language, helped with clearance work and performed yeoman service in pulling this all together. My agent, Susan Schulman, pushed and pulled me in many directions, revised my focus and helped me with a title to describe this all-encompassing effort. But the biggest contributors to this final version are my high school friend and Stanford MBA, Lennie (Leonora) Copeland and writer, professor and media technology guru (read: Goddess) Catherine Clinch, who edited the entire book. To all of these wonderful people, a profound "thank you."

Introduction

Companies rarely die from moving too fast, and they frequently die from moving too slowly. Reed Hastings, Netflix, CEO (September 2011)[1]

I was having breakfast one morning with a recently retired executive at a major Hollywood studio. He had been a divisional president, in charge of all things digital – from production to distribution to interaction with the studios' exceptionally limited database of consumer contacts. Still rather young, I asked him why he had left a very cushy job with lots of perks, a salary that would be hard to justify under any circumstances and a mandate to shepherd his company into a cross-connected digital universe. He shook his head and looked me straight in the eyes; "I had this strategic meeting with the CEO – just the two of us – so I didn't have to face the litany of insecure rulers of individual silos and fiefdoms. I could speak frankly with the guy who could force those insecure dukes to heel.

"I had worked months on a flashy business plan, lots of charts, trend lines and convincing numbers. Tons of research. It showed what we were doing, where we were missing the boat, behind the curve, literally leaving millions on the table. We didn't have metrics on our consumers, our communications were one-way and we didn't take advantage of introducing content to consumers in the new personal digital formats. We missed creating content for an entirely new spectrum of digital devices.

"My boss waited politely until I was finished. He grimaced and pulled out an old-world yellow pad, drawing a square in the middle of the page. His pen tapped the area outside that square as he said, 'This is where you are, what you just presented.' His pen moved to the middle of the page and drew a little circle inside the square, noting with a tap to that circle, 'And this is where you work and where your company wants you to be.' He looked up, and asked, 'Understand?' I was out of there within the week."

Change is threatening. Too many managers want the issues that arise from change to be the next guy's problem. Stop or at least slow down change, they say. They want to do their time, pile up the benefits and retire. Well today's men and women ascending the corporate or government ranks are those next guys. They don't have that choice anymore. The current universe of interpersonal communications is staggeringly different from even the very recent past. The world is splitting apart between those with

1

access to technology and those for whom daily life has not changed in centuries. Global warming, meet technology-access polarization.

When it comes to content and communications, we simply live in an entirely new world. "In 2012, for the first time, Americans watched more movies via the Internet (through Netflix, Amazon, and Apple's iTunes Store) than they did buying and renting physical DVDs. Apps like Angry Birds have become as profitable (on a cost-to-revenue ratio) as blockbuster franchises like *The Dark Knight*.

"Global smartphone and tablet apps were an $11.7 billion market in 2012, according to Forrester Research, a total larger than the U.S. box office [2012 U.S. box office, according to the MPAA, was $10.83 billion, a banner year, and despite a few dogs, 2013 box office actually exceeded 2012!]. If apps follow their predicted trajectory to a $38 billion business by 2015, they will surpass global movie ticket sales, which inched up slightly in 2011 (the last reported data) to $32.6 billion."[2] In the spring of 2013, adult smart phone ownership crossed the 50% line in the United States.[3]

Keeping up with such changes is often a seemingly impossible challenge. Many workers know the broad strokes of change but often supervise younger employees who have so embraced the new "new" that they easily outshine their bosses. The problem is that so many of those enmeshed in long-term jobs or vying for the fewer openings in an employment-impaired market don't really know what they need to know... and they don't want to look stupid by asking questions that they really need answers to. Change has just happened so fast that they fell hopelessly behind. So I wrote this book simplify what seems to be hopelessly complex, perhaps also as a reminder even to those who learned but have forgotten bits and pieces here and there. It's too easy to blame it all on technology, but human beings are also being rewired along the way.

With a crashed economy acting as a destroyer of unsustainable business models and an accelerant of change, the insertion of "new" technology into our social environment and information is flying at us faster and more pervasively than ever. We are seeing entire generations of people with significantly altered perception and learning skills, each receiving and processing "information" differently. The assumptions we make about "how to communicate effectively" can become obsolete so quickly that we can continue operating without the remotest hint of the ineffectiveness of our efforts until it is simply too late to correct an eroded business model or an ill-conceived creative effort. Just look at communications world around us.

We have recently witnessed governments fall from the diffusion of "seditious" information through the Web and mobile universe. The Arab Spring was born and nurtured in an ocean of digital communications. The rebranding and revaluing of creative content because of digital replication has taken its "piratical toll." We function in a fishbowl where privacy appears to be a distant memory.[4] Smartphones seem to be recording events everywhere, and the notion of interactive "hands free" wearable Google Glass (glasses that see, hear and are connected to the Internet) seem downright creepy to many.[5] The creation of outsourced business capacities from anywhere on earth – accessible with just a few keystrokes – has redefined work and the value of labor. The world of "top down" mandates has succumbed to "bottom up" empowerment.

But even in roiling seas of monstrous change there are moments of relative calm as people, governments and companies adjust to and digest the biggest sweeps of change. Social media exploded and rolled into our everyday lives, changed marketing seismically, replaced email for many and is now settling into a period of dealing with sustainability and monetization.

Aside from the new social and casual games that are sweeping players with mobile devices, too many entrepreneurs are shrugging their shoulders and complaining that they cannot think of what the "big new next" is going to be, that the big companies have all the advantages. But as Apple stock was sent reeling after the death of founder Steve Jobs, and mega-computer hardware manufacturers with billions of invested capital struggle to reinvent themselves, this momentary plateau is actually an opportunity begging for attention.

You can see it in the subtext if you will. Complexity has moved software into a more visible set of growing formats. Making the complex seem simple is a necessary trend. Touch screens let consumers see the complexity and interact with images as opposed to words to find the way. Visual paths make it easier. Growing from this visual capacity on smart phones, iPads made screen size more usable and touch screens a way of life. Microsoft's new Windows 8 allowed PC users to play with layers of functions and applications on visual planes, and adding this true full-functioning operating system to a touch screen tablet, the Surface Pro, seems to have erased the line that once divided laptops from tablets. Smart companies are helping us all digest the complexity, to understand it on a more basic and accessible level.

When myriad variables slam into the world at the same time – particularly the volatile mix of financial collapse with hyper-accelerating social and technological change – it is easy to confuse causation and quietly believe that when economic stability returns, so will the operating assumptions and social practices of yesteryear. Unfortunately, just as economic change has ended career opportunities and rendered entire businesses obsolete, the underlying impact of new communications realities and resultant brain rewiring has altered the direction of our very future forever. Yet, where deficits have crushed old models, so too have new opportunities sprouted in their place. The key is to learn to recognize the potential in something you haven't seen before.

From an era with too little genuine communication, we stepped into an ocean of too much information. We seem to be over-connected.[6] The tsunami of data, emails, advertising, social networking, television, digital media, etc. literally forced many people to narrow the spectrum of their communications and defer to ideologues who offered them underlying "comfort food" of facile slogans, redefining the world the way their followers wanted it to be, people perhaps sheltering themselves from contrary opinions and unwanted facts along the way. Many just stopped looking for truth in the morass of "information stuff" hurled at them by the truckload. Many outsourced their opinions to these purveyors of all-encompassing and simplistic solutions, giving such "peer leaders" incalculable new powers to shelter them from contrary opinions and unwanted facts.

People who were flooded with communications sought to limit what information reached them. Hundreds of emails became an easier-to-manage home page on Facebook or an assemblage of incoming and outgoing aggregated messages that were replaced with "tweets." People also learned to choose prescreened content through media dedicated to preserving their particular "take" on the world so as to limit the flood of inconsistencies that had previously battered their lives and challenged their beliefs. Yet, we seem addicted to our communications tools, unable to tear ourselves away.[7]

So what may have begun as a quest to learn how to navigate through the impact of social and technological communication changes became, for some, a set of survival tools to sort through piles of extraneous messages to find what they think they need to know just to make it through the day. By understanding how we communicate, how we filter and how people can be reached with effective messages, we can learn how to allow truth to seep through the crevasses of propaganda and marketing into the hearts and minds of all who really want to live a normal and productive life.

As technology floods our lives, trends are moving toward simplification, removing complexity and streamlining our choices. In a world of contracting home-size and an explosion of excessive electronic information, the idea of having a lot of stuff has been reappraised. Where consumers once treasured ownership of hard copies of content, today *access* to content is now king. Yet, through it all, we still want to feel and touch our fellow human beings, albeit it at a new level of connective tissue.

As social animals we have redefined what it means to be human by looking at our means of social connectivity. You might believe that – given so many links between and among people – we would get along better and understand our differences with greater tolerance. However, being able to effect noble and less-than-noble connections with our fellow man, in ways unthought-of a decade or two ago, comes with a price. Notwithstanding all the ways we can share each other's pain through horrific images of tragedy or disaster, enjoy each other's laughter and appreciate each other's culture through the miracle of television and film and the relatively easy way we can speak, text, tweet, aggregate our home page or email all over the earth – there *seems* to be so much more conflict and polarization in the world because we now experience it all in real time.

Perhaps the adage that "fences make good neighbors" is a good basis to comprehend what taking down the communication fences that distance and cost erected so long ago has done for a modern over-linked planet; we can travel instantaneously almost anywhere without leaving our homes. Those who take the time to learn the big "HOW TO" can exploit the new available communications tools and will continue to prosper in this rapidly evolving environment. Once we understand the changes that will never end, we can equally know how to use these very changes to make our lives more enjoyable and productive.

But the morass of easily accessible technological advances most certainly does not reach all people at the same time or in the same way. Today, for example, primitive cultures are attacking sophisticated nations with modern technology while clinging to beliefs created in the Dark Ages. Schisms are developing between generations within our own Western societies. We have literally been shredded apart and divided into social segments and political constituencies that either never existed before or were previously fragmented and powerless because of their relatively small size in a limited geographical area. Today, benign social networks with meaningful long-distance communications live side-by-side with their malevolent counterparts that are now empowered with modern technology, giving even small minorities the ability to threaten the majority with unprecedented force.

Inasmuch as success, economic and otherwise, lies significantly with marketing and communicating effectively, business models now require careful structuring around these new social groupings and evolving psychological mental processes that are inherent in our new and enhanced interconnectivity. To make matters even more complex for those desiring to reach audiences, constituencies or consumers, individuals almost always belong to multiple groupings, each with their own vectors. Ad hoc groupings often occur simply in reaction to a new issue. Increasingly, as change rips through our social structures, the subjects of that change (particularly the younger generations) literally see the world differently than preceding generations. We can even start with the gentler side of this fractionalization in our own back yard by examining the evolving impact of technology on perception and generational segmentation within the developed world.

We are left with too many questions. For the political leaders who are struggling to stay in power in order to maintain a healthy domestic economy in the hyperlinked world of global competition, these issues are nothing less than a quest for survival. History teaches us that all governments fall – the issues are always why, when and how. The commercial world also sees change at a more rapid pace; from the professional purveyor of content (within the full spectrum from rock band to major motion picture studio) to the chief marketing officer of a Fortune 100 corporation.

The answers are clear examples of what twentieth century economist, Joseph Schumpeter, described as perpetual business cycles sustained by serial events of "creative destruction" – destroying old business models and technologies followed by the birth and evolution of new ones. What is unnerving to many is the speed with which obsolescence strikes seemingly bullet-proof plans and practices. Even the once oppressive proliferation of email is already facing extinction as younger Web-users are turning away from that communications medium![8] As if we didn't have sufficient disruption from the Web, we are now deluged by the increasing penetration of smart phones and tablets, rapidly changing the way we communicate with each other and the world.[9]

It's hard to think of traditional Internet access as a "last century technology," but that is in fact what it is. It really didn't start rolling until 1994, but the *new next* is rolling in like an angry freight train. "[T]ech companies are scrambling to reinvent their business models now that the old model — a stationary customer sitting at a stationary desk — no longer applies. These companies once disrupted traditional businesses, from selling books and music to booking hotels. Now they are being upended by the widespread adoption of smartphones and tablets."[10]

Think Microsoft's Windows operating systems ("OS") will continue to dominate micro-processing for the foreseeable future? Think again. As mobile capacities explode, Google's Android OS (which outsells Apple's iPhones in the global market) is poised to rocket past Windows.[11] Will Microsoft's new full-function tablets – the Surface Pro and its little brother the Surface RT – stem the tide? Deep discounting on the Surface line in the second half of 2013 suggested otherwise. Microsoft CEO Steve Ballmer's announced departure also hinted that the company was looking for a new direction. Would the combination of tired old Microsoft with tired old Nokia wireless smart phones, an acquisition announced in the late summer of 2013, create something exciting and new? Critics were hardly holding their breath. Is Microsoft's new subscription plan for their popular Windows Office business system – adding cloud access to the mix – enough to push back and embed their word processing, contact management, spreadsheet creation and visual presentation software more deeply into the world of traditional consumers and business buyers?

Not that the Microsoft's competitors seemed to have all the answers. But the questions continued. Will the new tablet and iPhone multi-task-driven operating systems from Apple reposition their competitive place in the market? With fingerprint IDs? Will Apple's and Samsung's entry into the smart watch arena make a difference to hardware sales? Or will the Google tsunami overwhelm Microsoft's business plan? And which new company will dismember Google at some undetermined time in the future?

With data storage and even computing power lodged not just in the mobile devices themselves, but in easily-accessed remote processors and file servers in the "clouds," consumers are able to replicate their Web access with almost the same fluidity that came from traditional computer access to the Web. Still, challenges remain: (i) smaller screen size creates new issues in messaging and content and (ii) consumers tend to be more focused on their chosen tasks and less easily distracted when using mobile devices. What's worse, it seems only one in five smart phone users find mobile ads even "acceptable."[12]

As hordes of consumers move their online time from fixed to mobile platforms,[13] old-line revenue assumptions fly out the window. The handwriting is on the wall:

"Demand for Intel chips inside computers — which are much more profitable than those inside smartphones — is plummeting. At Microsoft, sales of software for PCs are sharply declining. At Google, the price that advertisers pay when people click on ads has fallen for a year. This is partly because, while mobile ads are exploding, they cost less than Internet ads; advertisers are still figuring out how to make them most effective. … Since its initial public offering, Facebook has lost half its value on Wall Street under pressure to make more money from mobile devices, now that six of 10 Facebook users log in on their phones."[14] Something had to change.

Facebook has contained their consumers' migration to mobile, but the fact that ad click-through rates are ten percent of fixed-platform levels has decimated their revenue model, causing a pull-down on the stock price that the company continues to struggle with. But Facebook knew that their value depended on attacking mobile advertising, where too many analysts fretted about whether consumers could find value in ads placed into this micro-sized medium, although tablet surfing moderates that issue somewhere. Mark Zuckerberg and his management team had a problem to solve, and they shifted their focus accordingly. Facebook continues to find new solutions to address the growing consumers' preference for mobile, reflected in rather stellar leap to Facebook's mobile profitability that took Wall Street by surprise in the summer of 2013.

Further, as noted above, Google is seeing similar realities for its search engine, and every major Silicon Valley player is rapidly coming to terms with the driving power of mobile computing. Mobile is the current "big disruptor." For those trying to reach consumers in this new universe, a series of challenges and opportunities marks the path. It took the Web nearly a decade and a half to disrupt the communications/marketing universe, but by 2014 mobile will itself eclipse every other form of Web access.

The fact that there are academic explanations doesn't help salve the wounds of economic change. Commercial content creators need consumers with cash. Marketers need to sell products and services. Politicians need followers. Amidst record unemployment, citizens demand job security. As terrorist threats proliferate, they ask their political leaders to assure them of protection from physical harm. Or from cyber-attacks that threaten to shut down our financial system and deactivate our power grids. There seem to be an infinite number of choices but no clear "right" answers at the time the decisions are made.

With all of the categories of needs/wants – from economic to political – each one is populated by smaller subsets of participants, and each subset is possibly dominated by even smaller subsets of trend-setting peer leaders. The margins of creating content and marketing it to these subsets may or may not be sustainable. What role does money have in determining which perspectives prevail? Exactly how can grass-roots sentiments overwhelm and trump well-funded incumbents? How does deep and profound moral and religious feeling fare against crass selfishness and atavistic survivalist practices? How much does the model vary if someone in their very early twenties is an evangelical Christian or a gang-banger from South Central Los Angeles? A passionate Roman Catholic gang member? Al Qaeda plotting an attack or an Islamist recruiting soldiers? Republican or Democrat? Big city or rural dweller? Stockbroker or schoolteacher?

What is the impact on traditional media models of millions of bits and moments of amateur content that find their way onto cell phones, home pages, computers, tablets – blogs written as truth and transmitted as if researched? Is there a difference in each generation's approach to the existing monetization models? How can these differences be addressed and still maintain economic efficiencies? How does a political system deal effectively with "connected" malevolent peer leaders seeking to alter religious and political destinies, attracting followers through the facility of global technology, searching out and accessing weapons that threaten to bring traditional organized societies to their knees?

Differing sub-cultures in different generations have often adapted in different ways to communication overload. We can't just look at the technological changes themselves, we also need to address the relatively new "science" (art?) of *psychographic* analysis (looking for non-demographic-specific commonalities of attitude and lifestyle) as well as traditional demographics and other determiners of consumer/ constituent behavior in general.

Because people don't fall into easy categories of social subsets – all college-educated-men over 60 do not behave alike – we need new tools to explain consumer/social affiliation behavior in order to implement the most effective messaging and interactivity. For example, you may discover a common psychographic message that impacts differing ages and genders in precisely the same way, but because media usage and sophistication may vary according to age, you may have to deliver that message through technologies that differ appropriately for each demographic segment you want to reach. Television and email may be the vehicle that drives to older constituents, while fan pages and social network linkage are necessary for younger adherents – even when the underlying message is the same.

Thus, when we find a group of human beings whose perceptions and habits give them a common approach to a given activity or content, even if those people are not distributed in clearly defined age groups or genders or regions, that commonality links them together into a single *psychographic* unit. Cultural, religious and environmental factors merge with education, economic success and individual priorities to determine consumer/constituent reactions.

This taxonomy becomes increasingly complicated because psychographics and other predictors of human behavior are not always the same when the activity or content changes. Change the context and the fact that an individual has a particular affinity for one group as to one issue in no way insures that this affinity will sustain when the issue changes. An individual may support an evangelical group, for example, because of its stand on abortion but wildly differ from that same group when it comes to environmental issues.

Because we seem to be living a state of utter chaos of never-ending change, getting a handle on it all requires some distilling into more simplistic analysis. There is no magical, ever-constant paradigm that will embrace the now and the next, but perhaps there is an organizational structure that can make understanding a bit easier. So this book applies a set of five basic "rules" to examine state-of-the-art techniques and technologies to manage and maximize effective communications skills – from a micro interpersonal level through mass communications and marketing.

Unless someone elects to live hermit-like – completely alone with no input from the outside world –being influenced by communications is a daily part of living. It's no longer just a study of communication to the masses but of masses of individuals communicating. The speed and reach of communications require new skills to enhance survivability and prosperity.

This book is a blueprint for us to understand what has happened in our connective tissue and how to use our new reality to move in a positive and constructive direction. Trend analysis is our guide; recognizing the relevant pieces of the puzzle is the challenge. We move from the "shredding" we often feel because of too many messages and too little time to connect with our fellow human beings, into a universe filled with opportunity – but only if the challenges are met with open eyes and a willing mind. All we have to know is how to *reach* those we want to communicate with – and be willing to   let   them   *reach*   back.

THE NEW RULES ON THE NEW PLAYING FIELD

"The opening up of new markets and the organizational development from the craft shop and factory ... illustrate the process of industrial mutation that incessantly revolutionizes the economic structure from within, incessantly destroying the old one, incessantly creating a new one ... [The process] must be seen in its role in the perennial gale of creative destruction; it cannot be understood on the hypothesis that there is a perennial lull." - Economist Joseph A. Schumpeter (1942)

"Revolution in art lies not in the will to destroy but in the revelation of what has already been destroyed. Art kills only the dead." - Harold Rosenberg, 1960's Art Critic and Author

Prepare to be a part of the new or die with the old! Not only must we constantly cannibalize our own world of work and play – if we do not, others will anyway. The sin is in our own reluctance to change, trying to preserve that which cannot survive. Time is not on our side. Because of the accelerating rate of change, we also need to design systems that are profoundly flexible and are not mired in bureaucracies of hardened stakeholders with rigid rules and assumptions. We need to experiment, develop a beta test that can grow, hopefully finding a new solution that we can scale upwards.

The words *scaling up* simply reflect our need for that flexibility – to expand when the necessity arises and to contract when smaller is more appropriate. The new rules are really skill-sets that can help you adapt to change and to use it effectively for your own benefit. Understand how to take a handful of employees or partners and scale up to the equivalent of an army utilizing a combination of technology and outsource partners. Scale down when the need no longer justifies the effort. Lean business structures with well-managed outsourcing have shock absorbers for economic downturns but still allow a small cadre of workers to respond to massive demand when necessary.

Success in this new world of enhanced communications requires a return to common sense realizations that things really are different. We cannot just shove the new round pegs into the square holes of our existing universe. Privacy is illusive at best. Online communications have permanence. Protecting creative content may be more about finding new economic models than simply embracing the latest and the greatest new piracy prevention systems.[15] We are witnessing a huge transition among consumers where they ignore schedules imposed on them by advertisers or programmers and eschew ownership of "stuff" – shelves of CDs and DVDs for example – in favor of ubiquitous access to the underlying content when and where they want. We now can socialize at a distance and still be intimate on a scale hitherto unimaginable. Our world can follow us around and fit in a purse or pocket.

Most people see right through huge volumes of communications that are hurled at them to find kernels of information that are relevant to them. Still, our new communications reality is ever evolving. It produces some of the most interesting new methods for problem-solving (whether through aggregation of expertise regardless of time or distance, the ability to "search" information or the new world of open source communication), marketing and personal communication. Business students and practitioners alike can study how to price goods and services, how to use promotions (sales and discounts) to generate revenues and how to apply various metrics to determine success.

The study of marketing has become a complex amalgamation of psychology, sociology, brain function analysis, economics, pricing theory, statistics, regression and trend analysis, testing theory, cognition, semiotics, and the aesthetics of audio-visual communication. And while I have glossed over the extremely valuable fields of traditional selling and applying active marketing research techniques,[16] this is simply an editorial choice based on limiting the breadth and scope of this book. It is time to find out exactly what is possible in this new environment and what limitations may still remain.

Even for grizzled marketing experts with decades of experience under their belts, the changes are legion and have occurred at every level. Fear not, everyone is equally overwhelmed. But if you break the issues down into bite-sized problems, if you recognize that those to whom a message might be directed could in fact help in the design of the actual message, and if you really understand honest and relevant targeting, the challenges can actually become a path to new levels of success, even in economically challenging times. The ability for an individual or a small group to scale up to take on the giants has never been more possible. This book is focused on "how to do it."

Rule One – The Medium is the Message (Still)

Back in the 1960s, a Canadian professor of English, Marshall McLuhan, coined the expression, "the medium is the message." When he wrote those words, he could not possibly have imagined how technology and accelerating change would alter the face of mass communications, twisting our notion of connectivity like never before. Strangely, his admonition poses the first great challenge in how to scale up communications to reach the right people at the right time. The second, Rule Two, will address the content of the message itself.

The most basic part of Rule One is to carry your message to the specific buyer or audience. It sounds easy, but as we examine human behavior through psychographic eyes (Behavioral Segmentation – Rule Four), we will understand the complexity of this process if it's broken down into a "checklist" process:

- ✓ Approach each communications task fresh (assumptions can kill you!).
- ✓ Avoid applying the same techniques just because you always have and are comfortable with them, and don't think recent can't be obsolete.
- ✓ Think "ground-up."
- ✓ Stop and look at your proposed message and the audience it should reach as if you had never communicated with them before (and understand it just might not be one audience).
- ✓ See what choices you really have and which you need to discover.
- ✓ Challenge and justify your assumptions every day.

With new content-delivery devices, there is a balancing act in sending the right message to the right platform at the right time – all within shifting sands. Messages are the focus of Rule 2, but transitions in platforms require constant rethinking as to which market segment uses which technology for what purpose. Statistics abound,[17] but a new platform or a new software content service can change habits with lightning speed. It is risky to assume that trend lines only go in one direction and that some technologies will perpetually dominate.

Think traditional marketing methods are totally dead? Maybe not. That's part of understanding Rule One. It will require us to examine entire communication structures, one by one, to see where validity remains, where change will kill off some of these media (or at least reduce the effectiveness sufficiently to have them drop to marginal values). Some folks actually watch all those ads on television! [18] Or, for example, a study of online charitable giving by Target Analytics, a unit of Blackbaud Inc., tells us that with the exception of spikes in donations due to major catastrophes, after an initial gift online, giving tends to be a one-shot event. Traditional forms of solicitation become more effective thereafter. Tobias Smith, director of online communications at CARE, punctuated this reality: "[H]ow you get people to routinely give online is a nut no one has yet cracked." [19]

This is just one example of the effectiveness of what's new versus the lingering value of what has existed for some time. What follows is a segment-by-segment analysis of what most communicators, marketers and purveyors of creative content have been using to deliver their messages – from individuals to as much of the world as they can reach.

Film

The art and science of selling theatrical films to the public is obviously changing. Traditional media advertising isn't going away anytime soon. However, the growth of ads on the Internet, with a heavy emphasis on paying large sums for favorable placement at the top of search engine categories and on ISP (internet service provider) home pages, has definitely changed the focus of American media buyers.[20] Even as U.S. consumers are over-saturated, a desperate advertiser – not just in the film world – has yet to find an analytical and effective marketing mechanism to rise above the clutter.

Older buyers tend to want to be *told* what's out there and make a decision. Younger viewers tend to want to *discover* what's coming up, pulling up only material that interests them and their peer leaders. For older movie-goers, tried and true marketing still works, but skeptical younger demographics want *what's next* or at least what they think is what's next. When a marketing campaign works – such as the Internet trail that led audiences to *The Blair Witch Project* film released in 1999 (an independent film that cost around $100,000 to make that generated worldwide box office of almost a quarter of a billion dollars) – old world marketers too frequently rush to replicate the experience with a parallel strategy for their next product or service. If they are targeting the "what's next" 15-35 world, they seldom achieve the same results.

Interestingly enough, the passage of time can make older marketing practices seem relevant to an audience unfamiliar with the original effort. For example, the thematic use of amateur home video makers tracking a horror mystery – the *Blair Witch* story – resurrected almost nine years later with the successful theatrical release of

Cloverfield, a film which adopted many of the Internet techniques that made *Blair Witch* the hit that it was. Then it happened again. *Paranormal Activity*, a $15 thousand-budget successor to *Blair Witch* but made less than a decade later (released in 2007), replicated that success and spawned hundreds of parallel theatrical film horror wannabes that died uglier deaths than the victims in those films. Recycling works if there is enough time for a truly new audience to discover this path. This explains why the Walt Disney Studios often re-releases (on screens or on DVDs) its classic animated movies every seven years – a new generation of youngsters comes along that has not viewed the original.

But time can also be the enemy. Saturating the Internet with stories, building up a frenzy before a product is available for purchase or viewing by the general public, carries with it a risk that when it actually becomes available the ultimate product is viewed as "old news" and not "what's next." When the pre-release "buzz" on the film, *Snakes on a Plane*, poured all over the Internet in March of 2006, the recognition factor and the "want to see" measurements taken at that time by marketing groups were quite high. But the film opened five months later – an eternity in the world of film publicity. The film grossed about half of its projected opening weekend. The disappointing results provide an example of how the passage of time can wreak havoc by exploding the marketing effort prematurely.

Confidentiality has become a big issue in the prerelease world of motion picture distribution. Controlling word of mouth is a constant challenge to the studios. If inside information hits too early and the word is bad, the "buzz" can kill a film. Think: Disney's 2012 *John Carter* debacle as Web–chatter decimated a film that really wasn't remotely as bad as the negative buzz suggested. But without some form of word of mouth at the right moment – from actual face-to-face recommendations to emails and tweets – a film doesn't stand much of chance of success. Building mystery can heighten the "want to see," but keeping a secret in Hollywood is anything but easy.

Lucasfilm and Paramount made secrecy a big part of their marketing campaign for *Indiana Jones and the Kingdom of the Crystal Skull*, a sequel effort mounted nineteen years after the last *Indiana Jones* film. *Crystal Skull* was released at the Cannes Film Festival on May 18, 2008. Two armed guards accompanied every print to protect against potential piracy and a premature leak to the public of the underlying story. Still, two days before the release, online reviews appeared, presenting the essentials of the film with particular accuracy. Stunned studio executives were determined to find the source of that critique. They were most surprised when the leak was traced to a reviewer who happened to be sitting at a restaurant table next to a gaggle of studio executives who loudly discussed many of the features of the impending release. The review shot virally around the Web.

With tweets, blogs and emails proliferating, studios have recently gone the extra mile to try to control temperamental actors and creative personnel from mounting disparaging campaigns or releasing confidential information about their films. Disney's new contracts, for example, limit contracting parties from releasing this news on "interactive media such as Facebook, Twitter, or any other interactive social network or personal blog." Although talent is released from these confidentiality provisions as the film plows into a public release, contracts often still prevent any disparagement of the film, the studio or the people involved in the production.

As test audiences are recruited to view various stages of a film's completion, participants are often required to sign non-disclosure agreements (plus provide their email addresses and Facebook accounts). The testing company tracks those accounts to see if confidential information about the film is actually being leaked. But today there are risks of losing the whole film to our digital universe. In mid-January 2013, Paramount announced it would only release digitally in theaters, a trend that has come of age.

So much for mainstream features. What about the thousands of independents seeking to turn the Web into the breaking ground for new independent features? They'd kill for tweets from stars that had any kind of following! Even bad ones. The big barrier to indies (independently produced full-length features) is the huge cost of marketing… and there are precious few American distributors around anymore willing to pay that bill except for the rare 1% or 2% of such films (in the United States anyway) that get enough festival buzz to justify the cost of a theatrical release. "Viral and free" just aren't enough to rise above the clutter. Hey, what about the Web?

Aside from using cloud-based subscription and download services as a source to view/buy traditional film and television fare – usually directly to a big screen television – there has been a parallel migration of original, commercially produced content to the Web. It may be a television series carried on Netflix or some of the new niche networks from entities like Amazon, Yahoo or Google.[21] What has eluded filmmakers, however, is the ability to make use of the Web as the basic and *initial* delivery system for *feature* films. Sure the U.S. "home video" market has significantly moved out of packaged media (hard copy DVDs, for example) into a digital universe that has generated a new name: "home media." But without the consumer awareness created by a theatrical campaign,

Web-driven digital viewing for features has remained almost exclusively an after-market to a theatrical release.

The first issue is that when filmmakers resort to the Web, it is usually because their film cannot find meaningful marketing and distribution from other media. Consumers seem to sense that reality and make that assumption automatically. So it's not just that there is no awareness; the fact that the film is premiering in that medium is itself a killer. The Web is a place for the unloved and unwanted – hardly the kind of product that sucks in consumers to a site.

Without any ability to generate real visibility, the Web as the source of original presentation of feature films seems to be an audio-visual cemetery of films that the Darwinian marketplace has already selected out. While there are sites for filmmakers to put their films on the Web (e.g., MoPix, getMoPix.com), absent sufficient consumer awareness generated by strong marketing efforts that just haven't been justified in the direct-to-Web-based market, the revenues generated to filmmakers here have been exceptionally paltry.

The second issue, getting over the inherent negativity which may change over time, is simply that the cost of generating sufficient consumer awareness is seldom justified given the limited upside potential in a Web-based opening at Web-based consumer price expectations. Without the ability to generate consumer demand, the third issue – monetization in a subscription, video on demand (VOD), ad-driven or a combination structure – becomes elusive. No eyeballs, no traffic, no money.

Since there isn't a regular flow of want-to-see original features on any online site, there just aren't appropriate go-to Web/mobile-based sites that consumers know to routinely access to view such films. Further, most of the sites that are experimenting with this format are generally accustomed to presenting original content in much shorter segments than a full-length feature film.

The notion of an "experiment" also suggests that only sites willing to play the loss-leader game to establish a new market can create sufficiently attractive content. But a feature film? Two plus hours? Yahoo has been willing to foot the bill to find out using established content creators with meaningful elements, but has broken up the feature content into separately-delivered shorter segments ("chapters") to fit their system with a film from the creator of the successful CSI television series.[22] This wasn't a notion of creating an instant path to profitability, just a question of how such content might be presented in the future. Yahoo was willing to market "Cybergeddon" as a feature "event" but still chopped up into a more traditional television mini-series format.

The big elephant in the room – generating a want-to-see consumer demand – has generally eluded independent feature filmmakers who are unable to access the larger, mainstream platforms. It's a chicken and egg problem. With only independent-level visuals and a dearth of commercially-viable production values or name performers, marketing money runs away. Without marketing support, there is insufficient consumer demand to generate any real potential for traffic to sustain a commercial site.

Indies have tried to find a traditional theatrical market through DIY efforts, although most of those have focused on an attempt to play the film by "four-walling" (essentially renting the theater) in a self-generated release to physical theaters. Direct online viewing as the primary commercial venue has still been a bust. Resorting to YouTube snippets from the film and massive attempts at viral campaigns in social media without real cash marketing expenditures have yet to create a financially-sufficient system that can sustain this art form, particularly given the increasingly hostile reception to the thousands and thousands of independent movies produced every year vying for a tiny success quotient. As noted, under two percent of such indies ever find a commercial release in the U.S. market in traditional media. This is a business problem in search of a commercial solution.

But filmmakers, don't relent! The marriage of content with solid sponsors – well beyond mere product integration – may be just around the corner. We've seen webisodes linked to sites for commercial products and services: Pure-play entertainment that *feels* compatible with the emotionality and personality of the product or service with which that content is associated. Associating with the right content, from coolness to reliability (remember the FedEx message in Tom Hanks' *Castaway*), may eventually motivate brands to expand their values to consumers by virtue of the entertainment they embrace and provide, perhaps even free, to the general public.

Major studios too have struggled with how to market to rise above the clutter. As jaded younger audiences seem to reject the old world mentality of hot leading men and women – movie stars – to determine what films to see, preferring to discover "what's cool next," studios have focused on films where trailers can be uniquely compelling (more probable with horror and comedy genres) or where there is a presold, built-in audience. The new "stars" are no longer the actors (although a good character actor can generate a "new next" character) the most consistent directors or pre-existing content with large followings. Think: *Harry Potter, Batman, Twilight,* and *The Hunger Games*, books that carried millions of loyal readers with them. Even for those living only in the notion of digital "Presentism," discussed in more detail later, the stars of the past are simply no longer on the radar of relevance in the *here and now.*

With excellent flat screen television quality these days, we can watch small (less visual value) movies on a small screen with no material loss in the viewing experience. Even some bigger films have sufficient appeal on a home TV. Consumers can access all kinds of content via robust home media subscription systems – perhaps using video on demand (VOD) for particularly higher value fare. Even pirated material is pretty much relegated to the small screen. Is the Hollywood's answer to this push to home entertainment to create fewer, higher budget, event films with production values that look and sound vastly better on a huge in-theater screen, perhaps in IMAX or 3D? Is this business plan sustainable?

Two filmmakers, associated with big movies and special effects, Steven Spielberg and George Lucas, stunned an audience at USC's School of Cinematic Arts in early June of 2013. Predicting that theatrical exhibition was becoming a niche market of very few films in very few bigger-screen theaters, these captains of the big film experience suggested that Hollywood is coasting on thin ice with too much money invested in these big experience motion pictures:

"'They're going for the gold,' said Lucas of the studios. 'But that isn't going to work forever. And as a result they're getting narrower and narrower in their focus. People are going to get tired of it. They're not going to know how to do anything else.' … Spielberg noted that because so many forms of entertainment are competing for attention, they would rather spend $250 million on a single film than make several personal, quirky projects.

"'There's eventually going to be a big meltdown,' Spielberg said. 'There's going to be an implosion where three or four or maybe even a half-dozen of these mega-budgeted movies go crashing into the ground and that's going to change the paradigm again.'…. Lucas predicted that after that meltdown, 'You're going to end up with fewer theaters, bigger theaters with a lot of nice things. Going to the movies will cost 50 bucks or 100 or 150 bucks, like what Broadway costs today, or a football game. It'll be an expensive thing. ... (The movies) will sit in the theaters for a year, like a Broadway show does. That will be called the 'movie' business.'

"There'll be big movies on a big screen, and it'll cost them a lot of money. Everything else will be on a small screen. It's almost that way now. 'Lincoln' and 'Red Tails' barely got into theaters. You're talking about Steven Spielberg and George Lucas can't get their movies into theaters.'... Both see 'quirky' or more personal content migrating to streaming video-on-demand, where niche audiences can be aggregated. 'What used to be the movie business, in which I include television and movies ... will be Internet television,' said Lucas." [23] The tanking or under-performing of major budget summer releases like Disney's *The Lone Ranger,* DreamWorks Animation's *Turbo* or Universal's *R.I.P.D.* shortly after this pronouncement made their words seem prescient.

What exactly does work on a big screen? Do major studios have a choice? Mass appeal films require mass marketing, a much more complex process in a world of highly differentiated marketing requirements in increasing numbers of defined cohorts, each one representing an increasingly narrower age-grouping (the reasons will be discussed later). Can escalating production values and special effects hold a big enough audience? What is a good script? Is there a difference in international acceptability? Disney's *The Lone Ranger* seemed to have missed the boat globally in the summer of the big budget movies in 2013. But Warner Bros.'/Legendary's *Pacific Rim* underperformed in the United States while eating up the box office overseas. In harsh economic times, do serious issue films have a chance where audiences may really be searching for escapism? Is the abysmal audience response to *The Fifth Estate* (the story of whistle-blower and WikiLeaks founder, Julian Assange) in the fall of 2013 a predictor for this genre?

Given high budgets and the need to reach mass audiences, movie marketing has taken on new dimensions in a changed world. Motion picture marketers are dealing with more segmented audiences required to justify a wide-release. They are still trying to identify their audiences and find those Rule One appropriate communications. Which audience segment gets what message... and later, how is that message delivered? Meanwhile, the business remains basically intact. As indies struggled, majors raked it in. 2012 saw the greatest increase in U.S. box office admissions in a decade, a solid 6% over 2011 with fewer expensive 3D titles and very few ticket price increases. 2013 numbers are even higher. Fewer films in wide release also generated a significant increase (22% between 2006 to 2011) in per title revenues for the biggest films. Somebody is still making a lot of money in this business.

If the change in "old world" books is huge, the impact on newspapers, including some of the biggest names in traditional journalism is astounding. Facing stiff competition from online dissemination of news, some of these journalistic giants have suffered catastrophic losses. The Tribune Co. – which owns newspapers such as the Los Angeles Times and the Chicago Tribune [24] – filed for reorganization under U.S. bankruptcy laws at the end of 2008. Chicago newspapers took another fall in March of 2009 as the Sun-Times filed for reorganization. In late February of 2009, Philadelphia-based newspapers took a big hit as Journal Register Co. and Philadelphia Newspapers LLC (which owns prestigious The Inquirer and The Philadelphia Daily News) joined the swelling ranks of print media filing for bankruptcy reorganization. Also in March of 2009, after reducing its news staff from 165 employees down to 20, the Hearst-owned Seattle Post-Intelligencer daily newspaper ceased printing paper copies and moved its existence to the electronic world, where it is still struggling to find economic viability.

Mega-investor Warren Buffet, himself a part owner of several newspapers and an avid reader of many periodicals, sees this paper medium as an obsolete source of "just unending losses." [25] According to an annual Pew report, the only sector of U.S. news media that remained and continues to be troubled as of 2011 was print journalism, which is still experiencing revenue and subscriber erosion.[26] Revenues and subscribers have been cut in half in recent years.[27]

A study commissioned by the U.S. Federal Communications Commission notes another negative impact arising from contracting revenues in traditional journalism: "An explosion of online news sources in recent years has not produced a corresponding increase in reporting, particularly quality local reporting, a federal study of the media has found. ... Coverage of state governments and municipalities has receded at such an alarming pace that it has left government with more power than ever to set the agenda and have assertions unchallenged, concluded the study. ... 'In many communities, we now face a shortage of local, professional, accountability reporting,' said the study, which was ordered by the Federal Communications Commission and written by Steven Waldman, a former journalist for Newsweek and U.S. News and World Report. 'The independent watchdog function that the Founding Fathers envisioned for journalism — going so far as to call it crucial to a healthy democracy — is in some cases at risk at the local level.'"[28] Nevertheless, it seems all but inevitable that electronic media will replace traditional newspapers completely. [29]

As media-giant News Corporation moved its print assets into a separate entity[30] and Time Warner spun off its magazine group into a separate publicly-traded company, the reality of plummeting values in traditional media, even with digital counterparts, is less-than-subtle. But the world still consumes news as well as targeted information and reportage, so how can this universe continue in some form that makes sense?

Some solutions to monetizing the newspaper presence on the Web, outside of individual newspapers having individual sites (with their own subscribers and/or their own advertising), include aggregating a number of periodicals through a common Web portal (as discussed further below).[31] These structures generate income either through a single bulk subscription payment by consumers for access to multiple periodicals, advertising aggregation or a combination of both. Revenue-sharing would be based on actual consumer usage.[32] The question is, can enough money be generated to sustain even a significant share of the news industry under this model?[33]

Does the elimination of paper, delivery and printing presses create sufficient economies of scale?[34] And as the aggregators themselves seek outlets as "apps" subscription services on cell phones, tablets, etc., can they even survive given the surcharge added by the app licensor/subscription service?[35] And will news in the future be nothing more than an RSS feed[36] or "one more app" versus traditional access to aggregated content via an online news provider site or even a newspaper or television program?[37]

Battle lines are being drawn. Others, like News Corp's Rupert Murdoch understand that the old revenue models are broken but reject aggregation and are determined to extract payments for access to individual periodicals from online users anyway: "The business model based on advertising-only is dead, Murdoch said, because it was 'founded on quasi-monopolies such as classified advertising – which has been decimated by new and cheaper competitors such as Craigslist, Monster.com, CareerBuilder.com, and so on.'… Murdoch reiterated his commitment to eventually charge for access to all his publications, including the *Times of London* and the *Australian*, just as News Corp. does now with *The Wall Street Journal* and Barrons.com. … 'The critics say people won't pay. I believe they will, he said."[38] Some believe business periodicals are different because either the company will pay for employee's access or because of the possibility of a tax write-off. Is Murdoch's perspective realistic?

Equally challenging to Murdoch is the extraction of articles (or substantial portions) from copyrighted periodicals by bloggers and news aggregation sites, which many claim is acceptable "fair use" under U.S. copyright laws: "Their almost wholesale misappropriation of our stories is not 'fair use.' To be impolite, it's theft," states Murdoch.[39] Others are watching Murdoch's experiment with great interest, hoping that they too can force sufficient numbers of consumers into paid subscriptions.

Believing that the public will pay more for high-profile periodicals, the New York Times entered the fray in 2011.[40] Premium periodicals like the Times are pushing hard away from the "free and supported only by advertising" online model, escalating their drive to mandate subscriptions with some success (discussed below). Many readers rebel and rely on the blogosphere or free news agencies or even sites with a sponsored bias rather than pay for what they were used to receiving for free.

And when Amazon entrepreneur, Jeff Bezos, bought the prestigious Washington Post in the summer of 2013, many asked why. FastCompany (August 7, 2013) speculated that there was indeed method in his madness. "He did it because he understands something about media the rest of us don't: distribution. Having conquered long-form, evergreen content (also known as books), he's now interested in distribution mechanisms for short-form, timely, and topical content. The fact that many before him have failed to find a workable business model for newspapers, the traditional delivery mechanism for this kind of content, only makes the challenge more interesting." In early September, Bezos himself confirmed the theory that this would indeed be an amazing experiment.

With ubiquitous and free news everywhere, charging subscription fees requires a particularly high bar of discernible quality, editorial excellence, unique research and specialized access and possibly the addition of some appropriate video inserts to compete with broadcast news. As noted above, one organization that seems to have moved into a healthy online subscription model is the prestigious New York Times. "Digital subscriptions [for the Times generated] $91 million [in 2012], according to Douglas Arthur, an analyst with Evercore Partners. The paywall, by his estimate, will account for 12 percent of total subscription sales, which will top $768.3 million this year. That's $52.8 million more than advertising. Those figures are for the Times newspaper and the International Herald Tribune (now marketed under the Times label), then already largely considered the European edition of the Times.

"It's a milestone that upends the traditional 80-20 ratio between ads and circulation that publishers once considered a healthy mix and that is now no longer tenable given the industrywide decline in newsprint advertising. Annual ad dollars at the

Times, for example, has fallen for five straight years."[41] But for small local newspapers that are heavily reliant on advertising, the opportunities are not so strong. Some have cut their daily efforts to less frequent releases; others are either shutting their doors or heading in that direction.

Further, as noted above, the potential of aggregated *subscriptions* (where content users can pay a single modest fee for access to a bundle of newspapers and other information sites) is on several corporate agendas.[42] Consumer resistance is still stiff absent compelling values or insider niched information which is a clear research tool and an obvious tax deduction. While Amazon.com, Zinio.com and Apple's Newsstand.com can manage your individual online subscriptions, NextIssue.com is a pricier alternative that gives you aggregated access to your choice of periodicals (assuming they are part of the Next Issue universe) for a flat monthly fee.

But even with these cool new alternatives, this market isn't going to get pretty any time soon. Perhaps the best expression of the fate of printed newspapers is embodied in this statement from then-Chairman & New York Times Publisher Arthur Sulzberger Jr., at a London summit of newspaper executives: "Asked about his response to the suggestion that the [New York Times] might print its last edition in 2015, Sulzberger said he saw no point in making such predictions and said all he could say was that, 'We will stop printing the New York Times sometime in the future, date TBD.'" [43]

The new e-reader formats seem to be creating another potential casualty for newspapers in any form – paper or electronic. The generic nature of information leaves newspapers saddled with the reality of surviving in a battle with the Internet. Since "information" (read: news) is ubiquitous on the Web, what exactly is the real future of newspapers, even good ones, in any format? Who is going to pay for what is readily available for free on the worldwide web?

Some experts don't believe that that news "papers" can even charge consumers for online delivery unless they some uniqueness (like *Consumer Reports*) or there is an expense account that covers the cost (such as *The Wall Street Journal*). Journalist Jeff Jarvis opines: "Once news is known, that knowledge is a commodity and it doesn't matter who first reported it. There's no fencing off information, especially today, when the conversation that spreads it moves at the speed of links … There will be no limit to competitors. Readers, like water, will follow the path of least inconvenience. It's impossible to compete against free. Have papers learned nothing from Craigslist?" [44]

Acknowledging that the subscriber and advertiser-supported models are broken, another journalist, Alan D. Mutter, suggests that without sufficient revenues, professional journalism cannot continue. However, he points out, the blogosphere is hardly a substitute for research and experience. He believes the uniqueness and credibility have dollar values: "Fortunately for publishers, for-pay content doesn't have to be the Watergate investigation of the future. People will pay for all manner of content on the Web, it if it is thoughtfully conceived and marketed … [Looking at the Wall Street Journal as an example] How does it get away with charging, when so much business information is available for free from places such as Yahoo Finance and 24/7 Wall St.? The answer is original, authoritative reporting and the power of its brand." [45]

Jarvis challenges the ability of journals to be sufficiently unique and notes that much special interest writing is of exceptionally limited value. As the debate continues, we will watch print journalism fade slowly (maybe not so slowly) away. [46] Strangely, readership of newspapers is on the rise, albeit that much of that consumption is generated from online editions, where advertising has yet to replace the revenues generated in the paper versions. [47]

Older generations, who are used to the Sunday paper or enjoy feeling newsprint in their hands – perhaps even those who still refuse to buy or are unable to afford a computer, will be frustrated. Billionaire-philanthropist, David Geffen, may have another model. Turn a major newspaper (notably the New York Times) into a tax-deductible non-profit corporation, simply because the cultural value of some newspapers should be preserved even if the economic model is forever broken. Can bloggers function without the hard-news-gathering old world media doing the legwork (for free?). After all, traditional media tend to beat the blogosphere by 2.5 hours on breaking stories.

Books

For book authors in search of elusive publishers, the "how to" may well be self-publishing, particularly in the new eBook format.[48] Every day hundreds of new books are posted in electronic versions only. E-tailers like Amazon and Barnes & Noble have fairly straight-forward processes for authors to upload their eBooks onto their sites.[49] Thus, with printing and distribution accomplished electronically, the only remaining publishing barrier is marketing, dealt with in later chapters.

With dedicated eReaders and all-purpose tablet computers, the book publishing industry is rapidly transitioning to electronic books in lieu of hard copies, even providing audible eBooks in a downloadable format. On its surface, this turn toward the digital would seem to make the application of Rule One a bit easier, since content and buyers are much more easily matched. But managing this massive change has become challenging for traditional publishers.

Are there sufficient remaining consumers even to sustain the old world hard copy book business? For those who prefer the look and feel of printed books, bookstores willing to shell out about $75,000 or more can save shelf space and create hard copy books on demand with a stand-alone printing system. The Espresso Book Machine can print on demand from about one million books in inventory or from a demand with a printing capacity of about 150 pages a minute. The retail cost of such a custom printed and bound book is $15 plus about three cents a page. The average 300 page book costs about $43. Small niche and out-of-print books can be brought to life. But with electronic readers clearly becoming the new standard, the market for such elaborate printing technologies is anything but clear.

Amazon, home to the Kindle and one of the biggest booksellers on earth, noted that the first half of 2010 represented the tipping point, where eBooks outsold the hard copies.[50] U.S. eReader purchases easily eclipsed tablet sales in the first half of 2011 as well.[51] But even Amazon jumped into the tablet business in the fall of 2011 with its 7 inch Kindle Fire, a Web-based platform that was introduced at a loss-leader price of $199 in order to facilitate Amazon's content marketplace for consumers. eBooks are increasingly becoming the norm in the United States, cutting hard into hard cover print editions but really slamming into paperback sales.[52]

Many experts point to electronic but non-Internet substitutes, like Amazon's large-screen (9.7 inch) Kindle eBook (the "DX"), and Kindle Fire where the content is downloaded directly to the device from the Web without an intervening computer, with a fee being charged to a designated account, [53] but the greater-functioning tablet appears to be destined to define this space going forward. Generally, experts agree that eReaders and tablets will only accelerate the obsolescence of hard copy books (with higher prices expected for limited run hard covers if they are still printed), particularly textbooks, [54] and newspapers.

The use of electronic "paper" is accelerating throughout the publishing world, and the projected dollar-volume is staggering. According to an August 26, 2009 survey from tracking company DisplaySearch, the current "$100 [million] e-paper market is expected to reach $9 [billion] by 2018." This reflects a growth rate from 1 million eReaders sold in 2008 to 77 million projected for 2018. The "green" effect of such low power devices and their overall convenience is winning converts at a rapid rate. While industry leader Kindle is resisting the path to a uniform formatting standard [55] most of the other devices (including the Sony Reader, iPhone and even Google) are creating compatibility with the EPUB ("electronic publishing") digital standard.

Do these new technologies enhance economic value of the written word or destroy it? Will most general textbooks or literature of the future be relegated to "free" open-sourced creativity at the expense of revenue-generating commercial production? And there is a darker side of eBooks – piracy. While electronic publishing is still very much in its infancy, the ability to place volumes of material online anonymously is easily accomplished. [56] If 95% of downloaded music is unauthorized, what will the book-publishing world look like when the majority of our publications are electronic? [57] Will publishers learn anything from the litany of mistakes committed by the music industry?

With all this change, how will the public library fare in the future – if there is to be such a beast? How will libraries fulfill their mandate of free public sharing and access to information in a way that differentiates them from the worldwide web? Does the combination of "information everywhere," the availability of digital books in special formats or online, and the current cost-cutting mania sweeping local governments spell an end to these cherished institutions? Even if libraries can embrace the future through technology, do government funds exist to fund the cost of this enhancement? Do they even require physical space? Is Google the replacement for traditional cataloging? [58]

Clearly, there are going to be big changes in library science, as well as in the ways that libraries remain relevant. To the extent that written content becomes ubiquitous over the Web, libraries may be forced to emphasize their "social gathering site," teaching and special program capacities as well as provide access to computer terminals and the Internet for those unable to afford either the hardware or the ISP fees. Many libraries have resorted to having a stock of video games with available console devices to play them to draw younger demographics to the library building. [59] Public libraries may even be forced create their own information-tracking and gathering capacities, encourage local creativity and interaction, but clearly what "libraries" must become will reflect the world around them. Or will they just disappear?

Public libraries are already in transition. They're not just for checking out hard-copy books anymore. They are places where people without computers can find access or where reading sessions for the young can spike a prioritization in the overall value of literacy. Meetings and cultural events, exhibits and lectures and even after-school tutoring have found their way into libraries across the land. But with pressures on government funding, a contraction in library personnel and a view from too many budget-cutting politicians that they are expendable, perhaps their functionality may someday be relegated to nothing more than a local website.

Some public libraries (5-6,000 in the U.S. at last count) are reacting to the electronic world by providing eBooks in their catalog. In the average process, a borrower signs up to "borrow" a book, is allowed only one electronic check out at a time, and the book automatically disappears from the download device at the end of the check-out period. Publishers wonder how this lawful "download" may impact the economic value of their publications in a universe where most books will in fact be electronic.[60] The response from many publishers is to sell their eBooks with an electronic limitation on how many check-outs are permitted before a new volume must be ordered.

U.S. downloads crossed well over the one million mark as early as 2009,[61] and the trajectory for the library lending segment may indeed provide a real threat. The companies that provide eBooks to public libraries are witnessing annual growth rates north of 20%.[62] But if you can download legally from a public library, even for a short time, isn't this the practical equivalent of piracy? Publishers understand the risk. Harper Collins, for example, now sells eBooks for such library use with a stipulation: a new eBook must be purchased for every 26 lending events, a practice that is likely to spread industry-wide. In November of 2011, the Penguin Book Group announced it would delay making its new books available electronically to libraries citing "security concerns." "Penguin joins Macmillan, Simon & Schuster and the Hachette Book Group, all major publishers who do not make new titles in digital form available to libraries."[63]

Textbooks

Some media have been more severely impacted by changes in communications technologies than others. The big loser in this space has to be print media. Major book publishers fired editors, closed smaller imprints and virtually stopped taking new submissions. A number of smaller publishers just folded, and there has been a parallel trend with bookstores, including major retailers.[64] From popular literature and business books to the printing of traditional textbooks, the shift in delivery is profound. Textbooks have also begun the migration to digital platforms, including small-screen smart phones.

Even though they require perhaps an impractical amount of "scrolling," eTextbooks[65] have an application that allows students and other heavy readers to download onto their iPhones. Apple's foray into this space (with an iTunes payment model) – particularly with its iPad platform – may present significant challenges to limited purpose eBooks. [66] School districts from Connecticut to Kentucky to South Korea are substituting tablet-based texts for the expensive hard copy versions, sometimes even providing their students with free tablets. We're even beginning to see a new form of a novel, reconfigured as an *application* for devices like iPhones and iPads, in which the user buys into a serialization of the story delivered over time in this "software" format.

Not surprisingly, the fact that different communications platforms are delivering the messages has actually had an impact on the content, vocabulary and grammar of the messages themselves. Younger generations, raised in a world of electronic media, are transitioning from textbooks into digital presentations and literature. Given the flexibility of today's technology, teachers and professors may want to have the capacity to edit and add to electronic textbooks, often delivered on eReaders and tablets, occasionally as noted above, even smart phones, at a net cost that averages half the price of the hard copies. With copyright issues abounding, indeed, some publishers already offer that potential.[67] At a minimum, particularly as the cost of computers continues to fall, school districts are increasingly buying electronic versions of texts (with certain rights to upgrades and new editions) instead of paper copies, ensuring a savings that is most necessary in these economically impaired times.

With an eye to keeping learning materials constantly current, "South Korea is taking a $2 billion gamble that its students are ready to ditch paper textbooks in favor of tablet PCs as part of a vast digital scholastic network."[68] At the January 2012 Consumer Electronics Show in Las Vegas, Apple announced a new app and a series of "exclusive" strategic alliances with major American textbook publishers to deliver interactive textbooks to iPads for under $15 each. Everywhere, lesson plans are already evolving into PowerPoint presentations, teacher-assembled Internet links, customized materials and interactive segments. Much of what will be disseminated is free information, readily available on the Web. Open source sharing of teaching materials will become commonplace among the teaching community.

"'Kids are wired differently these days,' said Sheryl R. Abshire, Chief Technology Officer for the Calcasieu Parish school system in Lake Charles, [Louisiana]. 'They're digitally nimble. They multitask, transpose and extrapolate. And they think of knowledge as infinite. … They don't engage with textbooks that are finite, linear and rote,' Dr. Abshire continued. 'Teachers need digital resources to find those documents, those blogs, those wikis that get them beyond the plain vanilla curriculum in the textbooks.' … In California, [then] Gov. Arnold Schwarzenegger [in the summer of 2009] announced an initiative that would replace some high school science and math texts with free, 'open source' digital versions."[69]

For old world textbook manufacturers, catering to the largest school districts in New York, California and Texas, the ability to release new versions of old texts, with barely enough changes to justify a new edition, is a lean, mean money-printing machine. For college texts, where students actually have to buy their books, the practice seems almost unconscionable given the extraordinary cost of higher education these days. But the new digital text offers a subscription-based alternative, appropriate for entire school districts, to the potential of a less-expensive digital version of hard copy texts.

Additionally, by eliminating the need to recycle old (and often out-of-date, used) textbooks, publishers should be able to maintain their net margins by providing single-platform texts for anxious and cash-strapped students at a significant reduction in costs per unit. Texts can even be updated and revised during the school year on a real time basis. Since most college students have laptops or tablets, the costs will be incremental and not economically destructive. For primary and secondary schools, older eReaders and tablets are cheap… and more than enough. If Korea can do it, so can most of the rest of the world!

Television

Is television next? It's easy to see the similarities between watching video material online or on a mobile device and watching a television. There's an image with sound on a screen. Invariably, these devices, even the underlying media, are converging rapidly. And indeed, even for Web-delivered content, the advent of "smart TV" or Web-connected devices for traditional television makes the old world TV screen the medium of choice for most consumers (in the U.S. anyway).[70]

The impact of "TV everywhere," as mobile platforms and gaming consoles become increasingly capable of providing additional outlets for audio-visual material, is also growing at a staggering pace.[71] If this trend continues or accelerates, as it is expected to do, the entire definition of television will require a ground-up re-definition. But because monetization through mobile platform carriers is easier to track and collect, there may be a very nice silver lining in this change. Tracking usage and creating the necessary metrics is, however, somewhat more complex for traditional Web consumption on personal computers.

We are already witnessing accelerating changes in the way subscriber and advertising dollars are measured. The currency of "eyeballs" exposed to advertising is changing in light of consumers' ability to time-shift out of commercials or filter out pop-ups. Audience metrics are now building in time-shifting viewing and Web-based consumption. 82% of television is viewed within three days of initial telecast (the so-called "C3" measurement),[72] but ratings agencies and networks are pushing for metrics based on seven day viewership ("C7"), even over 30 days. If you're advertising a time-sensitive event (like a movie opening), that hardly seems to be a relevant measurement! Per view pricing is quickly being replaced with subscription models with or without forced advertising viewing as the price to watch the desired content.

What's more, networks are readjusting their target "demographics" to sustain their advertising rates. Take this official network position from the summer of 2013: Dismissing the demos… CBS chief research officer David Poltrack said advertisers are moving past the A18-49 audience, and for good reason. Not only has the demo been in decline 62% of the population in 2002 versus 55% today but young adults watch much less television. 'I can assure you that the overwhelming majority of big advertisers care about far more than that audience,' he said, 'and are in fact no longer looking at age and gender alone.' When [Poltrack was asked] the big question- i.e., how close we are to having a consistent, billable, and metric of measurement across platforms[,] he said, 'We're getting there; One that we would all be comfortable with and rely on is still a few years away. But we're making progress.'"[73]

There is, however, an interesting and quite ironic side-note to this shift in media exposure and consumption. As advertisers drop, circumvent or materially reduce their large, traditional big budget marketing campaigns for any particular product or service (below normal expectations), the blogosphere often picks up on that fact and dismisses the underlying product, content or service as marginal and unable to secure a real marketing budget (the "unworthiness" factor). So for the time being at least, marketing even in this new world seems to require waste.

We are watching cable connections in the United States contract for the first time since cable became the powerful medium of today.[74] It's called "cutting the cord." We've already seen cord-cutting in American telephony, where 35.8% of American households no longer have land lines, but the trend in cable/satellite/teleco-delivered television has created a parallel reality. Younger demographics (or those who simply can't afford the luxury of cable) are finding ways to circumvent expensive cable subscriptions to find targeted programs on the Web.[75]

Just about every network program is rebroadcast on some Website, but it does take some effort to locate that content online. These younger buyers are able to bring appropriate messages to themselves, a self-directing version of Rule One. Because of the impaired employment market, a large pool of these younger consumers simply continue to access traditional television content on the Web even after graduating from their final degree. They don't even have a cord to cut.

Increasingly, entire networks are migrating into the on-demand, Web-based world. Amazon, Netflix, Google and Apple are well established in this space, but even Sony has announced a new Internet service and has already attracted media giant Viacom for "[o]n-demand content and traditional cable channels [which] will both be streamed to Sony's service if all goes as planned. This could mean everything from MTV, Comedy Central, BET, CMA, and Logo will all be streaming through Sony. [While] the agreement is only preliminary and Sony has also had discussions Walt Disney Co., Time Warner Inc. and CBS Corp."[76] Is this just an extension of pay-TV or the beginnings of a mass migration to the Web in an unbundled format?

Generally, the trend among those with satellite and cable access is clearly not news that the heads of the various channels want to hear: "According to ... The Diffusion Group (TDG), the number of US households that subscribe to traditional pay-TV has peaked in [2010-2012], and will decline from nearly 101 million in 2012 to less than 95 million in 2017."[77] It is also interesting to note that the programs that seem to have the highest rates of piracy were those where online versions of telecast programs were restricted. Take for example HBO, which, until October of 2013 (when HBO supplied shows to Google Play, a download-to-own service) accorded legitimate Web access to programs only to subscribers of their cable/satellite service: This service faced losses on programs like *Game of Thrones* and *Boardwalk Empire*, which are heavily pirated. And even though in June of 2013 HBO extended the availability of their parallel online portal, HBO Go, to outside sites like AppleTV, they still clung to the requirement that users also have a subscription to the HBO cable service to access this additional source.

With the ultimate cable/satellite value proposition – live sports – commanding increasing fees from telecasters, something has to give in a world where consumers have even less to spend on discretionary items. Those who don't care about sports or are willing to pay major leagues for Web-and-mobile-only access, cutting the cord is the easy button. We are even seeing Emmy-winning television from streaming-only entities like Netflix. But increasing costs and a desire to retain as many existing customers as possible has cable and satellite providers cutting marginal channels with fewer subscribers to soften the monthly blow from increased payments to team sports.

As cable subscribers rail at having to pay for bundles of channels they never watch, access to a la carte programs and even sports packages entirely online (the latter which account for one third of average cable bills) becomes compelling. Los Angeles Times editorial writer, David Lazarus, addresses the issues in changing the bundled cable channel model: "...I think it's an unfair and archaic practice that should be done away with... I'd have said pretty much the same [even] after a report ["The Future of TV"] issued by the New York Investment bank Needham & Co. warning that a switch to so-called a la carte programming would cost the pay-TV industry about $70 billion and leave viewers with fewer than 20 channels."[78] To Needham report author, Laura Martin, "The question is whether value to customers is measured by the quantity of choice or the price... I think choice is better." Lazarus suggests a middle ground of "mini-bundles" to assuage consumers who appear destined to get their way... sooner or later.[79]

But even as Millennials may not even have a cord to cut, traditionalists are serving up new cable offerings intended to lure them back into the fold: "The fledgling cable network Pivot — launch[ed] in a reported 40 million-plus homes [August 1, 2013](the 32nd anniversary of the launch of MTV) — took on the difficult task of convincing a group of largely middle-aged journalists at the [Television Critics Association meeting in late July of 2013] that they should take seriously a general entertainment service aimed squarely at the millennial (age 18-34) generation. Pivot certainly has ambitious plans, with a programming slate anchored by more than 300 hours of original programming for its first year. That includes an original scripted comedy (*Please Like Me*, created by then-25-year-old comedian Josh Thomas); an original variety show (*HitRECord*, from Joseph Gordon-Levitt and and Brian Graden); and a docu-talk series exec produced and hosted by Meghan McCain, John McCain's daughter."[80] Skepticism abounds on this seemingly eleventh-hour effort to buck the trend of cord-cutting; why would this network find its way as a basic cable offering as opposed to the more obvious and demographically consistent path of creating a Web-based channel? Some colleges are offering traditional content-rich web-based services free or at modest cost (e.g., Philo.com) for students to stem the tide of illicit access, but will this make any difference in the longer term?

Even in the premium content world, alternative delivery systems and higher profile original content is clearly becoming routinely available. Apple blows away the competition when it comes down to legitimate digital downloads of commercial film and television fare in the United States,[81] and Netflix is even more dominant in the world of streaming.[82] Streaming is also becoming the dominant "on demand" delivery system in the American market,[83] which makes Netflix the most important player in this space (in the fall of 2013, Netflix even passed HBO in the number of its U.S. subscribers).

Netflix not only has generated an output deal with major animation studio DreamWorks Animation for their future motion pictures (in lieu of cable!) but is generating high profile, expensive scripted television series (like *House of* Cards, which generated the kind of Emmy-recognition that once was reserved only for telecasters, *Orange is the New Black,* four new Marvel-character series or the relaunch of the former traditional series, *Arrested Development*) with more success than most pundits expected. A second agreement with DreamWorks Animation in mid-June of 2013 gave Netflix access to DWA's characters, stories and creative teams for a significant volume of potential television series as well. There is no question that consumers who use services like Netflix and Hulu find cable programming significantly less compelling.[84]

Following the lesson of premium content providers like HBO and Showtime, Netflix CEO Reed Hastings sees addictive scripted programming not as a source of money from the productions themselves but as a mechanism to insure subscriber growth and retention: "'In the beginning you're developing a foundation,' Hastings says. Still, he urged investors not to focus too much on *House Of Cards*' performance. 'It's our most viewed content today, but it's not the center of the company. It may be the center of the PR for a while. That's OK.' While he doesn't want people to 'think of us as the original content company,' Hastings made it clear that originals will be key to its growth."[85] For those who subscribe to Netflix, it is just as popular as the high-end cable channels in terms of competing for consumer viewing time.[86]

The notion of exclusive premium content is one approach that has paid off big time for Netflix, as "the company reports that [as of the first quarter of 2013, it] now has 29.17 million subscribers in the U.S. alone -- that's 2 million more than the number of subscribers the streaming video provider had at the end of 2012. Globally, Netflix reports more than 38 million subscribers [40 million by September 2013], an addition of 3.05 million new customers when compared to the end of 2012/previous quarter."[87] Unique programming can generate and hold subscribers to the entire service, where the value remains regardless of the value of the *individual* program.

But there's another approach, representing Amazon's foray into this space that uses the Web as a testing ground for potential series for its own digital networks as well as possibly mainstream television programming. Amazon began this new service in April of 2013 with 14 original pilot television programs, with consumers to cast the deciding votes. It very quickly picked two comedies for its own "network."

While the market expects Amazon to continue to expand into its own series and other premium productions, this format represents another value proposition to those in the industry seeking a more rigorous testing of the potential slate of new series. Google continues to experiment with narrowcast network and inexpensive programming, and the explosion of professionally produced content makes the Web look increasingly like old-world television. Smaller offerings abound all over the Web, building viewership on new series that seem to create a vast array of content choices.

Nascent attempts to move series-content into additional but more limited platforms have also already begun, notably as experiments in social media. For example, AT&T sponsored one effort that was premiered on Twitter, Tumblr, Instagram and YouTube: "@SummerBreak" follow[ed] a group of real-life graduating seniors culled from high schools in the Westside area of Los Angeles for eight weeks before they depart for college and elsewhere. Instead of the traditional 30- or 60-minute episodic format, the series [played out] out 24/7 as a series of tweets with photos and videos attached."[88] Is this really-short-form format likely to gain traction, find a path to monetization, compete with or supplement traditional television or morph into an entirely new form of mobile entertainment?

But there is a difference with such digital series, and the revenue models are anything but clear; most efforts are still in the experimental stage where losses are simply accepted. Further, the question of whether Web-based television is appropriate for everyone remains.

The idea of Internet-driven television may be fine for those who know exactly what they want, but for people used to surfing channels to find something they like or who simply turn on a favorite network and accept whatever comes, the Web might be just too much work. Once again, however, there are technology solutions that allow consumers to let Websites choose programs for them, either based on past viewing patterns or even following the viewing patterns of peer leaders or people who are linked as "friends" to a particular consumer.[89]

Thus, the seeds of network disintermediation (taking the network out from between the content creator and the viewer) and unbundling (where consumers don't have buy 120 cable channels but can access only the content they want) are being planted today. It may be more valuable to look at such networks merely as eyeball and sales aggregators (ads and subscribers), generating the economic values necessary to fund high value television programming.

Such aggregators exist in other media as well – movie theaters are aggregators of sorts – and are offering functions that can be provided by advertising agencies and their advertising clients as well as sites with major followers, like YouTube, Facebook, Netflix and Twitter. All of these forces are directed at the question of who pays for the creation of the content and for the marketing necessary to make consumers aware of its existence remains.

We certainly have more questions than answers. For example, if the proliferation of smart TVs renders the lower tier cable channels commercially obsolete, does that make the stronger channels with more desirable content more valuable or is it just the content itself that has value? Who or what will be the audience and advertiser aggregators of the future? Does the Web really offer competitive content at this time or does old world television still dominate? Are the selection of series programming on Yahoo Screen, the new comic book offerings on the Amazon Studios site or the reams of content on YouTube television or strictly Web-based formats? What's the difference? Is this the new replacement television system?[90] Is the old doomed?

For doubters, while viewership of live television in the United States is down, [91] there has been one strange anomaly in this prediction of the demise of traditional television. In this transitional period and even in impaired economic times, television ad revenues are still climbing.[92] Is it really the only mass medium left?

We can expect that older viewers remain a mainstay of traditional television.[93] Equally, the generation that follows the Baby Boomers seems to be likely to keep old world television as a relevant medium.[94] One of the most important factors would seem to be that *women* in that magical 18 to 49 age group still drive television viewing, and given their impact on consumer purchases,[95] not only are the major U.S. networks focused on this demographic, but entire cable channels are dedicated to or at least heavily focused on female viewership (e.g., We TV, Lifetime, Oxygen, OWN and Bravo).

But analysts are looking beyond the simple reach of the networks. They also care about impact and "stickiness." Ultra-conservative Fox News, for example, might have an older demographic reach outside of the target of most advertisers, but it really grabs the audience it has, making it the most profitable news organization in the United States. "For most of the television business — the segment that relies on advertising — that would be serious cause for concern because ad sales are almost always based on a target age of 25 to 54, and Fox News, for the last two years, has had a median age of 65-plus in its ratings both for the full day and for prime time.

"But up until now at least, Fox News has been more able than any other television entity to defy the tyranny of the demos, as they are known in the business. And the network, which has upturned traditions and expectations throughout its history, has earned consistently enormous profits, relying on the commitment and loyalty of its audience.

"'I don't think you can fully capture the value Fox News brings by looking at the Nielsen ratings alone,' said Craig Moffett, the longtime financial analyst who specializes in cable. Mr. Moffett, who heads his own firm, said that the key to Fox News's continued financial strength has been 'the level of passion and engagement' it inspires in its viewers." And while there are ups and downs in network revenues depending on extrinsic elements (election years, Olympics) which may push one year down, the general trend has been a reasonably stable ad revenue performance, even with some moderate growth in the near term.[96]

Is this revenue rise temporary or an interim retreat from the clutter of too many choices for too few eyeballs? With the massive assortment of advertising choices, old world broadcast networks and cable channels alike are able to make the case that they remain the most effective ad game in town, even as the Dish Network touted a new system to skip over ads in their delayed-viewing PDR systems in May of 2012. The telecasters' reach already extends to their parallel websites, and cross-platform packages apparently resonate with advertisers. With political advertising up in 2012, life appears to be solid in the television advertising world. But wait, there's more… lurking danger that is.

Not only is television falling down the chain of preferred entertainment for most Americans,[97] but even the successful aspects of traditional television are facing survival issues. With television generating revenues from multiple pots, a threat to any one revenue source could significantly erode the overall value of premium content, from the feature film after market to traditional television.

Except for premium channels (like HBO, Showtime and Starz in the United States) – which get monthly fixed "add-on" charges to consumer bills – today most cable and satellite-delivered channels generate roughly half their income from monthly consumer subscriber fees and half from advertising. The focus is on higher quality (expensive) content with messaging and entertainment tailored to significant and measurable audiences. But as tech companies begin to generate short-form and niche programming, much of it user-generated, the question is whether advertisers and traditional major television networks are even noticing.

Needham & Co analyst Laura Martin thinks they should: "The tech companies are 'creating short-form premium videos that are difficult to monetize, and therefore largely ignored by incumbents,' who'd rather create hit TV shows, Martin says. The big guns have to pay attention to conventional programming: Attractive shows help to keep pay TV subscribers attached to today's high-priced packages. 'Unbundling threatens up to 50% of the total revenue of the TV ecosystem,' Martin says. But media money follows time, and as mobile devices become more popular we could see 'advertising share shifts away from TV and toward the new premium-video online ecosystem."

The big producers are 'fighting over the 0-2% viewing growth pie rather than the 50% viewing growth pie.' Martin says that she'd 'feel better' about the long term prospects for Big Media 'if they were allocating 10% of their budget increases to short form premium video…designed to push young viewers toward their hit TV shows.'"[98] For smaller companies, perhaps, these new media opportunities offer both cheaper ad rates with more targeted programming, but those dependent on advertising, there are "issues" that must be faced.

To make matters even worse for traditional telecasters, younger demographics are used to a different way to access television content and have the technology to have television(audio-visual content might be a better description) everywhere, anywhere, all the time. Watching "television" may actually become ancient history if these technologies continue in their current directions.[99]

Considering so many attacks aimed at disintermediating the traditional network from its viewers, one would suspect that the prognosis for "old world" network television is not particularly promising. Indeed, the big four U.S. networks (CBS, ABC,

NBC and FBC) have taken to reporting their audience penetration "ratings" in a new "live plus 3" days (so-called C3, discussed above) format, which is being pressured to be expanded further to "live plus 7" days (C7, also noted above), aggregating the number of viewers to the original telecast plus those who view that content within three/seven days on their digital video recorders (DVRs).

For the fall of 2011 to the same period in 2012, the number of American households with DVRs has risen from 42% to 46% (among the 18-49 demographic, the number is 51%).[100] Without this fudge factor, these networks would have serious issues supporting their advertising pricing, even though it seems pretty obvious that many of those recording such programming do so specifically to skip the ads.[101]

Television content has parallel life online and in new mobile formats; it is already being aggregated – either streamed or presented in downloadable multiplatform formats (for sale or with embedded advertising) – on the Web through sites like iTunes, Amazon Studios, Yahoo, YouTube or Hulu. The latter is a joint venture between NBC-Universal and Fox, [102] which has added content from suppliers like Warner Bros., MGM,[103] Sony and Lionsgate.

But what is television anyway? Netflix reaches more people than any U.S. television network! Does it matter how programming is accessed, as long as consumers want that content somewhere? In later chapters, we will explore the trending of consumer preferences mandating their audio-visual when they want it, how they want it and where they want it (what some call television everywhere, but that is a very narrow description of reality). The subtext to all of these changes, of course, is exactly how is the production of content, at least the premium fare with the greatest production value, going to be paid for.

How we can assure that enough money can be generated so that those who are the best and the brightest content creators can be compensated to continue to create? Has even the concept of a television *network* simply outlived its usefulness? Perhaps, as suggested earlier, the amorphous concept of "aggregation" – whether it is the aggregation of eyeballs, subscription payments or ad sales – is a better word. True, networks are such aggregators, but since even television content has alternatives ways to reach consumers, perhaps it is becoming less relevant to focus on a single component in this content delivery wheel where content is the hub, delivered to consumers down alternative spokes.

Video Games

This pastime – thought to be an endless engagement of young males (and younger females) – has increasingly skewed older, now embracing a large number of people in their thirties and beyond. As *Angry Bird* apps and casual games are soaring in popularity, the mainstay of companies built on expensive console games are taking massive valuation hits that bring back memories of the rather dramatic fall of the music industry once the album model was decimated and file-sharing became de rigueur among younger users.

But the reasons for the console video game fall are quite different. Some blame the older consoles themselves, but this is probably not the real causation. Time impairment, the high cost of console games in an tight economy, the desire to flip quickly in and out of the long list of choices, highly addictive "short attention span" repetitive casual (e.g., the *Angry Birds* phenomenon) and social gameplay plus the intrusion of demands of the new social media environments have changed the gaming needs of all but the most diehard gamers.

Casual and social games have penetrated older demographics, otherwise wary of the complexity and speed of traditional console games. Simple, available "edutainment" gaming has created little virtual babysitters even for very young children, now able to engage with smart phones and tablets almost as soon as they are able to speak. Expect education even in modern school systems to reflect this "learning as a videogame" mentality in the coming years.

Thus, the downward slide in this sector is far from over. Console gaming seems to be destined for further contraction regardless of possible improvements in the economy.[104] While die-hard gamers will continue to embrace this segment, the most recent trends have suggested that the marketplace has generated shorter consumer time commitments to video games (thus generating interest in shorter games), migration to mobile platforms,[105] an unwillingness to pay for enhanced graphics, and an emphasis on "freemium" gaming (where entry is free, but where upgrades in levels, characters or character abilities may generate a revenue stream, albeit significantly less than expensive retail console games).[106] In fact the multifaceted capacities of gaming consoles to function as a principal delivery system for digital content in general is beginning to eclipse their primary use as gaming centers.[107] With the advent of social media, "casual gaming" has become the dominant player in this space.

The Web as the Film & Television Aftermarket

Within thirty days of its soft (experimental or beta) launch date (officially, March 12, 2008), Hulu's user base went from zero to five million, and 80% of the premium film and television content available on the site was viewed at least once a week. One year after its formal launch date, Hulu was second only to YouTube among online video providers, sending hundreds of millions of streams of requested video content to 42 million distinct users. [108]

By the summer of 2009, Hulu was one of the most watched forms of television, generating more viewership than most of America's large cable systems.[109] By the summer of 2010, Hulu was already talking about a possible public offering, although months later, it began entertaining interest from institutional buyers like Yahoo and Google, but nothing happened. As these potential buyers began demanding that Hulu's owner companies lock into unpalatable longer term content output deals in 2011, the talk shifted back to a public offering, morphing into simply "looking for a buyer" by the spring of 2013. Again, by that summer, the bidding fell apart as potential buyers balked at the lack of continued program licensing from the existing owners, who pulled the site off the market and elected instead to infuse a further $750 million of needed capital.

Hulu is and was different and seemingly much more consumer-friendly than studio-designed structures typically were. For example, Hulu gives consumers' the ability to create their own mash-ups (custom-edited blends of various types of content for use on their personal Webpages), assuming that the underlying content providers agree. This disharmony will eventually settle, and inevitably, the existing owners will repackage the site for sale to a third party.

Based on viewership, advertiser-supported Hulu is a wild, runaway success, [110] challenging the Silicon Valley skeptics who doubted a consortium of old world Hollywood companies could ever do anything right on the Web. Hulu's subscriber-supported premium upgrade also kept pace with the ad-supported service: "Hulu crested 4 million monthly premium subscribers in the first quarter [0f 2013] — and for the first time streamed more than 1 billion videos in the period — with Internet TV venture queuing up 10 original and exclusive shows to try to keep the ball rolling."[111] That "success" may be part of a new concern: telecasters who paid for content are now challenged in their "exclusive" television markets by the same Web-available programming. [112]

"Companies like Time Warner Cable Inc. and DirecTV Group Inc. pay cable networks billions of dollars each year to carry programming. Believing that they should have exclusivity because their payments support the enormous cost of producing TV shows, such companies have been pushing back against the Hulu freebies.... Investors also are wary that the media companies' embrace of the Internet-content-should-be-free philosophy threatens one of Hollywood's biggest profit centers: cable programming...'If you give away your premium content for free, you are basically hastening your own demise, signing your own death warrant,' said Laura Martin, a media analyst. 'There is a choice that companies have to make.'" [113]

Whole seasons of favorites were pulled from Hulu because of such contractual disputes over the meaning of "exclusivity." Rule One's appropriate consumers are being contractually barred from receiving appropriate content. Given the vastly higher revenues generated from traditional, old world television syndicators (with much more ad revenue from many more ads[114]) made their point. Even without a contractual mandate or court order to the contrary, Hulu's providers simply succumbed to their parent companies' pressures. Noting how valuable traditional television still is, the networks pulled the programs. [115]

Struggling to compete with traditional media and feeling the pressure from their parent companies, Hulu also blocked software that allowed users to move Hulu content from their computers onto standard televisions. Fearing cannibalization of a new medium by an old one, it seems that Hulu's providers are fighting a rear guard action that many believe will only encourage piracy. [116] Hulu's marketing pitch, with its minimalist volume of advertising, is predicated on offering network and high level programming with fewer commercial interruptions. Their assumption (which may be incorrect[117]) is that consumers will not tolerate significant commercial saturation in their Web-viewing.

Two years after Hulu's initial launch, Viacom pulled its Comedy Central programming off Hulu, removing the exceptionally popular *The Daily Show* and *The Colbert Report* from this site. [118] The company cited insufficient revenues for this particular premium programming even though Hulu itself was profitable. [119] As television stations and cable networks – which had purchased exclusive syndication rights to high profile programming – continued to press their displeasure with perceived cannibalization of their purchased values, Hulu's principal owners began talking about pulling some of their most desirable content from the site and offering such premium fare only to consumers willing to pay subscriber fees. [120] Was the model unraveling or just going through growing pains? Could the numbers be adjusted to work? [121]

And one more big change was in the wind. Cable giant Comcast took a controlling 51% interest in NBC-Universal, one of Hulu's principal partners. This provided some interesting new conflicts, both because Comcast owned networks that had output agreements for the content in question and because it is and was itself deploying a competing service. [122] Given this Comcast conundrum, Hulu generated some strong interest from potential buyers, but we already know where that process ended up as Hulu's owners just could not accede to buyer's requests to guarantees that these owners would continue supply programming to that service after it were sold.

Hulu wasn't the only Internet platform where multiple studios collectively shared exhibiting their content. Studios participated in other common platforms, seeking new marketing models for their valuable titles. Consumers and studios alike began to experiment with new formats where viewers are given a choice to buy, rent or receive ad-supported content online. [123]

By spring of 2009 a cavalcade of studios and networks, from MGM [124] and Lionsgate to Sony and CBS, stepped into the YouTube space to provide full-length, ad-supported older, "library" films and television episodes. Instead of fighting consumers over unauthorized use of copyrighted material, Lionsgate and its brethren reap the marketing benefits of placing their content in front of consumers. Their agreement with YouTube also calls for Lionsgate to participate in the advertising revenues generated from making their content available through this site.

In March of 2009, amplifying the Rule One connectivity, Google announced an expanded cross-platform advertising bundle where advertisers could blend search-based marketing [125] with Google's YouTube ad placement and combine that with traditional radio and television ads. Disney added its ABC/ESPN/ABC Family television clip rights to the YouTube mix with a twist: Disney would implement its own ads sales and remit a share of those revenues back to YouTube.

By September of 2009, major studios were exploring virtual rentals of full-length features through YouTube's streaming capacity. By 2011, YouTube was announcing that it would be organizing content into "channels" and even investing nine figures into the creation programming for at least 20 anticipated premium channels. [126] With a billion or more YouTube views a month as of March of 2013, and well over 72 hours of original content uploaded onto the service every hour,[127] the process of discovering new content is no longer a function of pulling down a barker channel or TV Guide.

Social media pitches from friends to gain traction to their latest upload, recommendations from Facebook players, search engines and the inevitable popularity tracking statistics drive people towards the snippets they ultimately watch, from cute kittens and babies doing silly stuff to a Gangnum style music video with well over a billion views. The variables impacting consumer receptivity to online video campaigns are complex, varying to length of the message to time of the week that the message is actually released.[128] Further, viewing trends suggest that video consumption may be growing faster overseas than experts had predicted. [129] Monetization is still the Holy Grail.

Where there is money, talent and their unions and guilds are sure to tread, and as early collective bargaining agreements with Hollywood's labor organizations often left the compensation issue fast and loose in these evolving technologies. If the past is any measure, the future for negotiations in this space is likely to be contentious. Back in the fall of 2007, the Writers Guild of America began what was to become one of the longest stoppages in the history of the U.S. entertainment business (12 weeks, although 1988 saw a 13 week walkout), in substantial part based on the promise of revenues of what was then described as "new media" (revenues that were going to flood the industry from the Web and mobile).

Writers wanted a pure inclusion of 100% of such revenues into the gross upon which their aftermarket payments (residuals) would be based, and studios insisted on the royalty structure that had applied to hard copy DVDs. A slight increase over their existing DVD residuals was accepted. Writers also wanted clear compensation for their original writing for the Web. While a payment schedule was negotiated as a part of the settlement, the level of the payments and the productions covered suggest that Guild members will not remotely regain the lost pay they had to sacrifice to get the result. Other unions left employment in these new media to be determined more on an ad hoc basis, but as television migrates increasingly to mobile and the Web, this will be a major battleground for talent trying to keep up with changes in content delivery systems. Will the mass of non-professionally-created content drive down the cost of Hollywood labor or is proven talent sufficiently valuable to sustain an increasing payday? Time will tell.

Cross-Platform Advertising

Getting consumers to watch the ads that support the online film and television aftermarket remains a core challenge. One of the latest trends in the online advertising model is giving consumers more control of the kind of ads they want to see or even allowing users to skip through ads to get to the desired program – while still placing an ad in or around the content itself. Again, this is nothing more than letting consumers pick their Rule One appropriate message. Since June of 2010, Hulu has been experimenting with allowing consumers to pick the ads they are willing to see. YouTube has a similar process with its TrueView format. They have discovered that consumers who have choice generate click-through rates [130] much higher than the industry average of 2%.[131]

Digital ad agency Panache uses another technique that allows consumers to "skip" the ad where viewers are "presented with a pop-up video featuring a large 'fast forward' button. Click it once, and the ad accelerates rapidly, while a hurried voice gives an elevator-pitch version of the message the ad intends to communicate... So while advertisers are allowing users more control, they're also looking to increase their frequency. The future of online video advertising, then, may look something like the typical TiVo experience: more minutes of ads, all seen in a rushed blur – though this time around, with branded audio to make sure the viewers catch at least *some* of the content they're trying to skip." [132]

Shorter attention spans, the willingness to skip commercial ads that aren't amusing and the need to interact, criticize and provide personal input on what was once a one-way marketing street will continue to change advertising at warp speed. Better short stories, losing the 30-second mentality of most audio-visual ads, the openness to interact (beyond the bribes for Facebook "likes") and the understanding of how to reach different (but appropriate) consumers, each in their own way, are critical. Real time or near-real-time tracking, discussed below, vet results and connectivity like never before.

Social Media

While we will delve more deeply into reaching and communicating with consumers and grassroots constituents through social media throughout the book, there is one huge void in corporate America that has yet to be property embraced and implemented: the use of social media within companies and their surrounding buyer/vendor base.

According to a report from the prestigious McKinsey Global Institute,[133] corporate America is far from achieving a meaningful understanding use of social media to maximize their economic goals. "While 72 percent of companies use social technologies in some way, very few are anywhere near to achieving the full potential benefit. In fact, the most powerful applications of social technologies in the global economy are largely untapped.

Companies will go on developing ways to reach consumers through social technologies and gathering insights for product development, marketing, and customer service. Yet the McKinsey Global Institute (MGI) finds that twice as much potential value lies in using social tools to enhance communications, knowledge sharing, and collaboration within and across enterprises. MGI's estimates suggest that by fully implementing social technologies, companies have an opportunity to raise the productivity of interaction workers—high-skill knowledge workers, including managers and professionals—by 20 to 25 percent."

If America is lagging behind the curve, it is indeed likely that the rest of the world is not up to snuff either. Perhaps it is because social media has taken its firmest roots among the younger segments of our society. Younger people are used to cross-platform information sharing, while older managers still use emails with limited targeted recipients. The opportunity to provide a more cohesive message to the entire company (and its related vendors and buyers), creating greater consistency and efficiency, lies in the effective use of well-positioned messaging through social media. Can older marketing executives fill this void, or is it time for the young turks (and what exactly is "young" in this space?) to take over, at least for those in their appropriately younger market segments?

New technologies allow instantaneous and wide-reach communication/value-sharing on an entirely new scale: "These technologies, which create value by improving productivity across the value chain, could potentially contribute $900 billion to $1.3 trillion in annual value across [U.S-based consumer packaged goods, retail financial services, advanced manufacturing, and professional services].

"Two-thirds of this potential value lies in improving collaboration and communication within and across enterprises. The average interaction worker spends an estimated 28 percent of the workweek managing e-mail and nearly 20 percent looking for internal information or tracking down colleagues who can help with specific tasks. But when companies use social media internally, messages become content; a searchable record of knowledge can reduce, by as much as 35 percent, the time employees spend searching for company information. Additional value can be realized through faster, more efficient, more effective collaboration, both within and between enterprises.

"The amount of value individual companies can capture from social technologies varies widely by industry, as do the sources of value. Companies that have a high proportion of interaction workers can realize tremendous productivity improvements through faster internal communication and smoother collaboration. Companies that depend very heavily on influencing consumers can derive considerable value by interacting with them in social media and by monitoring the conversations to gain a richer perspective on product requirements or brand image—for much less than what traditional research methods would cost."[134]

Whether it is a tweet from the chief executive officer, an internally generated social media site or easy-to-use collaboration platform (intuitive versus the overly complex traditional enterprise resource – ERP – software platforms that are often the plague of big business), the values sit there waiting to be unlocked.

Corporate paranoia, the fear of putting something in writing before it is vetted by a gaggle of legals, may also explain the reluctance of those at the top to take the plunge into social media. Not everyone is Mark Cuban, the dynamic billionaire and owner of the Dallas Mavericks (National Basketball Association) who engages his fans though tweets on a constant basis. "On June 6, Larry Ellison – CEO of Oracle, one of the largest and most advanced computer technology corporations in the world – tweeted for the very first time. In doing so, he joined a club that remains surprisingly elite. Among CEOs of the world's Fortune 500 companies, a mere 20 have Twitter accounts. Ellison, by the way, hasn't tweeted since … As social media spreads around the globe, one enclave has proven stubbornly resistant: the boardroom. Within the C-suite, perceptions remain that social media is at best a soft PR tool and at worst a time sink for already distracted employees. Without a push from the top, many of the biggest companies have been slow to take the social media plunge." [135] But change is in the air all across this space even, if there is such thing yet, in "traditional" web-based traditional social media.

With Facebook being the 10,000 pound gorilla in the room,[136] its early failures to embrace mobile technology fast enough and hostility in sharing data with advertisers ("monetization" issues) in what people believed would be the biggest "new" public offering for years very quickly tanked its shareholder value to half what was set when the company first went public. But there's a bigger trend that lies beneath Facebook's surface issues: it's too generic, too un-special and too much "everyone is doing it" to remain sustainable at the levels that most envision. The average Facebook user spends over six and a half hours a month on the site, [137] a number that has been growing slightly over the past couple of years, but the growth rates are slowing.

And there are signs that Facebook's need to monetize may have antagonized more than a few of its less-well-heeled business users who are finding it increasingly difficult to reach the fan base that they have built over time. In the first quarter of 2013 and despite claims from the company that the change did not create any anti-non-paying client bias, Facebook deployed a new News Feed algorithm that such business users claimed denied them access to their connected users… unless they paid for promotional posts (giving their posts a preference) at pretty stiff rates, well above those charged to celebrities for their fan base.

Is Facebook losing traction with both users and smaller advertisers? Has the site lost its "cool" factor? Is their connectivity to their own Instagram subsidiary, including their new video-sharing capacity[138] with this little picture-driven acquisition, enough to right the ship? Facebook has fought back with a vengeance as we shall see below.

The fear of advertisers and market analysts is not that there will be a fall from grace such as that which decimated the MySpace user-base or massive defections from Facebook to alternative sites, but that its users will find solace in more relevant parallel social media sites and spend less time on Facebook. Less time will create fewer revenue opportunities, a trend that could further erode shareholder values.

There are too many new specialized sites with their own attractive "stories," and there are only so many hours in a day. Google+ focused on creating smaller, more linked social circles of connected friends. Reddit, for example, has spawned thousands of sub-communities, drilling down on specialized interests, sharing values and links.[139] The emphasis in most of these networks seems to be increasingly dedicated to curating and sharing visual materials (so-called "social visualization"). The future of social media, as we shall see, will be how to identify and access audience targets … and what messages and content will be most effective in a sea of complexity based on too many choices. But real the elephant in the social media room is mobile.

The migration to smart phone and tablet apps has severely impacted social networking and the viability of their ad-supported platforms. With mobile generating less than ten percent of the advertising click-through rate of computer driven ads, and with well over 60% of Facebook's user accessing their accounts on mobile, these trends pose severe challenges to revenue generation. Further, "70% of mobile Facebook users return to the app daily versus only 40% on the desktop."[140]

With Wall Street valuations nipping at their heels, Facebook's executives moved to a "mobile first" reprioritization, opening up to third party apps (and marketing them). The results appeared in their the last quarter of 2011: "Facebook's new mobile advertising products accounted for 23% of its overall ad revenue, up from 14%."[141] The 2013 first quarter earnings results produced an improved allocation of 30% of Facebook's ad revenue to mobile. A significant gain, but still not proportionate to their consumers' shift to mobile. Would Facebook be able to kick those revenues sufficiently to relieve Wall Street fears?

But wait, as the announcer might intone, there's more. In early April of 2013, Facebook announced a new app for Android-based smart phones: Facebook's "Home" page. When the phone is initiated with this app, the user's Facebook page pops up to create an instant link. But the consumer is still able to use that device for non-Facebook communications; the app just lingers on the screen, showing updates in the background as the keyboard, texting and email can be continued in the foreground. While this may make it more likely that users will engage with their Facebook accounts more readily, early critics were skeptical that this application will "fix" the revenue problem that continues to beleaguer that social network.

Facebook finally found traction for mobile advertising in a strange place: "[The site] had particularly strong demand for ads that appear in its users' news feeds, the flow of updates from friends that they see when they log on. About 1 in 20 posts in the news feed is an ad, and advertisers cannot seem to get enough of them… [Facebook CEO Mark] Mr. Zuckerberg said Facebook's studies had shown that users were noticing ads more, and the company was working to improve the quality and relevance of ads…. Facebook is also studying when and how to introduce video ads, which are expected to command at least several hundred thousand dollars each."[142]

But the proof was in the pudding: "The social networking company [noted on July 24, 2013] that it had revved up its mobile advertising from virtually nothing a year ago to 41 percent of its total ad revenue of $1.6 billion in the second quarter. 'Soon we'll have more revenue on mobile than desktop,' [said] Mark Zuckerberg... The company's revenue soared 53 percent, to $1.81 billion."[143] The stock exploded to its highest point since the company went public a year before. Was this problem solved and getting better or was this a temporary until competitors reacted with their own mobile advertising blasts?

And mobile wasn't and isn't the only issue that vexed Facebook. It no longer has the same level of "hourly" attention from its users that it drew before the public offering. New players have entered the space, competing for both eyeballs and engagement time. As new social media sites rise, the prognosis for Facebook is challenging at best. No one expects the raw number of subscribers to drop significantly – it's free after all – but that its pervasiveness may be precisely its undoing: "With more than 1 billion users worldwide and an unstated mission to make more money, Facebook has become a social network that's often too complicated, too risky, and, above all, too overrun by parents to give teens the type of digital freedom or release they crave."[144] Indeed, as older people sign up with Facebook, the demographic reach is skewing accordingly.[145] Clearly, different social media sites have differing strengths depending on the targeted demographic.[146]

Facebook seems to be heading to that homogenized category that includes that old-world email address you don't abandon or even your listing in a telephone directory. People will probably still use the service, but expect increasing numbers of subscribers to spend the time once committed to Facebook to move to more specialized social networking sites.[147] For advertisers seeking an appropriate audience, these changes represent a flashing amber light.

Although statutes like America's Children's Online Privacy Protection Act might require parental permission for those under 13, some sites are stickier to younger adherents. Fortunately for Facebook, one of them is its recent acquisition, Instagram. "Instagram was the top photography [sharing] Web site among U.S. teens ages 12 to 17, with 1.3 million teens visiting the site during December 2012. By the analytics firm [Nielsen]'s count, roughly one in 10 online teens in the U.S. visited Instagram in a browser during the month."[148]

There are, however, battle lines forming between parental goals and children's actions to circumvent those goals: "[In 2012], 78% of parents helped create their children's Facebook pages and 7.5 million users are under the age of 13 and lied about the age associated with the account."[149] Amy Jo Martin,[150] writing in May 24, 2013

FastCompany.com, provides this anecdotal information that suggests how younger children are reacting to social media (and particularly Facebook): "[M]y team and I had 40 third graders come to the Digital Royalty office...When we asked how many of the third graders were either on Facebook, Instagram, or Twitter, more than half raised their hands. Facebook has a minimum age restriction of 13 years old to create an account...

"After getting into a discussion with the third graders, we learned that several of them had abandoned their Facebook accounts because that's where their parents were. They knew that the adult powers that be are a hop, skip, and a click away from monitoring the kid's accounts on Facebook. The third-grade solution was to hop from Facebook to Instagram (which, ironically, Facebook also owns). In some cases, kids said they created new, rogue Facebook accounts where they connected with their friends and used their old ones as a decoy for parental supervision."[151]

Parents are still concerned about their children's exposure to unsavory and predatory purveyors of content, wanting to limit and control what their kids can access. As we have seen in the above example with even younger American demographics, the " parent factor alone could send kids fleeing to other applications such as Snapchat, Pheed, and Tumblr, all of which appear to have strong teen followings. Investors are betting on Snapchat in particular, which sends more than 60 million short-lived messages daily, because they don't want to miss out on the next Facebook.

"'Teens are looking for a place they can call their own,' said Danah Boyd, a senior researcher who studies, for Microsoft, how young people use social media. 'Rather than all flocking en masse to a different site, they're fragmenting across apps and engaging with their friends using a wide array of different tools.... A new one pops up each week. What's exciting to me is that I'm seeing teenagers experiment.'"[152] Increasingly, uniqueness, access, specialized sharing capacity, relevancy and content will define those sites that survive and prosper. "Cool" is a fleeting and often elusive status.

But there is a phase of social media that may well revolutionize how we educate future generations. We've seen how tablets are replacing textbooks, but online instruction – a very pragmatic form of social media – might someday supplant traditional college and graduate education. There have been lots of courses and opportunities from smaller, for profit, online colleges, but the biggest and best are most probably the institutions that will have the greatest impact.

Today, major universities are now creating some very interesting online instruction. "From their start two years ago, when a free artificial intelligence course from Stanford enrolled 170,000 students, free massive open online courses, or MOOCs, have drawn millions and yielded results like the perfect scores of Battushig, a 15-year-old Mongolian boy, in a tough electronics course offered by the Massachusetts Institute of Technology [ranked first by U.S. News & World Report among U.S. engineering universities].

"But the courses have not yet produced profound change, partly because they offer no credit and do not lead to a degree. The disruption may be approaching, though, as Georgia Tech, which has one of the country's top computer science programs, plans to offer a MOOC-based online master's degree in computer science for $6,600 — far less than the $45,000 on-campus price."[153] Students may gather at the virtual student's union, and after class visits with the professor will online and from a distance. Room, board and travel may no longer be barriers to education, and the visa process for foreign students can be skipped altogether. Will professors become educational rock stars, measured by the vastness of their virtual classrooms? It probably still comes down to more than just access to a great mind...

Whatever the platform or delivery vehicle, of course, it really has no raison d'être without a message – content – to carry. To be effective, however, the message must also be appropriate to the audience. Further, in a dynamic world that embraces interactivity, where consumers believe they have a God-given right to complain, respond, reject and "like," this two-way street produces return messages, often reshapes the original communication and all-too-often generates reactions that fall heavily within the notion of damage control and the world of unintended consequences.

On to Rule 2.

Rule 2 – Scaling Up with Appropriate Messages Targeting Appropriate Audiences

The Challenge

We've looked at the platforms and the technologies. Each has parameters that define and shape the nature of communications. Maybe they're not all as limiting as a 140 character tweet or as all-encompassing as *War and* Peace in a book that never seems to end. Yet, one message does not uniformly ride across all platforms and different platforms reach different audiences with varying impact. The degree of interactivity within the medium of choice can also impact the message and, in fact, that interactivity might actually change the underlying message itself. Effective management and marketing have evolved with humanity.

But it all revolves around "communicating" and today, it's more of a two way street than ever before. Think about the earlier days of 20th century communications to the masses. Picture infamous dictators' making speeches to mesmerized crowds as opposed to more economically-driven figures grating with their "Head On – Apply directly to the forehead" or "ring around the collar" advertising campaigns. Mass communications have changed, cultures have intermeshed, population has soared and technology bears little or no resemblance to the communications tools we used just a half century ago.

At the core of this mass of complications is the perceived human need to convince, whether for social, political, religious or commercial purposes. Social interaction almost always results in one person asking (demanding?) something from another. This human proclivity to convince others operates at every level in our lives, from the microcosm of marriage or parenting, to running a multinational corporate conglomerate or marketing a product or a point of view.

As one generation grows up with a new and different set of social habits and technological realities, the way they process and interpret what they see and hear is different. Societies with less technology are less impacted between generations, hardly the case in the industrialized world. As we shall see later, even the notion of what a "generation" really is matters less as the relevant society embraces technology; as increasingly more rapid interval of change creates a world such that a fifty-year-old and a seventy-year-old may have more in common today than a thirty something versus a twenty-plus cohort. As change accelerates, we could see an effective "generation" – meaningfully age-related people who see the world and communicate under the same value and technology system in the same way – drop to below five year spreads.

Further, the younger and more sophisticated the consumer or constituent, the lower the susceptibility to the same repetitive marketing methodologies. Perhaps this is intuitive in a world of hyper-accelerating change, where younger sophisticates are heavily into a "what's next" mindset. Still, this need for something "new" seems to baffle traditionalists who are looking for a set of formulaic structures in which to insert their clever "new" slogans and audio-visual messages. Some of the old rules do apply – like the fact that sadness and emotional depression still have the ability to stimulate consumers to make a purchase. [154] There many more complex variables at work today; marketing is an evolving mix of "old" and "new" methods.

Another old world reality is the assumption that most people are comfortable with brands they know. A lot of advertising targets simply getting the public familiar with a brand. Sometimes we forget the obvious in a search for something more obscure. For example, consumers' drinking exactly the same soft drink are more likely to tell you they like that soda more if the cup they are sipping from has the soft drink's brand on it. [155] Hence, while tailoring doesn't always mean "new" communications techniques, it does mean using *appropriate* messages and methodology. Marketers don't have to abandon the old world; the "old world" simply provides one set of tools *appropriate* for certain communications. But they may also need to know how to find and use the new tools – evolving technology and social patterns – to reach other groups that might not be covered effectively by traditional communications.

Replacing Old Revenues in New Media

For those in industries where the economic models are becoming obsolete, the challenge is often a matter of survival. Hollywood wants people to pay for "appropriate" new content, but the young and the restless seem to want cheap-or-free online alternatives. No one from mainstream media has yet figured out how to generate sufficient new first-run entertainment-content revenues from the Web to replace those perceived to have been lost to "new media." Traditional after-market revenue bases have also found serious challenges from new media platforms.

The motion picture industry, for example, struggled with the plunge in per consumer revenues in packaged media (Hollywood-speak for hard copy devices like DVDs and BluRay discs) as their digital replacements take center stage. But underlying this trend is the offsetting reality that digital delivery is a whole lot cheaper than the old world of pick-pack-ship, and while the per consumer revenues are down, there are a lot more consumers enjoying content in some form of monetized digital platform or another. Even with a modest increase in BluRay usage, the last few years have seen a contraction of almost 30% in U.S.-generated consumer revenues from hard copy home media devices (mostly, the DVD market), rental and sale.

Until late in 2011, the overall trend for such home media – from DVDs to subscription digital delivery to video-on-demand – remained below the aggregate levels once commanded by the DVD market at its peak. Although the net margins to studios climbed from the vastly reduced cost of reaching consumers electronically, the per-viewer revenues had shrunk significantly, although the "you can make it up in volume" for home media of every variety finally kicked in at the end of 2011 and has been growing ever since.[156]

However, as films are now present in inexpensive online subscription services, a la Netflix, [157] or purchased by consumers in digital formats and either sitting in home computers, but more likely in cloud-based services, no one really knows what this lingering availability of films will do to the longer-term value of films on old world media, like television, where once exclusive windows determined pricing.

One version of this model of content monetization – getting consumers to subscribe to highly-niched entertainment content services with very limited choice – is probably unsustainable. Except for highly specialized data bases, primarily relegated to business and academia, the subscription model only works if the price is relatively low and the choice is rather large. And if there is a lesson to be learned from today's massive ubiquitous access to content, legal and not-so-legal, it may simply be that for most purposes, true exclusivity is simply not possible anymore.

Content providers, from cell phone carriers to telecasters, from home video retailers to internet distributors, need to embrace this reality and "just deal with it." Adaptation must replace intransigence. Simultaneous availability will increasingly be the rule, and for those who resist, an uptake in piracy will be their reward. No wonder the long-term value of audio-visual libraries is on the decline, particularly where the product cannot or does not generate new derivative (e.g., spin-offs) or ancillary values (like toys or video games). But monetization in many new media is still an uncharted path.

Some Hollywood executives have written-off the Internet and have fallen back on trying to control or stop change through legislation. Big media continues to believe that legal remedies will save the business. As Hollywood was unable to overcome the

Silicon Valley juggernaut in 2012 to pass the Stop Online Piracy Act, the echoes of voices past seemed to rant unchanged within the mainstream entertainment community.

For example, back on May 14, 2009, HollywoodReporter.com provided this classic example: "Michael Lynton, chairman & CEO of Sony Pictures Entertainment [the parent of Columbia Pictures]...decried what he described as the consistently negative impact of the Internet on the film business... 'I am a guy who hasn't seen any good come out of the Internet,' said Lynton, a former CEO of AOL Europe and president of AOL International. 'It seems to have done damage to every (part) of the entertainment business.' ... Lynton called on Washington to draw up rules that would protect copyrighted material instead of only focusing on expanding the availability of broadband across the U.S."

While Lynton acknowledged the promotional value of the Web in marketing movies, he was watching revenue projections erode as technology continues to change in ways that Hollywood has no capacity to contain. The merger of the Web and traditional television – as technology platforms, some even created and sold by his own parent company, [158] are charging ahead, sowing the seeds for the disintermediation of traditional television networks and channels.

Despite the fact that Hollywood keeps losing these "Congress please protect us" and "consumers have to stop being thieves" battles, the words still come out the same. The world of commercial motion pictures is rapidly morphing from a series of sequential and exclusive "windows" of exploitation into release in theaters and "other," with even these two alternatives on the verge of overlapping.

Mobile technology and bandwidth have improved, increasing screen capacity – size, quality as well as speed – which has generated a nascent creative industry that mimics old-world television and goes beyond the snippets associated with YouTube. Original, longer-form series programming have come to the Web, and the economics, once again, are driven by advertising and, except for sports, not subscriptions. But audience-building takes patience, money and occasionally dumb luck after lots of experimentation, assuming that the content is compelling.

Former *Friends* star Lisa Kudrow has a relatively successful comedy, *Web Therapy*, which has found traction, as has *Robert Townsend's Diary of a Single Mom*. Comedy remains the prevalent online series genre, but dramas have begun to find their audience as well. Programs like *Downsized* (a recession-themed program), *Anyone But*

Me (lesbian relationships) and *The Bannen Way* (a crime drama) have reached and captured a meaningful audience. The latter generated "a high-quality pilot to shop around before landing a deal with Sony, which eventually led to 13 million streams of the show on Sony's Crackle site ... and there are murmurs of developing it into a television series."[159]

Yet the path to revenues from Web-delivered video content still eludes the big players in both Hollywood and the Silicon Valley. Or does it? YouTube was supposed to be the platinum standard for monetizing video content on the Web. But notwithstanding the studio deal-making frenzy described above and the fact that when Google acquired YouTube, everyone marveled at what was perceived as an astute acquisition of a powerful content delivery system.

To some, YouTube still *appears to be* a massive loss-leader. The Web service reports two billion video streams a day and over 800 million unique users per year. Over seventy-two hours of videos are uploaded every minute! Experts believe this to be at an estimated delivery cost of $2.64 million per day ($753 million per year): "Depending on whose version of revenues you accept, Google is losing anywhere from $513 million to $663 million annually on YouTube," according to David Silverman of Internet Evolution. [160]

However, when I asked the "are you profitable yet" question of YouTube co-founder, Chad Hurley, at the end of May 2009, he just smiled and noted that while YouTube never releases its internal financial information, "revenues are going up as costs are going down." I can only image how much the bottom line has grown by 2013. The overall U.S. online content consumption numbers are staggering. For example, "182.5 million Americans watched 39.3 billion online content videos in March 2013."[161] Even by as early as mid-2009, YouTube had reached almost half a million daily video uploads and he had every reason to smile.

It is estimated that this video platform (also a search engine[162]) accounts for half of the video uploads worldwide, and 70% of YouTube's reach is outside of the United States. As of its fifth anniversary in the spring of 2010, YouTube had become a massive platform of mostly-user-generated content, but some ask if large-scale, revenue-generating, mainstream studio movies have still eluded this giant to date. Uploads have doubled and consumer usage increased by 50 percent from 2009 to early 2011. With growth numbers like that, it seems obvious that YouTube's time for substantial profitability is not too far off – assuming that this secretive Google subsidiary isn't already seriously in the black. Press reports in the late summer of 2010 "leaked" that

YouTube, contrary to assumptions of many in the financial press, might already be profitable.[163]

Looking for a "second act" to its mainstream search capacity, Google appears increasingly focused on monetizing YouTube by making it the "platform of choice" for pay-per-view Hollywood mainstream film and television providers and encouraging commercial copyright holders to opt for ad share revenues over take-down notices.[164] Overseas, YouTube already fares better with mainstream content. For example, in January of 2010, it premiered a Bollywood thriller day and date with the theatrical release in India, generating just shy of a million views of the movie (the company did not release the underlying revenues generated, however).[165]

The Web is also rife with efforts to create virtual networks online with several examples worthy of note. After leaving Fox News in the spring of 2011, controversial and conservative television columnist Glenn Beck opted to create a subscription-based Internet television network (GBTV.com) to carry his message and substitute for the revenues lost when he left mainstream broadcast and cable television. The subscription fee runs viewers "$4.95 a month for Beck's 5 p.m. show only, or $9.95 for full access to the network."[166] Whether this model succeeds may not easily be ascertained since the financials are not publicly available. But Mr. Beck is betting that his loyal following will generate enough to sustain programming and show a healthy profit.

Well-known media and technology journalist, Leo Laporte has taken one particularly interesting step with an advertiser-supported online television network. State-of-the-art equipment [167] allows a rather easy ability to aggregate content from multiple sources and air distant interviews via Skype. This highly cost-effective equipment allows Laporte to mimic a much more elegant broadcast network with minimal cost and present his tech-based programming to his extensive existing audience on TWiT.tv. Because programming is based mostly on Laporte-generated content and materials that are otherwise available without cost, the sustainability threshold for such a network is very affordable. But for others, the Web is a test-market for broader commercial potential.

Until a more linear method develops of marketing new series programming on the Internet, the value of tapped established brands offers a viable alternative. The Web may find that cancelled television programs, where a sufficient number of loyal fans remain, could find an online afterlife. In the fall of 2011, through the efforts of Webcaster Prospect Park in the fall of 2011, addictive television soap operas *One Life to*

Live and *All My Children* were contracted to move online with new episodes after being cancelled by ABC, albeit at significantly reduced budgets. Unfortunately, economic realities may have doomed this effort as premature when Prospect Park seemed to collapse. But the future melding of these media is inevitable.

Might the values for mainstream content providers lie in treating YouTube simply as a content incubator and evaluation system – an audience test-site? Presently, the path to commercial viability of placing mainstream content on YouTube as a primary medium of exploitation appears to be a very expensive mission (read: marketing costs) with seemingly insurmountable economics. Smaller companies with more focused (and cheaper) directives are better suited to mine grassroots creativity to find hot ideas for films that might find their way to your local theater or perhaps on old world television. One such company, California-based Blowtorch (with $50 million from venture capitalists), tried to create a mix of social networking with the production of short films and features by professionals as well as providing a platform for selected amateur videos. Unfortunately, the effort failed.

Blowtorch believed that professional features based on content and creative elements that have been selected and voted upon by its user-base could score big at the box office. The theory has yet to find proof of concept. Was Blowtorch too early or was the plan dead on arrival? As new audio-visual concepts fly out of the minds of those sufficiently creative to invent them, the new digital media does offer a way to test commercial viability, eliminating the traditional film or television distributor middleman.

Some advertisers have resorted to disintermediation out of necessity. The North American National Hockey League, for example, struggled to find national broadcast and local cable networks to carry its games. According to the September 23, 2008 *Wall Street Journal* (page B8), " The NHL's national broadcasts in the U.S. are carried on the little-known cable channel Versus; fewer than a dozen hockey games a season are televised on NBC Universal's NBC network." The NHL's answer? A new Internet streaming service, Game-Center Live, that charges a pricey $169 per year subscription fee to avid fans who might not otherwise have an opportunity to view their favorite team on television (because the team moved out of market or there is no local telecast).[168]

One way or another, the writing is on the wall for traditional network telecasters. Most certainly, the notion of a traditional prime time schedule as a part of the season line-up of programming is almost history. The big changes occurred before the economic crash. With a drop of over 21% in major broadcast network prime time viewers over one year (as measured in April of 2008) – 6 million people – the question is where have they all gone? Have they simply stopped watching television?

Cable networks saw *increased* viewership, but the bigger winners seem to be alternative opportunities to view the same program, or at least the "best" segments in many new formats, from mobile phones [169] to the Internet. *Time-shifting* continues to gain ground. Viewers are increasingly determining when and where they will be consuming their favorite shows; younger demos have even cut the cable cord entirely and view their programming though online and mobile access wherever and whenever they choose.

But television content is no longer simply a message delivered within a specified time via one medium, even if it is time shifted. "Since viewer entry points are more numerous than ever, content producers have attempted to drive increasingly diminished audiences between media platforms as a means of feeding sponsors, the network, and parent media conglomerates. Broadcast networks are also increasingly using these different platforms to establish and reinforce ties between their content and branded identities." [170]

Supplemental information, additional programming, behind-the-scenes views, click-through links to further site and advertiser websites are often found on networks' parallel websites, but oddly, it is the website that often generates the initial (and often only) viewing of the subject matter. U.S. broadcast network NBC amplified its reach during the 2012 summer Olympics to numerous parallel websites and commonly-owned channels, offering advertisers myriad hooks to reach targeted consumers.

 But metrics still terrify traditional telecasters, especially when applied to individual television ads. They still stay steer clear of such ratings for individual commercials (very easily measured), and advertising revenue models often embrace cross-platform packages (adding Web and mobile-based components to a standard media buy on the telecaster), estimates on DVR usage (but isn't this an ad-skipping model?) as well as so-called "product integration." [171]

Nielsen and Google[172] are tracking DVR viewers, and what they are finding is not entirely all bad news.[173] As advertisers create images that intrigue consumers as they fast-forward through commercials, occasionally, they stop and look when a well-designed image (something that looks good in a fleeting moment) catches their eye.

Movie trailer-ads and teasers for television programs were the most likely to be "stopped and viewed" by consumers zipping through commercials.[174] The campaign for the film *Forgetting Sarah Marshall*, for example, scored particularly high in this arena. Even ads for certain products (e.g., Glaceau Vitamin Water) have enough imagery to draw speeding viewers to stop and watch. Thus, it behooves those who do create ads to create attractive visuals that work at fast forward speed to lure viewers.

In the United States, election and Olympic years can be the drivers of change, with deep and desperate coffers ready to spend to deliver a critical message to defined demographics. 2012 saw both phenomena, amplified with the uncorking of SuperPACs' wallets,[175] and ad sales were up at major networks by high-end single and even low-end double digits as result. The same result occurred four years earlier, albeit at significantly lower dollar numbers because the floodgates of SuperPAC contributions had not yet been unlocked.

Despite predictions of doom and gloom and the depressed ratings noted above and the reality of DVR time-shifting,[176] up-front traditional network ad sales for the fall 2008 major network broadcast season actually rose by almost 10% over the previous year. But even with good ad sales numbers, the atmosphere was still tense as everyone seemed to feel that the existing telecasting model was approaching an uncomfortable paradigm shift. With neither events occurring in 2009, exacerbated by one of the worst years of the recession, ad sales plunged. It seems that good TV ad years are no longer based on overall economic growth, but more on specialized events that are television-friendly.

Numbers had already begun to slide before the crisis. The near term economic realities that decimated the financial markets were certain to create massive cutbacks in advertising and marketing expenditures [177] – a most significant driving force in media, communications and entertainment – well beyond a short-term negative blip in this market. [178]

The huge reduction in automotive advertising, due to the obvious economic catastrophes besetting automakers, was just the tip of the iceberg. Businesses targeting consumers reluctant to spend money on non-necessaries contracted their ad budgets to reflect economic reality. Despite network claims that the recession would only drop buys by 10%, those on the inside projected vastly steeper declines. Some suggested triple the losses).

Rates for single spot ads placed in the biggest network live events (e.g., Super Bowl, Academy Awards, etc.), seemed to fall as well. While NBC touted a record sales year for the 2009 Super Bowl, the program was peppered with ads from Universal Pictures and General Electric; three affiliated companies, which report consolidated earnings, were effectively paying *themselves* for these ads. Ad *rates* fell slightly to a still whopping $2.5-$3 million per 30 second spot. That ad-rate was sustained by CBS for the Super Bowl 2010, selling all its spots a few weeks before the February event. Over time, the numbers crept up. With more pre-planning needed to coordinate parallel social media campaigns and an uptick in the economy, Fox's Super Bowl 2014 sold out all of its ads by early December 2013 (at $4+ million per 30 second spot).

Still, the networks have become masters of deceptive financial reporting. They prevent "apples-to-apples" comparisons by changing the labels and packages they use, year-by-year, in selling ads. It makes comparison of like kinds of statistics more difficult. First, It's important to understand how networks report increases in ad sales: on a cost-per-thousand ("CPM") viewers reached basis. Thus, even if a network's overall viewership (ratings) might be contracting (as most are), their cost-per-thousand number might still be rising. As networks reported increases of 10-12% in up-front ad sales in 2011 over 2010, [179] for example, this was not a reflection if the total pie, just the CPM.

When a network sells out up-front ads [180] at a particularly high dollar value, those sales are dependent on programs' generating significant ratings. Remember, they are selling CPMs. If the programs fail to meet expectations as they very often do, the network then has to deliver free "make-goods" to the advertiser who made the original purchase in order to fulfill the cost-per-thousand promise. Since only the original numbers are high, statistically, it looks as though the network had a successful year. However, after the adjustment for actual performance and a reduction in total viewers, the actual average revenue-per-ad winds up being significantly less than the numbers might otherwise have suggested. Thus, the true economic "gain" – according to insiders – drops to pretty much "flat."

Further, the occurrence of non-annual major events – such as the Olympics and election years – can have material impact on aggregated dollar ad spends, making correcting for recessionary variables that much more complex. To make matters even more difficult, telecasters have moved to a practice of selling advertising attached to a particular program in bulk, traveling as the program is telecast on sister networks or even on the network's own Website. Without elections or major events, the writing for traditional broadcast networks is on the wall. "[In the first quarter of 2013, a] combination of low ratings and a sluggish ad market accounted for the 9% drop in the average price of a 30-second primetime spot on broadcast network TV versus [2012's] Q1."[181] Cable, Web-driven and broadcast networks continue to slant their metrics to reflect "success" at reaching consumers, but one must be increasingly skeptical of the numbers without a deeper analysis of their true meaning and accuracy.

Of late, traditional broadcast networks also focused slightly less on the "reality" programming and added much more in the way of advertiser-friendly scripted series to their fall schedules. [182] Closer examination of many of these numbers suggests a lot of activity between related companies as well as sales based on higher-than-expected ratings contingencies. For those in the know, however, there is still little reason to expect a massive resurgence in television ad sales, [183] although the broadcast networks have been successful in convincing many advertisers that they are the only truly national medium with a large-scale reach.

Even successful companies are re-examining big broadcast network spending practices. Their media allocations are gravitating away from the mega-costly, annual-event-driven advertising blasts. In 2009, for example, soft-drink-maker Pepsi spent close to $33 million creating commercials and buying media time in connection with the Super Bowl. [184]

In recession-plagued 2010, Pepsi downsized that money to $20 million. The soft-drink giant also elected not to sponsor that American football classic and instead mounted a non-traditional campaign in which consumers were asked to vote online as to how Pepsi should spend that sum in the form of charitable grants. Calling their effort the "Refresh Project," Pepsi asked the U.S. public to vote regarding potential contributions "to a number of health, environment, culture, and education-related organizations.

Pepsi [gave] away multiple grants each month, including two $250,000 grants, ten $50,000 grants, and ten $25,000 grants. Visitors [were] also encouraged to submit their own organizations and grant ideas."[185] The campaign provided direct interactivity between potential consumers and a sponsor enhancing both Pepsi's general reputation and its perception in the press plus the general public, benefitting local charities aimed at veterans and returning troops, local "green" projects, literacy as well as programs targeting obesity and providing food and shelter for the poor, to name a few.

For most in broadcast television, the writing is seared onto the wall. According to the second quarter of Emmy Magazine: [186] "In 2009 the owners of more than 150 TV stations [in the United States] either declared bankruptcy or were in severe danger of defaulting on their loans … When Comcast Corporation recently bid to buy NBC Universal, the plum of the deal was thought to be the venerable peacock network [NBC]. But Comcast placed virtually no value on the network or its stations, says analyst Chris Marangi of Gabelli & Company … In the face of this financial storm, it was still rattling when Brian McNeill, managing director of Alta Communications, a venture capital firm heavily invested in media, told the FCC [U.S. Federal Communications Commission] at a recent public hearing that the owners of 90 percent of all [U.S.] TV stations are on 'the cusp of default or in [default] workout or already in bankruptcy.' Later he said he 'doesn't know if there is a solution, other than a long, painful financial restructuring of the whole industry.'"

These trends generate obvious questions. Why actually buy ads on specific programs anyway? Isn't that very old world? If advertisers want to release campaigns at specific and targeted psychographics, wouldn't it be more efficient to use a new kind of aggregator – one that aggregates content across many platforms that have already been predetermined to reach defined psychographic segments? The aggregator knows the psychographic weight of specific programs, networks and media based on extensive behavioral analysis.

When an advertiser wants a particular reach, the aggregator takes the message, modified for different platforms, and places that campaign through a complex spread across various platforms that all converge on that specific psychographic. Media time and space is no longer bought and sold the old way on a television network or on a group of Websites. Rather, advertisers typically buy a scattered and computer-generated placement, through an aggregator, across many platforms that all have one thing in common – they reach the targeted audience. More than one psychographic? The scattered placement is weighted according to audience priorities, and the computer automatically sends the ads to the right consumers, whether on network television or MySpace depending on where the most likely potential buyers are.

The future will generate increasing sophisticated psychographic placement aggregators, but they already exist today, often in an "ad exchange" model. [187] The old simple television ad does not seem to fit in this more modern environment. A television network may soon be relegated to history books. In August of 2009, YouTube widened its monetization model and brought amateur videos closer to a mainstream television model. Up to that point, YouTube had only accorded revenue-sharing to professional content suppliers.

The Web service announced that – as long as there are no issues with underlying rights – the makers of high-traffic amateur videos (even "one-hit wonders") will be asked if they will accept advertising to be associated with the video. The content creators would then share in the resulting revenue flow. This arrangement had only been accorded to those who produced consistent hits. But with this democratization, YouTube would be giving benefits even to amateurs. This revenue-sharing structure (though ad sales aggregation) looks a lot like the defining value of traditional television, though what is an ad *associated* with the specific content (vs. the overall site) is still up for debate. In a world where media are converging, the YouTube model suggests that the program and ad sales aggregation of "television" are no longer special or unique.

Disintermediation of Traditional Television

Even highly placed industry insiders see the end of traditional television networks: "Warner Bros. TV's president said the studios will bypass broadcast networks next decade using broadband and cellular. 'We will go directly to consumers with content,' President Bruce Rosenblum said [February 19, 2008] in a notably candid insider's talk to Stanford law students. 'Your generation' is witnessing 'a complete disaggregation of the networks,' he said. Warner leads in supplying prime-time shows to the networks, and going around those big customers will usher in an era that will be very expensive for this business but offer it exciting prospects, said Rosenblum, [then] 50. 'The sad part is, I won't see it,' he said. 'That's five to 10 years away.'" [188]

We actually might not have to wait that long. As the market crashed in the fall of 2008, Wall Street sent a resounding message to the old world of traditional media: we don't believe in the sustainability of your economic assumptions anymore.

The disruptive transitions in media were only hastened by the economic downturn. Traditional broadcast television, for example, had seen decades of erosion, both as to the number of viewers and the particularly harsh loss of the younger demographics. Cash-strapped advertisers fled in droves from their network advertising commitments.

When the market crashed in 2008, CBS was the only stand-alone broadcast network stock. It fell through the floor to a whopping 70%+ below its then-recent high share price. [189] This was in spite of the fact that, when compared to the other broadcast networks, CBS had a relatively reasonable ratings experience in the fall season premier. [190] NBC announced that it was considering revamping the very nature of its network programming, perhaps reducing the hours in prime time or the actual number of evenings covered by the network at all.

NBC moved late-night talk-show host Jay Leno into the third hour of what was still referred to as weeknight "prime time" to meet new budgetary restraints. The news was hardly greeted with uniform enthusiasm. Some affiliated stations simply saw the move as NBC mounting an underwhelming and transparent cost-savings experiment at the expense of mainstream ratings. An NBC affiliate in Leno's hometown of Boston initially balked at carrying this 10 PM program at all, but finally relented. [191]

It was clear to industry experts that the traditional broadcast business model was lingering on fragile life support systems. The prognosis for a "resumption of business as usual" when the markets correct was relegated to the category of unsustainable mythology. [192] While the Leno "experiment" failed and the program was pulled from prime time and moved back to its late-night slot in February of 2010, broadcast network television was already becoming a second class citizen in a universe populated with rapidly growing cable networks, generating revenues from both subscribers and advertisers.

The old world broadcast behemoth's ability to pay for the high budget dramatic programming on which they built their reputations seemed to erode, literally disappearing, in the big meltdown. [193] As advertisers decreased their advertising expenditures, the high-value, bigger budget production network programming theories – already age-challenged – seemed to be in the throes of a "dance of death."

Viewing trends reveal the decline of traditional broadcast audience appeal over the decades. Since Fox wasn't around at the beginning, let's look at the overall reach of the American networks that did exist at the time: ABC, NBC and CBS. These three major networks reached 75% of the American audience in the 1950s, 51% of that audience in the 1980s and 18% of the audience today. [194]

The New York Times [195] distilled the conundrum facing the traditional broadcast networks: "The business model of the big three networks — which became four when Fox began prime-time programming in 1987 — has for decades relied on a simple formula: spend millions on original programming that will attract advertiser dollars and later live on as lucrative reruns in syndication … But ratings are going down. In the 1952-53 television seasons, more than 30 percent of American households that owned televisions tuned in to NBC during prime time, according to Nielsen. In the 2007-8 season, that figure was just 5.2 percent."

The Times also makes the most obvious and fundamental observation: "Most analysts and many executives agree that the economic model of broadcast television — which relies much more heavily on advertising than cable — is severely fractured. What they are wondering now is if it is irreparably broken." Costs for scripted dramas on these networks have soared to an average of $3 million an hour. Reality programs have seemingly saturated the airways to the breaking point.

There is a very real question whether the standard advertising-driven broadcast model can sustain against the cable network model of some advertising mixed with subscriber revenues, and whether any type of traditional "network" model – including cable – can sustain against ubiquitous content distribution channels. [196] Previously relegated to advertising revenues (often shared with affiliates), the broadcast networks have therefore begun to press cable systems that carry their signal for a share of subscriber fees.

The major broadcast networks are now just a couple of selections in a vast ocean of available channels. Too much choice actually results in consumers' weeding out entire channels of content that they never access. Rule One again, enforced by the consumers' own determination of what is appropriate for them. But as consumers narrow-focus which channels they really watch, subscriber and advertising values, already slammed by a tough economy, fall further. Cable and satellite providers often try to generate additional consumer activity by grouping similarly themed networks (e.g., documentary-type channels) in adjacent numbered slots.

The Wall Street Journal[197] noted: "It is doubtful [American] viewers want as many [channels] as they have. In 2007, the average household tuned into only 16 channels of the 118 channels available … Indeed, the explosion of channels was driven by cable operators' need for a marketing tool to convince people to pay for more choice, given the presence of free broadcast TV. That gave rise to a system where channels developed for cable are paid affiliate fees by cable and satellite operators. Broadcast networks, which individually draw much bigger audiences, generally don't receive fees [a fact which is beginning to change]."

But what happens in a digital universe, particularly post-June 12, 2009 (when U.S. analog broadcast television went all-digital) where the dividing line between Internet-delivered and traditional telecasting blurs? Google TV was announced and implemented in the last quarter of 2010, appearing on Sony's newest flat screens almost immediately. It allows viewers to use their television sets to search the Web (through Google TV, of course) for streamable versions of their favorite shows. ABC, NBC and CBS responded immediately by blocking full-length episodes of their primetime shows from the Google platform.

But the ability of viewers to access Web-seated programming is going to be normal in most new television sets coming onto the market.[198] Is it just a matter of time before networks and channels are simply replaced by direct access to specific shows? Perhaps that's why cable giant Comcast focused on buying control of content-heavy NBC/Universal.

Every year, the number of cable and satellite subscribers in the United States who "cut the cord" and go directly to the Web for programming increases. 2012 saw a decline of over one million such former cable/satellite consumers. While online access to televised content generates revenues in most quarters from paid downloads or subscriptions or advertiser-supported sites that parallel network programming, cable content providers like HBO who offer their content online only to their cable subscribers face spikes in piracy over their restricted and proprietary content.

This trend has effectively begun the process of "de-bundling" the mandatory basic package of networks that cable and satellite subscribers have to purchase from their local providers and augurs badly, particularly for those niched channels at the bottom of consumer preference list. Consumers thus would only pay for the channels or programs they actually watch. With the cost of sports programming demanding huge fee increases, the pressures on consumers is approaching a very hard wall. Even among mainstream channels, current conditions are anything but comfortable.

With monthly cable and satellite bills rising to levels that actually encourage consumers to cut the cord (or avoid ever having a cord), the battle of channels seeking higher retransmission fees has gotten downright ugly. When Time Warner Cable dropped U.S. broadcast network giant CBS (including its Showtime affiliate) from its cable service in the summer of 2013 over that network's per subscriber fee demands, TWC's offer to let consumers decide by offering CBS as an a la cart choice was instantly and powerfully rejected by an angry Les Moonves, CBS' CEO. And while this dispute was eventually settled, the road to a la cart service seems increasingly inevitable.

However, Lazard Capital Markets' Barton Crockett maintains that such de-bundling would not have as great an impact as expected: "Crockett bases his conclusion on two assumptions: Consumers would continue to spend $78B a year on pay TV. And, in a post-bundle world, content creators could collect all of that instead of settling for the $32B in program fees that they currently receive from distributors. Actors or producers wouldn't try to appeal directly to consumers, cutting out Big Media companies, because they need someone who will 'write big checks, and take care of the administrative hassles of marketing and distribution,' he says. 'Anyone can make a singing competition, but networks like Fox and NBC can make them popular by touting them to large audiences, and investing large sums for the highest profile judges and best production values.'" [199] Crockett sees more money going to the high-value channels with serious erosion at the bottom of the channel list.[200] Nevertheless, it is hard to believe that such standard cable/satellite delivery will remotely survive into a future of consumer-constructed "personal networks" based on individual choices and software that guides appropriate content, based on observed preferences, into that consumer's wheelhouse.

Indeed, if you look at YouTube as an audio-visual superhighway, the backbone for anyone with the financial resources and reach to configure a new media network, the possibilities are endless. It is indeed the "great disruptor," the medium that has made the greatest inroads in bringing TV-like content to consumers from a different medium. What's more, it seems as if the ad linkage to even their short content has been relatively effective. [201] Heavy YouTube content suppliers are often able to generate their own sales, even amplifying the values that they can generate with successful content.

Demand Media – which launched a "content farm" of very cheap "how to" programming over YouTube – was successful at first. They generated a ten figure public offering providing users instructional videos (e.g., using its eHow library of videos). Complex algorithms tracked and analyzed what Web consumers were searching for, identifying demands for information and then creating the responsive low cost content. Demand had its own ad sales staff with a negotiated a reverse revenue sharing agreement with YouTube. Could this format be the next generation of "television?" Did its ultimate failure to compete with quality completion teach us an additional lesson? Even without the losses inflicted when Google's search filters vastly reduced Demand's access to consumers, its share price quickly fell.

Yet *television isn't dead*. Far from it. Higher quality content matters. While traditional broadcast networks have dropped in audience reach, Americans (and the rest of the world) are spending more hours in front of that screen. [202] A bad economy might reduce the capability of advertisers to buy ad time, but that same economy produces an incentive for people to watch a free or relatively inexpensive medium.

As people grow older, not surprisingly, television viewing increases and the average age of American television viewers rises. [203] We may only select an average of 16 channels out of the universe of cable networks, but that may in fact help identify audience segments to potential advertisers. After all, it's not the same 16 channels for everyone. The latest trends place television everywhere; programming availability is spreading beyond the broadcast, cablecast spectrum or even computer access onto our mobile phones. [204]

The trend lines say it all. "Consider that the average American household consists of 2.7 persons and contains 2.9 television sets, in front of which we sit for record-setting spells, according to Nielsen figures. In the quarter ended Sept. 30 [2008], the typical American watched 142 hours of television monthly, up about five hours from the same quarter the previous year. Internet use averaged more than 27 hours monthly, which was an increase of an hour and a half, according to Nielsen." [205] By 2011, the extra "free" time from hefty unemployment numbers kicked average U.S. monthly viewing averages up to 154 hours and 5 minutes according to Nielsen data.[206]

Sitting and watching traditional television in the United States still skews towards the very young (children), those over 30 years of age with pockets of certain demographics, notably African-Americans, still heavy consumers. With cable networks (e.g., BET, OWN and Aspire) focused on strong African-American demographics, programming acquisitions like Paramount Home Media Distribution's buying product for its "Brown Sugar Saturday Night" weekly presentation and BounceTV's over-the-air network programming targeting African-Americans, U.S. advertisers are eager to reach a market segment that watches more traditional television than any other.

"The demographic also tends to be tech-savvy. African-Americans are 14% younger than the American population as a whole. Additionally, the median age for African-Americans is 32, and 54% of the Black population is under the age of 35, according to Nielsen/NPAA. African-Americans over-index on cell phone use, and a growing percentage watch television while multitasking on their mobile device, laptop or notebook, according to BET's EVP of corporate research Matthew Barnhill." [207] This is just one example of how cultural patterns impact appropriate messages in appropriate media.

Program consumption is developing new viewing patterns across the entire demographic spectrum. Even Internet usage overlaps television-watching. "We are so smitten with screens that we often can't bear to choose one over another: 31 percent of Internet use occurs while we're in front of a TV set. We are also taking an interest in watching video on our phones: 100 million handsets are video-capable ... Hulu [the Internet service that re-"broadcasts" television programs, which tends to have a younger audience], which was created by NBC and Fox, offers many TV shows online and had a 57 percent increase in viewership in the last six months of 2008." [208] While under-30 viewers are increasing intrigued with Internet and mobile delivery of television content, numbers suggest that the death knell for traditional television may be a ways off; "cutting the cord" hasn't yet destroyed the old model. [209]

Some claim that the Web is a place where only pirated materials can succeed. Indeed, the path to monetizing content is a very uncomfortable road, as the music industry has discovered. While purveyors of content try and find new ways to make money from Web-delivered product, DVD-mail-order-rental-house Netflix is already at the forefront. Netflix used its U.S. subscriber base to stream films to their existing paying consumers, an experiment which has become one of the Internet's greatest success stories. Netflix dominates the American Internet in the evening, accounting for slightly below one third of all consumer traffic at that time period. [210]

In the case of one motion picture production company, Relativity Media, this streaming model substitutes for the traditional (but now-difficult-to-obtain) premium pay cable television output arrangements (where a cable system buys pay television rights to an entire studio's film output for a given term, typically provided by HBO, Showtime and Starz in the U.S.). DreamWorks Animation quickly followed suit, with a new U.S. Netflix deal kicking immediately after its current traditional pay television deals expire, potentially generating as much as $25-30 million a title according to inside sources. Then art film supplier, The Weinstein Company, joined this mini-bandwagon in substituting Netflix for such traditional cable deals.

For others, notably the Epix venture (between Lionsgate, MGM and Paramount), Netflix' Web streaming is postponed until at least 90 days after titles debut on premium pay services. This generates a whopping $1 billion over five years to these Epix partners. [211] As of March of 2013, according to its own Website, "Netflix is the world's leading Internet television network with more than 33 million members in 40 countries enjoying more than one billion hours of TV shows and movies per month, including Netflix original series." Over 80 percent of those subscribers are, however, U.S.-based. Funny how they describe themselves as a television *network*. Sometimes old world terms just take a very long time to die.

Netflix' deal with Relativity has one other component that enhances its impact: It "did not place any restriction or where or when [Netflix] could offer its content for streaming to other platforms, unlike [major] studios' output deal with HBO and other pay cablers." [212]   If disintermediation is to wreak its havoc on the system, content owners need to be able to place their products on any and all available platforms without restriction. But aftermarket buyers (like television syndicators) are still fighting for that elusive exclusivity that appears to defy the very essence of modern digital delivery. Such platform agnostic deals remain a rarity in Hollywood.

On one small and perhaps overlooked disintermediating moment by the Finnish company Rovio Entertainment – the creator of the mega-successful mobile *Angry Birds* casual game – was its launch of its own "Angry Birds Toons" content platform in March of 2013. Essentially, this new capacity turned every app that offers the game into an outlet for its new short (about 3 minutes each) animated series. Thus, Rovio's content will find its way onto virtually all mobile platforms and travel equally well to in-home televisions via Web-connected sets.

Rovio claims access to 1.7 billion screens around the world, but the big news is how they completely skipped over (disintermediated) traditional Hollywood telecasters (and their international equivalents), thus retaining the entire value proposition for these productions. Spin-off values for bigger productions will rise as Rovio has both marketing and delivery access to audience levels most entertainment companies can only dream about. Is the handwriting on the wall to so-called "syndicators" that their life expectancy is in serious jeopardy? Content aggregation seems to have taken one giant step away from traditional gatekeepers!

But even in the world of traditional television, old world "broadcast networks" are finding technological challenges that seem to betray their quest to protect their unique content delivery platforms. For example, Aereo provides a service to consumers in New York, Boston, Denver, Atlanta, Baltimore, Dallas, Miami, Houston, Detroit and

Salt Lake City, enabling fee-based subscribers to view and/or time shift over-the-air local broadcast programs over consumers' more convenient platforms and mobile devices.

The catch is that Aereo began its service without negotiating for specific rights from the telecasters, claiming that since the content was free over the air, this was not taking something away from them. So far, while there conflicting decisions elsewhere, several courts have agreed with Aereo, which has prompted some major sports leagues to threaten withdrawing from TV and more than one network to rethink over-the-air transmission completely.

In early April of 2013, at a National Association of Broadcasters event, News Corporation (owner of Fox Broadcasting and now part of the 21st Century Fox spin-off) CEO Chase Carey suggested that his over-the-air network might have to considerer dropping that transmission technique in favor of the new streaming technology used by companies like Netflix or simply to become a pay channel in the satellite/cable/telco world.

"'We need to be fairly compensated for our content,' he said on stage at the NAB Show in Las Vegas. He added that it's not an 'ideal path' for Fox but one that might be necessary if a company like Aereo continues to 'steal our signal.' In a statement released by News Corp. following Carey's NAB session, the company said: 'We simply cannot provide the type of quality sports, news, and entertainment content that we do from an ad-supported only business model. We have no choice but to develop business solutions that ensure we continue to remain in the driver's seat of our own destiny. One option would be converting the Fox broadcast network to a pay channel.'"[213]

In a world where content can be taken and redistributed by convenience re-packagers, is there a value proposition to such mainstream telecasters that might actually enhance their revenue positions? Take for example Boxee TV, a hardware solution to aggregating all form of television (from Web to over-the-air), linking social networking and consumer-to-consumer communication with content, to enable consumers to see it all on their home screens. But Boxee faced resistance from content providers, and they have been constantly changing their approach since they first entered the market in 2008.

Their newest solution focuses on moving their digital video recorder functionality from the living room to a massive off-site file server (the "clouds"), offering consumers a monthly subscription service with much more storage capacity.

Boxee CEO Avner Ronen responded to News Corp's CEO's complaints about Aereo at the April NAB gathering with a better economic opportunity: "Our pitch to [telecasters] is if we move the DVR to the cloud, we can do dynamic ad insertion, so instead of losing the ability to monetize that audience if they're watching a week later or binge viewing if they've recorded the entire season, if you could serve fresh ads whenever somebody is watching it … that is a better way to monetize DVR."

Clearly, their technology has gathered traction despite industry challenges, and we can expect to see these capacities incorporated in the next generation of televisions; in 2013, Boxee found a little salvation by being acquired by electronics giant Samsung. With change, some must die so that others can live. War is hell, but the underlying pressure from mobile seems to be an even bigger disruptor in audio-video content delivery than anyone could possibly have imagined just a few short years ago.

Specifically, mobile is taking on more significance as telephones and tablet technology improves. It is not inconceivable that a significant portion of the viewership will come from this delivery system versus the Web. Even Web-driven telephone services, like Skype and ooVoo, offer the potential of becoming content platforms on their own someday. There are obvious values to getting more content to more consumers, even if the revenue models need to be revisited and reworked. The dynamics of the various socio-economic strata and their preference for one platform over another also impact how messages are formatted for differing age and economic cohorts.[214]

But the gold doesn't stop with the ability to deliver content on the go anywhere at any time. The nature of the individualized connectivity provides an additional feature that should serve advertisers very well: Big Data on the consumers who are sucking up the content. In the output deal described above, Netflix is sharing valuable consumer data with Relativity. But the competition out there is fierce. When Warner Bros. announced a pay-per-view alliance with Facebook in March of 2011, for example, Netflix stock took an immediate 5.8% hit. [215]

Watching audio-visual content on an electronic screen sure mirrors television viewing, but is it *in fact* television viewing? Exactly what is "television," or "cable television?" Are people watching content focused on what platform is providing the service anymore? Does it matter how you get the signal? Are tablets or mobile phones that different from small televisions? Are such devices simply alternative screens, an entirely new medium or somewhere in between? Does it matter that they get a Wi-Fi signal from your home, office or a 3G or 4G wireless link? If a traditional television series starts out on a network but is canceled and it is continued in another medium, is it still a television series? [216] And what media rights do you have to own or control to content to have the right to create an app [217] and deliver programming to these "new" media?

In early 2011, Time Warner Cable carried quite a few of their available cable channels into the new format via an app, only to have the underlying cable networks scream like stuck pigs that TWC didn't have that right. Rather than test the theory in court, Time Warner blinked … just as Cablevision announced a parallel "app" making a similar claim. [218] Yet another "new media" battle line was being drawn.

But is content becoming truly de-linked from the media that delivers it? Is there some practical value to putting content on a network, where consumers know that they can find entertainment? Is a search engine really a sufficient replacement, particularly when viewers aren't really looking for specific content? What happens when they're just surfing and looking for something interesting? And isn't the networks' ability to maintain ad sales staffs to service all of its programs more efficient than having producers sell their own ads for single programs? Aren't there companies that can aggregate ad sales and placements as outsource vendors? [219] Isn't there a value proposition with telecasters paying for and presenting clear formats of comparable programming? Can the Super Bowl and the Academy Awards thrive on Web-only availability? The ability to market programming to an audience cannot be underestimated.

Even some big studios and networks are migrating their traditional content, particularly television programming across multiple platforms. They are letting the consumer decide when, where and how to watch their favorite programs. [220] The smarter ones understand the benefit of playing the same program on multiple platforms. Will powerful content creators eventually circumvent networks and go directly to consumers or through aggregators that aren't traditional telecasters?

If studios think that they may be able to address consumers without the network "middle man," is it possible that content creators will also disintermediate studios as well? Social networks, which define and segment individuals based on interests, taste and personal characteristics, would seem to be a more likely source of relevant content aggregation than traditional telecasters. We're watching a trend toward smaller niched social networks and niches forming within larger structures (by groupings of "friends" for example on Facebook and MySpace).

Some social networks have evolved into middlemen by aggregating consumer-friendly thematic content. There are networks for pet lovers, [221] models and their photographers, [222] Muslims, [223] bloggers, [224] African-Americans, [225] and even shopaholics. [226] Through linkage, the large social networks are increasingly allowing the export of audio-visual material and text from users' home pages to parallel social networks, perhaps of a more specialized nature.

It is precisely this specialization that creates the opportunity for revenue-sharing between the product/content supplier and the social network to target its specific demographics. It would work much like a theater owner splitting box office revenue with the studio supplying the film. In other words, getting rid of the television network as a middleman may not necessarily result in more direct access between content creators and their audience. There may simply be a different intermediary, such as a social network.

Sometimes, events and grassroots responses to such events skip television completely. The connective tissue is often a home page on a social network where mobile phone videos are uploaded and shared. Specific Twitter networks have evolved in response to a crisis, such as those that reported the explosive attacks in Mumbai, India or the protests in various countries in the Middle East. The connections are often created for the relevant moment and fueled by communications technology. While the habits of social media continue in these changed societies, nothing like the storm that brought down entire governments have yet to resurface.

Responding to crisis is one example, but there are specialized commercial applications that can arise in the strangest arenas: "Thanks to the advent of Twitter — a forum for updating the world on what you are doing at all times — the days of chasing down the ice cream man, frantically waving dollar bills, are a thing of the past. A few clicks of the mouse will reveal the current location of your favorite mobile dessert truck and, if you're lucky, also what they are serving, how long they will be there and the secret to getting a special discount." [227]

Even the giants, like AOL, [228] are getting the message. This online behemoth, noted: [229] "A company rooted in bringing the Internet to the masses, AOL is shifting its focus toward serving niche audiences with the launch of dozens of specialty Web sites. The latest specialty site – ParentDish for parents – formally launched [in mid-May], with The Boot for country music and The Boom Box for hip hop and R&B [shortly thereafter].

"The sites reflect a growing sophistication of Internet users, who are spending less time at portals like AOL.com and Yahoo.com and directly seeking specialized content at more focused sites. Examples outside AOL include Boing Boing, which keeps tabs on technology and the Internet; The Sartorialist, on street style; or Mom Logic, on parenting and being a mom. While these mini-networks continue, they have yet to generate business plans that justify their existence on commercial terms... yet.

"'The consumer market is clearly fragmenting,' said Bill Wilson, AOL's executive vice president for vertical programming. 'We wanted to give people many front doors, not just one front door to come in."

AOL isn't alone: Yahoo Inc. recently launched Shine for women ages 25 to 54. In mid-May of 2013, outside of its content programming strategy, Yahoo addressed its growth vulnerabilities with the $1.1 billion all-cash purchase of rapidly-expanding social media/micro-blogging site Tumblr. That Tumblr's investors and management avoided taking an equity stake in Yahoo suggested a lack of faith in Yahoo's longer-term prospects. For Yahoo, the acquisition represented a new story for its own investors. Yahoo is telling everyone it will let the existing Tumblr CEO continue at the helm of his operation. But Wall Street is still trying to figure out whether Yahoo is a technology or a media company. Does adding an over-50 personality, Katie Couric, as Yahoo's "global anchor" matter? Too little too late or a real turnaround with a new path?

But, as the No. 4 Internet property behind Google Inc., Yahoo and Microsoft Corp., AOL has been more ambitious. "The current problem with an awful lot of the mega sites is the fact that they aren't well targeted," said Rob Enderle, an industry analyst with the Enderle Group. "The material is written and designed for a general audience, and the reality is we are all individuals." This appears to be a rising sweet spot for advertisers. But the challenges of marketing to a massive number of separate niches will test the mettle of more than one marketing executive.

Programming on the Web

Isn't the Web the most obvious place for appropriate consumers to link to Rule One appropriate messages? Or is the Web just too vast and diverse to make the economics work? Making money from Web-originated content has occasional winners, such as the Unilever-sponsored spoof that followed nerdy comedians "Evan and Gareth" in a series of "webisodes." As they roamed the country, Evan and Gareth wrote the book on how to score with "chicks" on behalf of Axe brand men's body care products. However, except for such sponsor-directed programming, finding a consistent revenue-generating formula has remained elusive.

Nevertheless, a glimmer of an exception occasionally hints at the "maybe" of the future. Actress Felicia Day decided to produce a real Web-based series with better production values than typical webisodes. It was a big gamble: "In three years, *The Guild,* a homemade comedy series about gamers playing a *World of Warcraft*-like virtual role-playing game, has gone from cute one-off to full-fledged phenomenon. The show's run so far has garnered an estimated 65 million views, and has even spawned its own comic book … In fact, she just may be the only person who has figured out how to make a living by producing, writing, and starring in an original online series." [230]

A few early episodes – produced for less money – were teased on YouTube and found traction until a loyal fan based seemed to sign on for the duration. Spurning mainstream Hollywood offers to sell the series, Day's agents seemed to have turned a very big corner in licensing arrangements with several major players, not the least of which was Microsoft. "Microsoft pays an undisclosed fee to debut each season exclusively on the company's Xbox Live, MSN, and Zune platforms (season four debuted in mid-July [2010]) … Day's company shares in sponsorship revenue from Xbox Live's 'branded-destination environment.' [Her agent] has secured similar distribution and revenue arrangements with Amazon, iTunes, Netflix, and New Video Group, which distributes the show on DVD." [231]

There is a nascent movement, likely to accelerate into the future, of using Internet bandwidth to mirror the channel capacity available on cable or over-the-air. Trying to redefine its role on the Web, for example, Yahoo! has migrated heavily into advertiser-supported Web-original programming, mirroring traditional seasonal slates favored by the traditional broadcast networks.

Introducing eight new shows in the fall of 2011, Yahoo! is focusing on selling "shows to advertisers targeting women on a 'share of voice' basis using its data and insights tools to measure reach and targeting … Yahoo said its original video programming already reaches 26 million people per month." [232] Whether this combination of Web-original programming with targeted demographics (and solid metrics) is economically sustainable has yet to be determined. Getting consumers to pay directly for Internet-original content, however, has been somewhat more elusive.

While there are a few pay-for-play models in use, for the most part, alternative reality games [233] have provided sponsors with an ability to use multiplayer games to engage, interact with and entertain relevant consumer groups in connection with their products and services. Generally, Web-viewers seem loath to pay subscriber or per download fees for the snippets offered online. Building a model based on advertising, even the YouTube short-form content aggregation site has not produced the advertiser-generated revenue explosion that the entertainment industry had hoped for; at least not yet.

For example, even mainstream studios, such as Time-Warner's Turner Broadcasting System have failed to monetize this new format. In January of 2007, Turner launched Super Deluxe, a Website that featured short videos from up-and-coming comedians. "[Fourteen] months after Super Deluxe had launched, Turner announced the site would sleep with the fishes. At its peak, it corralled only 400,000 monthly viewers and didn't win substantial ad revenue (a paltry $10,000 in the first quarter of [2008]). With a fat staff and a fatter roster of outsourced talent, the site was bleeding money. Turner fired the entire staff save one employee and very little, if any, of Super Deluxe's content [was] expected to move over to AdultSwim.com when Turner formally [took] the site down [at the end of 2008]. So the whole enterprise (and the $15 million or so spent building it) will completely evaporate into cyberspace " [234]

Clearly, this interim transition between Internet and television is both awkward and fraught with risks. Pricing structures are illusive and revenue models have not translated well from business plans to consumer behavior. There are hurdles to be conquered, but the movement into a merged television-Internet universe is inevitable. Money is pouring into this new medium, even if it might not be exactly in the manner some might wish.

Maybe Mark Cuban's theory about monetizing cable versus the Web is correct; when you want to monetize elegant audio/visual content, stick to high-bandwidth cable and satellite and add two-way interactivity. Yet AOL's acquisition of the Huffington Post added not only printed stories, on-camera news stories, and live updates but an ability for viewers to join in the process. The BBC's global radio service embraces entire programs based on listener participation, through Skype but even via Facebook and other online audience input.

The audience literally becomes the programming. But all of this is either advertiser supported (Huffington Post) or provided as a government service (BBC).

Consumer resistance to "pay-per-use Web-formats" is strong and building, which is one of the reasons advertising is so important to Web-based content. Even subscriber formats (sometimes combined with advertising) feel consumer resistance unless the body of content is so vast that it is viewed as providing almost unlimited access to a category of established commercial entertainment.

Addressing Fortune Magazine's Brainstorm Tech conference in July of 2009, mainstream media-moguls such as Barry Diller, IAC/Interactive Corp CEO (and former Fox and Paramount Pictures CEO) see the Internet as having only three basic monetizing models: transactions, advertising and subscriptions. Diller suggested that the struggle to monetize Web content was likely to get "bloody" before the dust settles. The Recession slowed the online retail market in 2009, but the market is back in spades. In 2013, people are truly back shopping online like never before, a trend that is accelerating. [235]

Mobile is the new focus, however, as this form of access is now passing every other form of Web access. The reality is that with the growing penetration of smart mobile platforms, if you want consumers, that's where they are spending increasing amounts of time: "[As of late] 2012, U.S. consumers [spent] an average 82 minutes per day on their mobile device, which is more than double from 2010 … And by 2016, there will be over 10 billion mobile devices, creating 10 billion opportunities for marketers to get closer to consumers. Marketers need to rethink the value of mobile marketing to put their brands in the hands of consumers." [236] There are already more mobile devices than people!

The first 6 months of 2012 also showed U.S. ad spends of $1.2 billion on mobile platforms (tablets, smartphones, etc.), plus Web-search alone – which unfortunately for content providers [237] makes up about half of the $17 billion ad revenues in this space – clocked a mighty $8.1 billion [238] in the same time period (up from $280 million in 2006). [239] The first quarter of 2013 exploded to a massive increase, $9.6 billion.[240] This isn't new marketing money; it's a reallocation of existing marketing budgets.

Google is still the advertising lion in mobile as well, [241] but because the click through rate is a fraction of comparable traffic directly on the Web, advertisers spend less per ad on mobile. [242] People just use their mobile devices differently from their computers. Marketers are struggling with how to configure their mobile efforts to get results. Even online versus mobile search seem to be different. Online allows more detailed comparisons and clearer visualization, better suited to more complex quests.

Mobile tends to be more location based, where consumers tend to address "where" more than "what." [243]

Mobile is also driven by "apps" (downloadable applications that provide the user with a functionality defined by the download), but even in this space utility is generally perceived by consumers to be more valuable than entertainment or social connectivity. [244] With cost inefficiencies due to lower ad clicks in the mobile space, advertisers are trying to find advertising that fares well across the digital media landscape, a challenge given the different emphasis in each category.

So exactly how do consumers use their mobile devices when shopping? The results in 2012: "eMarketer found that 41% of shoppers will use their mobile device to check Amazon for competitive pricing, and 42% will check for sales prior to entering a store. Additionally, 21% … [used] their smartphone for holiday purchase – nearly double from 2011. There is ample opportunity for brands to interact with mobile … shoppers from awareness to search and purchase." [245]

With mobile GPS functionality, many merchants can access mobile-enabled shoppers in their vicinity with instant coupons and specially tailored sales. The key seems to be understanding the narrower and shorter-time focus of consumers when using their phones for commercial purposes. They are questing on a device that may not offer the same visuals of a larger screen. But mobile isn't the only recent game-changer in the marketing space.

Direct access to social network members for shopping is expanding as well. In April of 2008, three record labels (Universal Music, Sony BMG and Warner Music) opened a store on MySpace – a little first step in what could be a long march towards this shift. Advertisers are watching these trends and exploring all of these new directions. Many firms still view much of this Internet advertising (brand-building and online selling) as experimental, even though it has been around in force for well over a decade! But with almost 20% of all global marketing money being spent online, this medium hardly seems experimental anymore.[246]

The key concept is "aggregation" – aggregating *content* or *eyeballs* or *advertisers* – to create economies of scale, such that administrative costs can be amortized over increasing numbers of elements. Television networks can be viewed as such aggregators, but the range of available structures grows every day. For example, iTunes aggregates music that is delivered electronically just as the first stage of the Netflix model aggregates motion picture DVDs, renting them in hard copies (which are mailed back and forth from company and consumer) as well as through their streaming service.

We are watching the evolution of new forms of cloud computing. [247] The cloud enables consumers to play an infinite array of PC video games without having to buy game consoles and hard copies of expensive cartridge games. Yet, it still generates a constant stream of revenues to the companies supplying the content and the service. Many of the above examples are based on per use or subscriber revenues. Still, advertising remains the mainstay of most of in-home digital entertainment. The Web has been just one of the latest highways to deliver content at virtually every level, but parallel platforms are tearing away even at that "new" medium.

Mobile

Mobile connectivity has permeated the above pages, but it's time for this ubiquitous technology to have its own section. It seems pretty clear that mobile devices are rapidly becoming the primary communications device on earth. Growth has been spectacular, leap-frogging to the fore in developing nations, pushing landlines out of the way, and accelerating in the most developed nations. Even in the U.S., the growth of mobile data traffic, up 123% from 2010 to 2011, tells a powerful story. [248]

Let's look just at cell phone usage in the U.S. With 85% of American mobile phones able to reach beyond traditional telephony, the number of cellphone owners who text on their phones has grown to 80 percent from 58 percent in 2007. [249] The number of smart phones in the U.S. accounts for two-thirds of new cellphones sold and half those in consumers' hands today. [250]

The number of U.S. cellphone owners who use phones to send e-mail has jumped to 50 percent from 19 percent in 2007, and those using phones to shoot video has risen to 44 percent from 18 percent five years ago. [251] With 37% of American teens owning a smart phone as of the spring of 2013, and with girls accessing the mobile universe significantly more than boys, the power of this new medium is beyond obvious. [252] And that's even without considering the new larger-screen tablets that are invading the marketplace in unprecedented numbers.

The pervasive use of mobile phones and tablets, with increasing screen size, bandwidth and applications, seems to be a meld of Internet and "something else." [253] Experts predict that the computing power inherent in the devices themselves or the availability of "software as a service" (where the computing power is provided outside the device by a third party vendor) will eventually replace the laptop as the mainstay portable computing device. [254]

There's even a hybrid laptop-tablet – represented handily by the Microsoft Surface that offers consumer full-on Windows 8 processing in its upscale "pro" model. Consumers increasingly access stored content "in the clouds" that once required a sizeable hard drive normally associated with at least a small laptop. Now, mobile computing offers a new level of sophisticated interactivity. Further, the ultimate in Rule One connectivity are mobile apps, where consumers direct entire fields of functionality and information to themselves. This makes the mobile space one of the most prized values for advertisers seeking to find their market. The market literally identifies itself.

Mobile consumption of content is clearly a mega-growth business, [255] but early trends suggest some unexpected "gender-oriented" results. According to a music industry analysis, females out-downloaded males two to one in all forms of content sampled, with the heaviest usage coming, not surprisingly, in the 18-35 year-old bracket. [256] When it came to apps-heavy iPhone downloads, the numbers tended to even out with women edging out men by a lesser 6%.

In 2009, when Apple introduced a $9.95 operating system upgrade to the iPhone Touch, the dividing line between laptop and cell phone blurred even more. Functions such as "cut, copy and paste," greater file-sharing capacity, multiplayer gaming and even an "internal" search engine were added. When embracing the largest possible audience is factored into the equation, advertisers note that the cell phone follows the user into almost every facet of life.

Tablets fall between laptops and smart phones, but there is an overall blending of mobile capabilities across platforms. This ability to deliver information and entertainment – especially immediate information (see the discussion of Twitter above) inherent in news and sports – affords the mobile platform increasing relevance to advertisers. Even whole movies and television programs are now commonly viewed on these mobile platforms. For those at the lower rungs of the American economic spectrum, often unable to afford a full-on computer, the mobile phone may be the *only* way they access the Web. [257]

Owning a computer and having high-speed access to the Web is definitely linked to income. [258] Although public libraries and Internet cafes also provide computers with access to the Web, the cell phone's ubiquitous presence is a solid choice for advertisers seeking the broadest reach.

It also seems reasonably obvious that the smart phone [259] is very likely going to be the credit card and even the electronic house key [260] of the future. Every post-2011 Nokia smart phone, for example, will have the "charge my account – waive and pay" NFC (near field communications) technology that currently enables short-range financial data exchanges which you have seen work in for concert tickets, subway fares, etc. Google's and Apple's mobile operating systems are heavily into this capacity.

The personal data contained in credit cards and other comparable IDs – currently carried in a wallet or purse – may routinely be (already are) stored on your phone. Of course, having such storage introduces a new level of security risks. A user could lose credit cards, the health insurance card and driver's license when the cell phone goes south, although replacing them might become easier. At least your cell phone can have a password; wallets can't. There is a big battle brewing between the carriers (who enable the relevant apps to land on their platforms) and the credit card companies as to how to carve up the revenue pie.

Apple's most successful iPhone has generated user loyalty partly because of intuitive integration between and among other Apple products, but because the business of supplying "apps" (applications) to iPhone users (and now iPad freaks) has allowed their owners to exploit the greater memory capacity to customize both content and capabilities. The addition of GPS (global positioning satellite) technology has added an obvious relevance making the cell phone valuable in more ways than stationary computing. The user's physical location now becomes relevant to advertising, and the response rate to location-targeted advertising on mobile phones has been stunning, particularly among iPhone users. [261]

Evolving geolocation software provides advertisers with the opportune moments to offer incentives for consumers who avail themselves of the relevant offers. [262] Privacy advocates just quiver in fear, particularly as the U.S. National Security Agency's once top secret massive Prism telephone/Web traffic spying program spilled into the headlines in June of 2013.

As bandwidth accelerates into the mobile phone world, there is a blur between the Internet and mobile. A cell phone is often the preferred device to access the Internet. Japanese subway passengers can be seen glued to the mobile devices, catching up on their favorite television programs and even motion pictures. We are seeing a rapidly growing version of that trend in the United States, where mobile subscribers can buy access to certain programs provided by their carrier through strategic alliances. MobiTV and CBS Mobile, for example, have joined forces to provide millions of high bandwidth mobile subscribers with the opportunity to view many of their favorite CBS shows and even major sports events on these tiny screens.

On April 14, 2010, a consortium of twelve major telecasters announced a new venture aimed at delivering mobile content across a vastly larger cross-section of cell phone users. [263] Ubiquitous television delivered on mobile devices, from cell phones to 3G/4G-linked tablet computers, appears to be headed for standardized mass consumption. In a few years, such mobile access will be just a part of daily life. For users who have grown up with small screen viewing, it's often the best available platform of the moment, where convenience trumps the quality of a better visual experience. But the entire field of electronic "delivery" is exploding in all directions and can only accelerate as the Obama administration plans to roll out more fiber optic cable and create greater Broadband access in the U.S.

Asian markets are layering increasingly elegant bandwidth capacity and, with European Union approval secured in November of 2012, Britain is announcing a plan to supply broadband to every household, an effort that has slowed slightly by that nation's self-imposed austerity measures. [264] The fact that virtually all forms of television content are available online or via mobile access may account for the fall in the number of people who even own televisions in the United States. [265]

A study by Horowitz Associates – entitled Broadband Content and Services 2009 – reveals that 61% of broadband users watch video online on a weekly basis. This is up from 45% in the year 2006. According to the study, using the web for *video* is preceded only by checking/sending email, getting information such as news, weather, or directions and doing financial-related activities. News clips and YouTube-type user-generated video still dominate the online video landscape: At the time of the survey, 22% (up from 16% in 2007) of consumers reported that they watch an entire television show online at least on a weekly basis (see chart below). [266]

To date, usage of the web to watch television shows online is driven by convenience. Seven out of ten of American broadband users who had watched a full episode of a TV show online had done so because they missed it on traditional TV. As more branded, TV-type programming becomes available on (or is created exclusively for) the personal computer (and ultimately the cellphone), the audience for long-form programming online will certainly grow.

Younger consumers are really driving the adoption of online rich, video-oriented media: 84% of 18-34 year-old broadband users view video online at least on a weekly basis. Indeed, we can hypothesize that these younger broadband users who were born into this interactive medium, might find online viewing more enjoyable – and more oriented towards their on-the-go, multitasking lifestyles – than traditional, passive television viewing. Just about everything and anything that can be found online has been tailored for delivery on smart phones as well.

And while the data on the effectiveness of ad click-through rates suggests that people use their phones at one-tenth the rate of online users, people are beginning to discover that there is a solid interaction between initial ad reaches via mobile to ultimate purchase via a more traditional Internet connection. But mobile is clearly the go-to new medium of choice for advertisers, and the dollars are ramping up significantly.

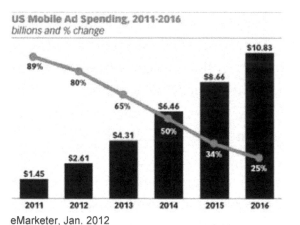

US Mobile Ad Spending, 2011-2016
billions and % change

eMarketer, Jan. 2012
Note: Includes display (banner, rich media and video), search and SMS/MMS/P2P messaging

Advertising on the Web

The Web still offers the ability to identify Rule One appropriate consumers to be targeted with appropriate messages, but only if advertisers are able to harness this incredible capacity. Internet numbers were growing before the recession at almost three times the rate of cable television and five times faster than broadcast television.[267] In the United States, for example, 13.2 billion consumers viewed online ad in March of 2013 alone, a number which continues to grow. [268]

These statistics remain of particular interest to advertisers even in a contracted economy. The Internet is the new pervasive growth technology, attractive to younger demographics and capable of selective targeting. The ability to reel in consumers from the Internet is a driving force in the new age of advertising. The Web is definitely picking up a very large segment of users who might have, in past years, addressed the same content solely through their traditional televisions with hard links to a particular website which often generate sales or at least precious "eyeballs" which attracts advertising dollars.

To many, the new Internet advertising model may be the emphasis in future ad spends. But is this really where new companies will prosper? With an over-saturation of advertiser-supported Websites and a contracting economy, the mix has had a significant impact on pricing. There are barriers to new companies to find a mix in this ocean of over-supply that spurred a search for new paths to profitability for Internet startups. If a Website doesn't reach 5 million viewers, It's not In the game – unless it is able to reach a particularly coveted niche. Small advertisers who can sell into the market at all are watching the ad rates plummet by 75%. Time spent on ads is as much of a factor as the initial click.

Just looking at the money spent creating and placing ads is only a part of the new revenues being generated by these changing ad placement trends. How that money is spent is also mission critical. For example, using for key-word links from emails and then generating a "related" unsolicited offer on the Web to a consumer who couldn't cares less is exceptionally ineffective. Whether it's old world, direct-marketing snail mail or unwanted "modern" electronic spam, the effort is mostly a waste. "Since only 1/10th of 1% of people respond to unsolicited email advertising, and under 3% to physical junk mail, most of the $170 billion spent yearly by direct marketers simply 'annoys people, creates landfill and clutters spam filters.'"[269] Communication without value to the recipient misses the mark by a wide mark.

The alternative revenue list for new media marketing, when properly applied, is still substantial, beginning with selling software to businesses to enable them to create consumer values (information and/or entertainment) on the Internet/mobile sites to tracking and analytical software to let them know how effective a campaign might be. Targeted search with built-in incentives creates another revenue-generator. This is a prime revenue driver for companies such as OpenTable.com, which sells its restaurant reservation software to participating restaurants to allow customers to use the site.

Other advertisers, hoping for subscription fees or customization charges, employ techniques such as the "freemium" model (offering free online services, but charging a fee for premium upgrades), generating referral fees for linking customers to other sites, and of course generating profits from eCommerce transactions (including the sale of "virtual" goods in virtual worlds).

As a side note, analysts watch Google's online success at selling priority positioning to advertisers in connection with key word searches as the barometer of the future. However, my friend and former co-author Professor Peter Sealey (former Coca-Cola chief marketing officer), notes, "Search is great, but you can't advertise Coca-Cola in search; Google is going to try to compete there, but they don't have the same algorithm that they had in search." In a rich media (read: full audio/visual quality), broadband universe, where the lines between Internet and television blur, there may be a value limit to what may soon become "old world" search engines.

Content is still the driving force for all media. With so many choices, driving a message home means finding who might be truly interested in that message in the first place. The next generation of ad-targeting software has been forced to embrace a new reach to deliver value.

But even Google has recognized the limitations of simply relying on search to find appropriate messages for appropriate consumers. And there is growing resistance from advertisers against simply paying for access to eyeballs or limited-result "hits." Key word search, paying for priority positioning on the relevant lists based on such click-through "hits," can be prohibitively expensive for smaller advertisers, and prices are soaring.[270]

Some of the newest techniques focus on the "maybe" consumers, not just people who killed their purchase midstream (and were clearly interested) but those whose cursor hovers over a possible link long enough to suggest serious interest. Google's Lightbox family of interactive display ads, introduced in late 2012, actually expands to a full visual canvas when a consumer hovers over that link for two seconds or more, and the advertiser only pays when that expansion occurs.[271]

Where eyeballs go, marketing dollars are sure to follow. But that growth is not as evenly distributed among business sectors as one might assume. There are earlier adopters and heavier users. Traditional "old world" broadcast media are still holding their own – but for how much longer? The Horowitz-generated tables in the preceding section illustrate what consumers are watching on broadband. These numbers are changing almost as fast as we can write about them. Let's look at a eMarketer's analysis as to exactly how quickly ad spends are migrating to the Web and directly into mobile:

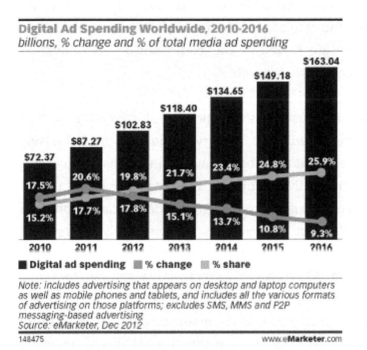

Digital Ad Spending Worldwide, 2010-2016
billions, % change and % of total media ad spending

Note: includes advertising that appears on desktop and laptop computers as well as mobile phones and tablets, and includes all the various formats of advertising on those platforms; excludes SMS, MMS and P2P messaging-based advertising
Source: eMarketer, Dec 2012
148475   www.eMarketer.com

U.S. spends on mobile are even more startling (particularly as you see the relative position of old-world print ads by comparison):

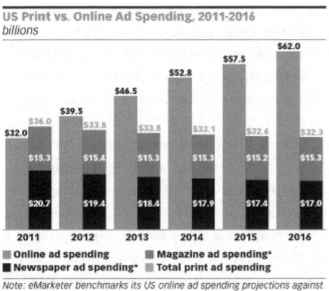

US Print vs. Online Ad Spending, 2011-2016
billions

Note: eMarketer benchmarks its US online ad spending projections against the IAB/PwC data, for which the last full year measured was 2010; eMarketer benchmarks its US newspaper ad spending projections against the NAA data, for which the last full year measured was 2010; *print only
Source: eMarketer, Jan 2012
136019   www.eMarketer.com

The question many companies are asking is: are we deploying that marketing effort, at massive cost, in anything that approaches logic or efficiency? Increasingly, we have the ability to "near real time" correlations between marketing efforts and results. Quantum analysis is *de rigueur* in corporate vetting of their rising costs in this area; we must determine the rate of return on our marketing spends. New measurement systems, some of which are driven by bar codes and RF identification tags, are making those correlations increasingly accurate.

Take, for example, beer-maker Anheuser-Busch, which uses local distributors to deliver its product to retailers. Salesmen keep track of every bottle of every Anheuser-Busch product sold by visiting key retailers at least once a week and transmitting their measurements of shelf space and competitive efforts at the retail level by satellite uplink. The local distributor and Anheuser-Busch use extremely sophisticated software to correlate (literally by sub-zip code) the effectiveness of every advertising and marketing effort deployed in and received by the relevant neighborhoods that are serviced by the relevant retailer. This produces a cost/effectiveness analysis that was unheard of a decade ago. The ability to have sales efforts reported from the field and tracked by satellite back to corporate headquarters has made companies like candy-manufacturer, Mars, Inc., one of the largest consumers of satellite uplink and downlink time in America.

Measuring effectiveness of advertising on social networks had been problematical until August of 2011. While "hits" could be tracked, advertisers were not comfortable unless they had some way of measuring who actually watched the entire ad. In August of 2011, Facebook and Nielsen began Online Campaign Ratings (OCR).[272] While this joint tracking service might make privacy advocates squirm, it generates detailed information, hence increasing the value where ads actually reach their targets.

Surprisingly, parallel efforts in bricks and mortar retailers, where specialized electronic equipment has used customers' cell phones to track their movements through the store, have met with much more in the way of consumer outrage than online tracking. "'The idea that you're being stalked in a store is, I think, a bit creepy, as opposed to, it's only a cookie — they don't really know who I am,' said Robert Plant, a computer information systems professor at the University of Miami School of Business Administration, noting that consumers can rarely control or have access to this data."[273] Sophisticated computer programs *infer* patterns to such consumer behavior, online or in-store, a fact which seems to trouble more than a few people.

But the bottom-line measurements are talking to corporate America, and these monetary mavens are not so happy with the results. As the above numbers illustrate, the cost of advertising is rising faster than the rise in the cost of goods, a trend that has continued unabated since the 1980s. Between 1982 and 2002, for example, as inflation increased the cost of consumer goods and services by 160%, the cost per thousand ("CPM") of prime time broadcast network television increased by more than 400%! When the cost of goods and services sold does not rise fast enough to absorb the concomitant marketing costs, something's got to give, particularly in an economic environment produced by the global financial meltdown.

Even before the financial crisis (and the bankruptcies of two of the three largest U.S. automakers), we had already seen established brands, like General Motors' Oldsmobile, shut down to eliminate a marketing budget that did not produce adequate sales. Television and radio spots have become shorter. Gone are the infamous 60 second spots of days of yore. New products must hover around a brand name. For example, there are approximately forty "Crest" products – from toothpaste to mouthwash – trying to pick up legitimacy and stickiness when consumers reach across a shelf in their supermarket.

While targeting has long been an art form, it is rapidly becoming a science with new media, social interconnectivity and real time or near-real time consumer tracking systems. Consequently, the Web has become a huge part of the future of marketing. Yet targeting assumes that one knows the target, and therein lies the biggest issue in marketing today: identifying those appropriate for the content, product or service and not wasting marketing dollars on those who are unsusceptible to the message. Increasingly, however, those "targets" are proving illusive and fickle, associating and dissociating with almost unpredictable patterns.

Even after the targets are identified, the next task is to figure out which consumers fit into each of the "marketing vectors" – thereby, defining the psychographic groupings. This effort becomes even more problematical when dealing with the youngest members of society who have literally been born and raised into the "next" world. Change is so rapid that lumping younger consumers into generational (twenty-year) or even ten-year cohorts actually serves no useful purpose, as will be discussed further on pages 96 and following below. Among younger demographics, a ten-year age separation is monumental. Further complicating the matter is the fact that only after each of the above variables is tracked and identified can the "marketing materials" be created and applied.

The thought process for marketing in societies with deep penetration of state of the art communications bears little or no resemblance to past analytics. Thus, even psychographically appropriate messages that span many age groupings may have to be delivered through different media to reach targeted demographics. For example, an advertiser may have the same message delivered in a television ad for an older demographic, while younger users find that message through a social network.

It seems as if all of those social, legal and brain-shifting realities are literally shaking up the very meaning of marketing worldwide. The word itself, will mean "communicating with an intention to convince," whether we are talking about social activism, political causes or simple commercialism. It is interesting to note that the notion of "psychographics" (grouping people by personality, values, attitudes, interests, or lifestyles) is increasingly replacing "demographics" (grouping people by more clearly objective criteria like age, gender, race, ethnicity, geographical situs and/or income, etc.) as the analytical tool for targeted marketing. This appears to be an obvious recognition of the fractures that have occurred in society as discussed in detail above.

To exacerbate the analytical complexity further, different causes, products and services also have their own psychographic relevance. While some matters may provoke consistent responses, such as an anti-abortion stance from both devout Catholics and Evangelical Christians, this doesn't mean that these two religious groups would necessarily share the same attitudes regarding environmental issues. Nevertheless, demographic analysis on the same issues might produce either no or very limited valid predictive statistics. Thus, different issues and target information might indeed require a complete reconfiguration of the relevant psychographics to enhance meaningful marketing and communication.

Additional variables, such as the relative naïveté or sophistication of the user base (which can include literacy, technological competence, access to media platforms and communications devices, range of experience with viewing and understanding communications, relative importance of predispositions in comprehending and processing complex messaging, etc.) must then be calculated. The more primitive the society and the less sophisticated the user base, the simpler the psychographic analysis becomes. For example, in communications in rural parts of Sub-Saharan Africa, the low penetration of computers, telephone,[274] televisions and even radios is compounded by the relative importance of tribal and religious affiliations. In this environment, there is a relative dearth of differentiating psychographic segmentation.

You can expect technology to step into the developing world with surprising rapidity, sometimes jumping into state of the art without intermediate steps. The transition from new to commonplace to old is the story of mankind. But will the range and depth of psychographic segmentation that currently adhere to sophisticated communities today – as opposed to just the technology – also seep into all facets of society? Clearly, there will be shifts in who the next generation of sophisticates and naïve users will be.

The hyper-modernization of China is evidence of this phenomenon. Yet other than who is able to learn the "next new," it is not so linear and simple to determine future psychographics. The communication patterns of today may suggest the future, but accelerants (like leap-frogging over landline telephones directly into mobile phones evident in the developing world) might produce some surprising and unpredictable results.

Today, mass communications through more traditional media are both more practical (cost-wise) and are still viewed as "credible technology" among a wide socio-demographic basis in this universe of naïve users. It embraces diverse psychographics which would be impossible in a more sophisticated society with fractionalized and myriad psychographics (in a world of unlimited "connected" media delivery systems).

With "new media" (which could be "old world" media to a more modern social structure) presented to technologically less sophisticated users, media skepticism is not well developed, and simple messages take root quickly and effectively (as we have seen in our discussions above). But will this trend necessarily continue as connectivity is no longer dependent on traditional means of distribution? Wires and local broadcast antennae are being replaced with satellite and cell tower transmission. Is the only barrier economic?

Polarization through Technology

As modern nations accelerate with technological advancements and even citizens of emerging nations use digital communications to implement political change, a vast pool of the world's population remains mired in a pre-technological-revolution past. Wikipedia tells us that 61% of the earth is not connected to the Web, but the United Nations tells us that there are still more mobile phones than toilets! The new complex marketing paradigms that work in the West clearly don't apply everywhere.

Rule One becomes particularly basic in this environment where consumers (or people whom the government or other factions work to influence) have limited capacity to understand messages and few appropriate vehicles by to which to deliver them.

While currently of limited impact, there are new programs that offer hope of opening the technology door to previously excluded groups. With the support of such notables as the U.N.'s Kofi Annan and media-mogul Rupert Murdoch, Nicholas Negroponte (from the Massachusetts Institute of Technology – MIT – media lab) has developed an ultra-cheap, almost indestructible, laptop computer. It can work off solar power and can be linked to the Web in small rural neighborhoods through local wi-fi wireless networks. The devices are distributed for free among the children in third world and developing nations to address, encourage and enhance literacy and general learning skills. The cost of these laptops began at approximately $200.00. Intel, which originally resisted the technology, is now fully on board.

The "One Laptop Per Child" (OLPC) project is often funded by local governments or charities (discussed further on page 96 below). In areas where the program has been widely deployed, the results are astounding. Children are motivated into literacy and exploration over the Internet. This enables them to be self-directed in a universe of limited classroom teaching. As laptops are brought home from these local, often one-room schools, some villagers have taken to the practice of sharing this exciting new access with their children.

Detractors point to the black market of OLPC laptops misdirected by corrupt officials and the use of these purloined devices as communications tools for criminal elements. Whatever the risks, the potential for advancing knowledge and opening minds to a universe beyond local indoctrination is gigantic. But this program still represents a drop in the technology bucket for most in nations where poverty is the rule.

For now, the use of traditional media in emerging regions remains effective. Health and science journalist, Corey Binns[275] offers a concrete example of this in a study that examines the socio-cultural impact of serialized dramatic radio programming in HIV-ravaged Ethiopia. The non-profit, Vermont-based Population Media Center ("PMC"), produced *Yeken Kignit* (literally, "looking over one's life"), a serial that follows the lives of a typical Ethiopian woman and her handsome husband. When infidelity results in her husband's contracting HIV, the Ethiopian heroine overcomes her own reluctance to seek out medical testing. Happily, she did not contract the disease.

This program has a loyal following and reaches more than half of Ethiopia (population. 70 million). The report noted that those who faithfully listened to this series were four times more likely to seek medical testing for HIV than those who did not. PMC has offices throughout Asia, Africa and Latin America. It has similar programming (on radio and television) with equally positive results dealing with dominant issues in other nations, such as the Philippines (domestic violence), the Sudan (female circumcision), and Nigeria (teenaged and pre-teenaged pregnancy). Web accessibility at any level in such regions is markedly lower than found in more modern nations and bandwidth often hovers at the most basic level.

We've seen how street protests have been driven by cell phone linkage in places – like Egypt in 2011 – where the Web simply would have been impractical. But even for more peaceful access, impoverished regions often still have some form of local wireless telephony that can provide at least texting options and primitive social networking where there is no widespread Internet. In late 2011, for example, news network Al Jazeera sent the following text message to a database of 5,000 Somalis whose phones were known to have texting capacity (translated): "Al Jazeera wants to know — how has the conflict of the last few months affected your life? Please include the name of your hometown in your response Thank you!"

An explosion of responses – at least 2,000 by mid-December, 2011 – painted a bleak picture of war-ravaged Somalia. Conditions of starvation, brutality and wanton injustice were far worse than many had imagined. The growing use of this novel, crowdsourced news gathering process may redefine reportage in such remote areas. Indeed, many of the images provided during the suppression witnessed in Syria in late 2011 were texted from deep within violent cities where reporters were banned.

Sometimes, the problems of third world access can be found even in technologically advanced nations. For example, many in the United States believe that the difficulties in and cost of wiring distant rural areas and small towns have stalled broadband penetration in the United States to two thirds of total households. They point to the 95% plus penetration of broadband in the world's leader, South Korea, as an example where heavily concentrated urban populations make wiring easy to accomplish.

There is, however, another more disappointing reason – poverty. A report from Bernstein Research analyzed Web-access as a function of income: "At the low end, customers aren't just choosing between one provider and another ... They're often choosing between these services and a third meal."[276] While South Korea has global bragging rights, its elegant Internet access is heavily government subsidized – a factor that is not as prevalent in the United States. To some social theorists, such access to communications and information becomes an additional polarizing factor and now rises to the level of a basic necessity in a modern society.

Following the One Laptop per Child policy discussed above, former U.S. Ambassador Nichlolas Negroponte, has worked to provide low-cost, often solar-powered laptop computers with local Wi-Fi connectivity to poor village children as "teaching machines." There is significant evidence that the attraction to these devices generate self-instruction and even literacy among isolated and otherwise impoverished youth in developing countries. "Sugata Mitra gave street kids in a slum in New Delhi access to a computer connected to the Internet, and found that they quickly taught themselves how to use it. This was the moment he says he discovered a new way of teaching.

"He calls it the grandmother technique, and it goes like this: expose a half dozen or so kids to a computer, and let them have at it. The only supervision required is an adult to listen the kids brag about what they learn. It's the opposite, he says, of the disciplinary ways of many parents—more like a kindly grandmother, who rewards curiosity with acceptance and encouragement. And it is a challenge to the past century and a half of formalized schooling."[277]

However, to believe that all is vastly better in the more technologically-advanced nations is to miss the impact on how brains in such societies are being rewired to cope with the massive deluge of information. Inventor and futurist Raymond Kurzweil has applied the mathematical concepts in "singularity theory" to the exponential growth – between our own mental processing of massive amounts of newly generated information to data generation from digital processors – of information that is generated every day.

In Kurzweil's analysis, the greatest change in humanity in the last thousand years has been the acceleration of the rate of change itself. Machines will eventually outrun the human ability to reason and invent, according Kurzweil, and human brains are being rewired to anticipate change and expect the *new next* as inevitable. "So we won't experience 100 years of progress in the 21st century—it will be more like 20,000 years of progress (at today's rate). The 'returns,' such as chip speed and cost-effectiveness, also increase exponentially. There's even exponential growth in the rate of exponential growth. Within a few decades, machine intelligence will surpass human intelligence, leading to The Singularity."[278] Living for the next suggests a diminishment of the past and present, but there are others who explain this brain rewiring phenomenon – at least in those aspects of society that are fully immersed in technology – from a different perspective.

There is a countervailing theory – "Presentism"[279] – that suggests that we are so overburdened with digitally induced sensory overload that we are incapable of living anywhere but the present, having lost the time-linked narrative among past, present and future. With instant and massive electronic communications in the now, the focus on anything else has vaporized, says theorist Douglas Rushkoff. People are so presently-focused that they even forget about the future consequences of their online posts. Rushkoff notes: "Our society has reoriented itself to the present moment. Everything is live, real time, and always-on. It's not a mere speeding up, however much our lifestyles and technologies have accelerated the rate at which we attempt to do things. It's more of a diminishment of anything that isn't happening right now--and the onslaught of everything that supposedly is."[280]

Rushkoff's analysis digs one level deeper: "[He] breaks down other symptoms of our current condition. They include: Digiphrenia ('the tension between the faux present of digital bombardment and the true now of a coherently living human generates... digiphrenia--digi for 'digital,' and phrenia for 'disordered condition of mental activity.'); Fractalnoia, dealing with how the volume and now-intensity of information causes us to create patterns that don't exist; and Apocalypto, 'a belief in the imminent shift of humanity into an unrecognizably different form'..."[281]

But are Singularity and Presentism theories that divergent? Aren't these simply two views of the same phenomenon? Perhaps the current generation's obsession with searching for the "new next" is really about disavowing the icons of the past and bringing the cool new into the present.

And what is a "generation" anyway? Does that term hold any relevance for marketers anymore? If the underlying theme that defines a *generation* is a commonality of culture and shared history, once thought to be a 20-25 year cohort, doesn't this acceleration of events effectively shorten that commonality of culture into decreasingly defined cohorts?

While a fifty-year-old may feel culturally linked to a seventy-year-old, among younger technologically sophisticated ages, the relevant cohorts would seem to be defined by a decade or substantially less for everyone born after 1980! What, after all, would a thirty-year-old have in common with someone a decade or more younger?

And if there are more such cohorts as a result, there would seem to be a parallel increase in the cost of mass communication. Each such group, needing its own tailored message (or invitation to communicate), has its own methodology that would be delivered by means of its preferred technology. Mass communicators must understand the moving target of reaching such diverse segments of our society with constantly changing campaigns and metrics.

What's more, the instantaneous feedback loop has indeed changed everything from storytelling to marketing, particularly in the younger generations – cohorts – who have lived during the most exponentially-accelerating times in human history, at least as to change and body of available information. Anyone who believes that they have it "all figured out" will meet obsolescence almost instantly. Grappling with the *now* in a rapidly-changing universe is the ultimate challenge for mass communicators.

Can technologically "pushed" brains remotely connect (and vice-versa) to the minds of those who have been mired in societies where technology seems to have bypassed locally impoverished societies? Does this polarization help explain the disconnect between the recent trends in poorer nations towards religious fundamentalism against those societies where hyper-accelerating change driven by state-of-the-art technology defines life? And exactly how does all of the new "here and in your face" technology impact those in society, good and bad, who wish to communicate to (with?) children?

Marketing to Children

This effectiveness of communicating with naïve users also makes younger children more vulnerable to suggestion. This explains the heavy emphasis in Western legal systems of child protection legislation – the U.S. Children's Online Privacy Protection Act. The ability to understand and question commercial marketing messages (skepticism and critical thinking), even in the connected United States, does not, on average, even begin before a child reaches seven years of age.[282] The Rule One questions of appropriate recipients of appropriate messages take on particularly sensitive significance in this vulnerable demographic.

Brain processing experiences its greatest growth and mind shifting in the earliest, developmental years. It is of profound social significance how many deep and life-impacting commitments are made by the young. For example, most people have settled on their religious beliefs by age 13, and the *average* age that people begin cigarette smoking is 14.5.[283]

Thus, in countries that do not have strong child-protection legislation, or where "indoctrination" is an integral part of constructing social networking, attitudes and lifetime habits can be created with relative ease simply by addressing naïve users, particularly by beginning early enough in a development cycle. An example of such early-stage indoctrination would be the Taliban "schools" – called Madrassa – in the tribal districts of Pakistan, which turn out Muslim extremists by the thousands every year. To many children, such fundamentalist schools are their only hope for literacy. This vulnerability is not lost on those who wish to spread their message of hate and intolerance with willing new recruits.

The more intense and consistently these efforts are applied by marketers and proselytizers alike, the easier it is to create minds that are compatible with an underlying commercial, political or socio-cultural message. Furthermore, these tactics are most effectively implemented by addressing these minds in their pre-adolescent years – and even more effective if those patterns can be imprinted on those under the age of seven.

When one sees interviews of elementary school children in Palestine hoping someday to be suicide bombers or middle-aged patients suffering from emphysema or lung cancer who took their first puff at age ten, one fully understands how life vectors are seemingly set in stone in these early formative years. In many communities and social networks extremist views predominate – extreme, at least, to the average Westerner or Asian sophisticate. Absent some strong early-year countervailing force, it is easy to see how societies polarize and become irreconcilable.

We have evidence within our own society where children are force-fed one overriding social value or religious belief to the exclusion of diversity or even considering the perspectives of others. One has only to view the "comments" or "blogs" from young men and women old enough to frequent the Web and literate enough to engage in debates in reaction to reports carried on the news services of their Internet Service Providers. The words used against someone who expresses a value or perspective different from that of the commenting party are often laced with vituperative and circled with intolerant rage.

Yet defining what society or parents should teach or how they should raise their own children is a very complex issue. Clearly, the question of social responsibility can be addressed; but those who influence children often see their proselytizing as their moral responsibility. It might be easy to criticize the R.J. Reynolds Tobacco Company for their use of a cute, child-attractive, camel for their earlier Camel cigarettes ad campaign. But how do you keep a passionate Taliban father from pushing his son into a Madrassa, even if the result of that effort results in placing his child in harm's way years later as he "volunteers" to become a suicide bomber?

As modern societies create technological sophistication, provide almost unlimited access to information and foster new levels of linkage through social networks, children grow up faster with a mental capacity that eschews undistracted focus needed for complex problem solving. Some distractions may help to create some interesting "ah ha" moments,[284] but when the problem is sufficiently complex, focus loss is detrimental to discerning a critical solution, often the case with more complicated scientific or mathematical problems.[285] Instead, they jump from communication to distracted communication, and except for recessionary unemployment realities, mirror that behavior in frequent job changes. Technology is only accelerating into increasingly younger Americans that will only exacerbate these issues. The December 23, 2013 New York Times tells us half of U.S. parents were giving fairly sophisticated electronics to their 2-to-10-year olds as holiday gifts. A 3-year-old with an iPad? It's just the way it is.

But the openness of children to messages that bombard them from everywhere, from innocent Instagram picture-sharing to more nefarious sexting and pernicious communications from media of all kinds, can easily be a parental nightmare. Cults can recruit, perverts can search, extremists can indoctrinate and advertisers can lure, despite the fact that Western (and other) nations have taken extra steps to create privacy mandate for their youngest members.

With the plethora of Western-oriented storytelling in mass media, children in very different cultures are developing Western tastes and habits that may erode their own traditions along the way. Does the future suggest that even children will establish primary peer relationships based on global communities and values or will traditional communities endure unscathed? The issues will consume historians, political scientists and sociologist for decades.

The determination of what is "appropriate" when a strong political power sends a message – and suppresses contradictory messages – has more than social significance. There are deep psychological factors at work as well. Societies that enforce strong codes of behavior obviously get the job done. Depending on the extent of the various punishments for violating social norms, rebellion from these dictates becomes indirect and sublimated. But what exactly is the natural human response to being told what to do? When a communication is directed at mandating or proscribing behavior (perceived as a limitation on freedom) the natural human tendency is often to buck the directive.

Psychologists call this "psychological reactance." We can see obvious examples like the "rebellion" of an adolescent or the "boomerang effect" of over-zealous marketing. Even powerless toddlers resist in their own way, and seemingly empowered Americans might say, "I just don't like to be told what to do." This feeling is inherent in all phases of social engagement across all cultures, particularly if the message is a negative directive ("don't do that!"). The effectiveness of such a directive is a function of the relative sophistication of the prospective recipient, what the message is and how it is delivered, "including argument quality, severity of the consequences associated with the message topic, and magnitude of the request made in the message."[286]

Nothing makes the point like one of several recent experiments at Duke University's Fuqua School of Business. Participants were asked to name a significant but controlling person in their lives whom they believed had wanted them to work hard, and another significant yet still controlling person who wanted them to have fun. Test subjects then performed a series of cognitive tasks (creating words from jumbled letters – anagrams) on a computer while the name of one or the other of these people was subliminally and repeatedly flashed on the screen (so quickly that their conscious mind did not see the name). The result: people who were flashed the name of a person who wanted them to work hard performed significantly worse than did participants who were exposed to the name of a person who wanted them to have fun.[287]

The more sophisticated the listener, the higher the effectiveness of the cognitive, logical aspects of the directive. With a less sophisticated listener, the most important elements would be the emotions used in the delivery and the perceived threat by the recipient. Further, the degree of this reactance behavior varies greatly among people. Some refer to a low reactance person as being easily influenced. Being raised in a highly structured environment, laced with strong punishment for rejecting commands, can exacerbate the degree of reactance. In short, reactive behavior appears to be innate, varies in strength from one person to the next and can be conditioned out of people. Yet the image of a repressed individual – the perpetually susceptible milquetoast – reacting with murderous rage when the pressure point is exceeded is all too common in our local evening news programs.

Politicians have long used the punishment/fear response to get elected or to secure unwavering support for their policies. Where governments control speech, this feat is more easily accomplished. Simply, control of what people know about the world shapes their opinions. North Korea's leaders control information inflow so completely that their people have almost no real knowledge of the outside world. Brutality reinforces the message.

Reactance against governmental policies will be severely punished. Efficient control of all communications and communications devices – a legacy that the next-generation leader, Kim Jong-Un, seems to have embraced – has resulted in the growth of a popularly-held mythological belief of a North Korean safe harbor within a malevolent view of the rest of the world.

Controlling the release of fear-inducing information that is generally unavailable to the public is equally powerful. For example, making it known that the "punishment" is a risk of death or physical harm. Or the notion that an American might be labeled as unpatriotic: "You're either with us or against us." You might remember the infamous statement from C.I.A. director George Tenet at the end of 2002 immediately prior to the invasion of Iraq? He said that the government's case for proving the existence of weapons of mass destruction in the Saddam Hussein's military was a "slam dunk."

The public was still stinging from the imagery of the 9/11/2001 attacks on the World Trade Center building and the Pentagon, so they accepted these words without question. Statements of this kind overcome both reactance and skepticism because there is no independent methodology for an ordinary citizen to challenge the veracity of what was later proven to be an unfounded governmental assumption. The government builds the fear and then positions itself so that the government conveniently becomes the only agent capable of allaying that concern.

Picture these same emotional sets in common marketing situations where the message is focused on creating consumer demand. When one combines skepticism and an over-saturation of messages trying to get people to do or not do something with reactance behavior, the challenge of marketing or convincing becomes even more complex. For example, a marketing team charged with selling an "edgy" theatrical horror film would be met with a wall of skepticism if they tried to sell the movie by an old world "don't see this motion picture" tactic.

But if a religious group banned the film, an edgy audience in their late teens or early twenties might be impressed enough to go! One wag put it this way: "Perhaps it is better to replace 'No Smoking' signs with ones that state: 'Please Enjoy Your Cigarette Somewhere Else.'" We may not see this trend any time soon, but for those trying to communicate without instilling fear it is certainly a lesson worth learning.

"Spin" is how facts and events are depicted in the press. Applying Rule One logic, spin is a matter of repackaging information that might not be appropriate (or appropriately received) into a format that seems to be appropriate. Public relations firms are often referred as "spin doctors" or "damage controllers." When a government puts the spin on a story we call that "propaganda." Governments that wish to diminish the truth or deny it altogether must be able to create one of three possible situations in order for the message to be effective:

1.   control of the underlying assumptions (unchallengeable since the data is not available to the public), or
2.   control of the mechanisms of communication, or
3.   a mass predisposition against the truth and a belief in a contradictory mythology.

Governments may have one or more of the foregoing handed to them at the time that a political party/faction takes control.

In the United States, C.I.A. Director George Tenet's "slam dunk" statement is an example of how our own government used the "unique control of underlying facts" structure to foment its policies. Most governments — whether liberal or conservative — are masters of creating mythology to foster their goals. A walk back through not-so-distant history provides examples of "lying through statistics" by simply picking the rights "statistics."

Those who are old enough to remember the Vietnam War will recall the consistent images showing military victories with ever-growing but usually exaggerated "body counts" of enemy killed, as well as undue optimism as to the expected outcome of the war. War used to be measured by territory captured and under control not dead bodies, but in Vietnam that "land taken and held" statistic didn't generate the kind of positive picture the spin-masters wanted. Instead, the story shifted to one of a victorious democracy flourishing against a communist foe based on this macabre and generally meaningless number.

This sobering quote appeared in the New York Times, years before the fall of South Vietnam and the total collapse of the very government that was so "freely elected": "According to reports from Saigon, 83% of the 5.85 million registered voters cast their ballots yesterday. Many of them risked reprisals threatened by the Vietcong … A successful election has long been seen as the keystone in President [Lyndon] Johnson's policy of encouraging the growth of constitutional processes in South Vietnam."[288]

Controlling access to information can often be a subtle gesture, but the effects can have significant impact. During the Vietnam War, the government faced difficulties because the press was permitted virtually open access to the theaters of war throughout South Vietnam. Failing military results were making the daily news and public support fell accordingly. Having learned the "spin" lesson gleaned from the Vietnam experience and understanding the need to secure public support, the U.S. government carefully controlled how journalists were introduced to the conflict in the earliest days of the 2003 Iraqi invasion.

Single journalists, sometimes accompanied by a camera or sound technician, were "embedded" (literally "assigned" with no other reporters tied to the same unit) into small units of U.S. fighting forces. They were not permitted to move beyond their specifically approved military microcosm. If their reports were slightly critical, reporters were immediately removed. At the same time, the message being sold to the public via the media was that the press was gaining unprecedented access to the real story.

As the rest of the world questioned the reasons behind the U.S. military efforts in the first place, the U.S. press turned the war into the *individual* stories of the men and women in the U.S. military involved in combat. The press literally turned macro-issues into micro-focused stories. The ability to use satellites brought audio-visual images instantly home to the American public. This "Living Room War" offered the vastly more visual impact of seeing the young men and women in the front lines versus the "talking heads" of "suits" discussing the underpinnings of why the U.S. was there in the first place.

The embedding of press with the troops shifted the perceptions of most Americans into how these soldiers, sailors and airmen were succeeding in their efforts, staying safe where possible, and triumphing quickly against an unprepared (but visually interesting) foe. Popular support grew rapidly as these personal reports flourished and increased. Live news reports amplified the excitement shared by most Americans. This "personal" micro view is further amplified as combat soldiers in the field use their cell phones and computers, often in defiance of military orders and policies, to send information, images and even "blogs" from the field.

To understand the emotional connectivity of messages, it becomes valuable to begin this analysis by looking at one of the most emotionally impactful parts of human existence: religion. Understand how people use and misuse religious messages, an emotional extreme, and perhaps there will be a glimmer of recognition on the risks and values of finding how to resonate emotionally for lesser and perhaps more commercial messages. What used to emanate from the pulpit (sometimes televised) or the local religious library (books and tapes) now spreads through the Web, with much accessed on smart phones. Better educated leaders, capable of biased editing of audio-visual content, can deploy compelling if inaccurate imagery that has an even greater emotional impact on naïve viewers who consider such content as immutable evidence.

The most effective political spin imaginable occurs in societies where organized religion is widely practiced and where political leaders manage to create a perception in their followers that they represent the "Will of God." In situations where peer pressure and group solidarity create an environment where dissent is not possible (very much present in societies with fundamental religious beliefs such as Shiite Iran) the results have been profoundly destructive. Tenets and policies which may begin as secular political philosophies can become tsunamis of religious passion over time in the hands of skilled politicians working in partnership with religious leaders.

But religious "spin" can also literally spin out of control. A badly-selected descriptive term, ill-conceived and spoken without thought, can fly through the mass media and sear through the Web, destroying careers and setting major defensive denials in play. Todd Akin, once the Republican Senator from Missouri, lost his reelection bid in 2012, for example, by trying to convince the world that "legitimate rape" victims rarely bore children as a result of the assault and thus did not need any exception in his quest to ban almost all abortions.

Would Akin have uttered those words if he has simply asked himself how his opponents would use his statements? What was spoken as evidence of his socially and religiously conservative profile wound up being read as a mindless, factless attack on women! It is always relevant to ask in advance how various social segments, from consumers to competitors, are likely respond to any given message.

What is equally relevant is that the absolute axioms of one era can shift to polar opposites over time. Awareness of trend-shifting, not assuming that social consciousness is static, is an essential part of appropriate messaging. Back to history for an example. During the Spanish Inquisition in the late 15th century, for example, Jews fled to Muslim controlled areas for sanctuary against Catholic Christians who were bent on killing non-believers.

Though is not a particularly tolerant religion, in the early 20th century, Palestinian Jews and Muslims lived side-by-side in peaceful coexistence. The creation of Israel in 1948 created a new opportunity for galvanizing political power against a new and convenient common enemy. In the 1950's, Egyptian President Gamal Abul Nassar used this new nation to distract his people's attention away from his failing economic policies. His rhetoric spun him to the top of Middle Eastern leadership (including a short-lived effort to unify Syria and Egypt into a single country – The United Arab Republic). Oil hadn't yet empowered the Arab world. Hating Israel became a *secular* issue intended to unite the region under Nassar's *secular* (pan-Arab socialism) leadership.

As time passed, Middle Eastern leaders sought to galvanize vast populations behind their push for control, particularly at the expense of elected secular leaders. They began a slow but accelerating process of blending the notion of anti-Zionism with a perception that this was a correct and devout demonstration of a belief in Islam. This factor was present in both Shiite and Sunni factions, despite their mutual disdain. As the decades passed, entire religious-political movements grew around support for the notion of the destruction of Israel.

The matter morphed away from being a secular issue, which would subject the relevant leadership to the vagaries of an ever-changing political landscape. Gradually, it developed the immutable constancy inherent in religious beliefs, where the populace supports a leadership that reigns for very long periods of time as purported spokesmen for "God."

Muslim religious leaders increasingly cemented the notion of devout Islamic beliefs with the disdain if not out-and-out commitment to the destruction of Jews, not just those in Israel, but wherever they lived. Transitory political power became inseparable from "correct" religious tenets. Hamas was elected to the leadership of Palestine in January, 2006. It is a military Sunni Muslim political party – deeply rooted in the Qur'an – that was founded primarily on the promise of destroying Israel.

Look at the cyclical trending that is switching impressions and emotions as quickly as events unfold. China, once an isolated and global pariah, is now an international role model for growth and lifting people out of poverty, while Western capitalism is finding decreasing traction around the world. The notion of permitting gay and lesbian marriage, unthinkable a decade or two ago, is now a majority view in the United States according to a Gallup Poll.[289]

So when creating a message for any particular market segment, It Is not enough to *believe* that social and moral values remain constant. They actually change all the time. Find out! Younger demographics, used to the fast pace of change, are often the most vulnerable to change their positions on key values. So much for looking at the segment you are trying to reach, but do you send messages – the old world of advertising – or do you *communicate*?

Thus, when one applies this notion of emotional commitment to down and dirty commercial marketing and entertainment, the linkage we see is creating a *relationship* between marketer and the consumer. Older marketing was a built around sending messages to consumers without expecting much in the way of a return message, other than mere sales or poll metrics. But defining "brands" and consumer/ audience relationships have evolved in our hyper-connected universe. Marketing executives are grappling with change, learning harsh lessons along the way.

We see a great deal of discussion in the advertising and marketing community using terms like "connected" or "integrated" campaigns. Integration is about a consistency across platforms and messages that coordinate a uniform brand message to consumers. But it is more important to find relevancy to the individuals in the consumer base, even if the communications are over more limited platforms. "Connectivity" trumps integration, but requires a deeply responsive communication with the target audience.

The obsession with brand-building, consistency, needs to overcome (balance if you will) a natural skepticism in the eyes of the general public that adheres to most new messages. It is more important to be *authentic* than brand-consistent. "Beginning with the Bible many centuries ago, brands often times came up with stories to distribute, to 'build a brand.' However, in the age of radical transparency and hyper-informed users, people are now more aware of inauthenticity than we have ever been… If you choose to tell stories as a brand, don't make it about you. Make it about the real people. Use the power of your brand and reach to reflect the truth."[290]

What's also even more important than brand awareness is the *emotional* connection that audiences and consumers associate with a brand: "Melanie Dempsey of Ryerson University and Andrew A. Mitchell of the University of Toronto demonstrated this when they exposed participants to made-up brands paired with a set of pictures and words, some negative and some positive. After seeing hundreds of images paired with brands, the subjects were unable to recall which brands were associated with which pictures and words, but they still expressed a preference for the positively conditioned brands. The authors of the study labeled it the 'I like it, but I don't know why effect.

"In a follow-up experiment participants were presented with product information that contradicted their earlier impressions, offering them reasons to reject their brand preferences, but they still chose those with the positive associations. Conflicting factual information did not undo the prior conditioning. The associated feelings superseded rational analysis."[291] Make it authentic and focus on the emotional message, which consumers often cannot articulate but most certainly experience.

Further, overwhelming people with messages all around them – that 360 encirclement – can backfire to the point where resentment builds or people just look past the flood. Creating additional values, where the product or service becomes part of daily life, for the individual constituents in the campaign creates the stickiness that makes marketing work. It's about smart and relevant communications, rather than massive and simply consistent brand messages.

And let's face, the *Big Idea*, solving a major issue in a new and inventive way, often creates positive spin that amplifies the product and the brand along with the idea. It's the difference between being a disruptive "shock jock" (different but not necessarily relevant) to becoming a game-changing "value jock." "For instance, a retailer may opt to run a campaign to build awareness or even a sales promotion. The real problem is the high cost of their business itself and the structure around it. Enter Everlane, a digital luxury clothing design manufacturing company that drastically reduces its product costs by completely cutting out the middleman. Instead of hiding the problem, they invented a business that solves it...

"Creativity and innovation are about finding unexpected solutions to obvious problems or finding obvious solutions to unexpected problems. We should use our creativity to provide better businesses and solutions rather than constantly trying to disrupt what people are doing.

"Campaigns or products, if they are not worthy of people's time, will end up polluting the world--literally and metaphorically. As we forge ahead into the post-digital, all-mobile era, 360 Degrees of Integrated Campaigns to tell Brand Stories via Media Disruption may no longer be as effective--and quite frankly, as necessary - as we thought... Brands should aim to solve real problems by providing Connected Services over 365 Days and by Inventing new Businesses that benefit People, not just the Brand."[292]

With two-way interactivity, we have entered the *Relationship Era* of marketing. Companies fight to get *liked* by consumers on their Facebook page, but the underlying tussle is to have consumers accept an emotional tie to the purveyor of the message that is *and remains* positive. Exactly how do you approach this new paradigm?

"The methodology here may not be especially rigorous, but the results dramatize three immutable facts of contemporary marketing:

1. Millions of people will, of their own volition, announce to the world their affection for a brand. Not for a person, not for an artwork, not for a dessert but for a good or service. Congratulations. People care about you.
2. Your brand is inextricably entwined in such relationships. If you were to type in 'I hate Exxon,' you'd get 2.16 million hits--not counting the 'I hate ExxonMobil' Facebook page. People are decreasingly listening to your messages, but that hasn't stopped them from thinking about you and talking about you. And each of those expressions of like, dislike, ardor or disgust has an exponent attached to it, reflecting the outward ripples of social interaction.
3. What used to happen in the privacy of your own boardroom, plants and C-suite is now extremely public and common currency on the Internet. People in glass houses shouldn't do anything illegal, embarrassing, hypocritical, offensive,

tasteless, vulgar, excessively greedy or otherwise incorrect--especially when getting caught being honorable and constructive has such benefits. Perhaps by coincidence, but most likely not, this sudden vast availability of information corresponds with a societal megatrend of judging institutions not only on their offerings but on their conduct. Thus, for the first time in commercial history, there is not just moral value but asset value in being a mensch.

"This is the Relationship Era, the first period of modern commerce when your success or failure depends not on what you say, nor even on what you produce, but increasingly on who you are. And it isn't hard to discover who you are. Just Google yourself. Take your time. It's all there, in perpetuity.

"Except for a handful of industrial juggernauts mainly removed from public view (including ExxonMobil, truth be told) doing business in the Relationship Era has many requirements. Ethical conduct. Seamless customer relations. Constant contact and cooperation with all stakeholders, including not just investors but also employees, suppliers, distributors and retailers, neighbors, governments and the society at large. It must be an all-pervasive imperative to earn the trust of all concerned--not as a means to gain advantage in a sale or negotiation but as an end in itself."[293] In short, it's a never-ending process that needs constant attention and correction.

And sometimes the approach is to blend ("bundle") your message with something that already resonates with your audience or consumer base. Just as there is guilt by association, there can be benefits as well.

The Power of Bundled Messages

Sometimes, we can take a message that may be totally Rule One inappropriate for a particular psychographic and make it not only palatable to that segment but have them rallying to the cause, simply by associating the "inappropriate" so intimately with a strongly desired value that the bundled effect carries the message home on all fronts. When you represent a minority seeking majority clout, sometimes it is wise to marry the values you wish to foster with other values already held sufficiently widely to make a difference.

The strategic ability to pair a value shared by very few (for example policies that positively impact less than five percent of the nation) so that it is intimately an inseparably linked to wider and more accepted views is a marketer's dream. Emotional linkage between a product or a point of view, on the one hand, with some bigger, more positive values, on the other, is a critical in marketing. How consumers *feel* about what you are messaging is usually the difference between success and failure. In the United States, history shows us how this worked on our own political stage.

In 1964, social conservative Barry Goldwater was soundly defeated as the Republican nominee for President of the United States. His platform was not founded on religious beliefs but a combination of libertarian disdain for an intrusive Federal government and a generally fiscally conservative belief set.

How could a party that championed tax reductions and deregulation ever generate enough votes to win a national election? Their platform almost entirely catered to corporations and the highest income brackets (a clear minority of voters) at the expense of social programs that benefited the lower and middle classes. There was seemingly no way to develop a national constituency. That would have required vast numbers of lower and middle class voters be willing to vote against the very programs directed at providing them with economic and "quality of life" benefits (Social Security, Medicare, consumer and environmental protection) at the expense of business not anxious to pay for the cost of polluting, etc.

Then the Republican Party hit upon a stroke of marketing genius, blending the notion of fiscal conservatism with embracing the most fundamental social issues that Democrats were seemingly unable to espouse: policies against abortion, gay marriage and rights, embryonic stem cell research as well as favoring public school prayer and teaching intelligent design as an alternative to Darwinism. Finding themselves at the center of "conservative" political power and invited to meetings at the highest levels, the leaders of Evangelical Christian movement were now politically empowered; they reciprocated from the pulpit.

The Democratic machine that had called all the political shots since the Civil War was now trumped by a machine with wider reach and appeal: the conservative southern Evangelical church, which we now call "The Base." Evangelicals voted for the "Neo-Con" Republicans, supported tax cuts for the rich, and prospered as governmental policies and new judicial appointments tracked their core beliefs. They remained steadfast even though the political promises of their party did not substantiate the reason for the Iraq war, or deliver a solid victory in Iraq, and the economy fell into a recession. As this conservative movement felt that some Republicans were moving away from their socially conservative values, a new Tea Party movement reinvigorated conservative values, reacting to counter American demographic trends showing a majority of Americans were now really a growing amalgamation of urban ethnic diversity.

The results in media were quite astounding. Fox News television used a strong Evangelical/conservative platform to become the most profitable television news organization in the United States.[294] Conservatives used new media both to communicate as well as to galvanize social action, making sure that their constituency was properly focused and informed to use sheer numbers to influence governmental policy-makers. Social and fiscal conservatism blurred into a unitary theme. Once the conservative constituency had been sufficiently identified – either online or by their choice of media – it became relatively easy for conservative action groups to respond quickly and effectively to any issue that contradicted their beliefs.

Of necessity, Democratic candidates were drawn into this sweep of more fundamental Christian religiosity. They made sure cameras were present as they attended Sunday services (including the President) addressed myriad congregations as a part of their campaigns and professed their dedication to their deeply-held belief in Jesus Christ. But their stance on the most conservative of social issues – which were most important to the Evangelical movement – created an uncrossable chasm with the true Evangelicals, who now constituted approximately 30% of the U.S. electorate (Wikipedia tells us three quarters of American call themselves Christian). Just imagine the prospects for a U.S. presidential candidate who does not actively practice Christianity.

Given our ability to filter messages, ranging from "spam" to choosing channels and Websites that already embrace our core values and avoiding contradictory sites, this notion of linkage becomes mission critical to marketers seeking tangible results. If you are filtered before a message can even be consumed, your efforts are wasted. If the message appears in a friendly venue or is delivered to a consumer in response to a search or other direct request, obviously it will be better received than a bolt from the blue. Hanging with the right crowd especially in marketing, makes a big difference. We call this "affinity marketing."

It is interesting to note how the power of some social groupings – particularly those based on a fundamental interpretation of faith – will trump the power of inter-generational and geographic affiliations. Thus, where there are strongly held religious beliefs, the bonds that hold people together within that group are extremely difficult to break absent a new and often individual catastrophic vulnerability. Religious belief will supersede the dictates of virtually any other social grouping – even family. Affiliating with a preapproved social segment may help to rise above the clutter and reach people who have barriers to outsider messages. An examination of social groupings that might have relevance to your message or product is a path worth exploring.

Rule Three – Master Damage Control

A dozen men in good suits and women in silk dresses will circulate smoothly among the reporters, spouting confident opinions. They won't be just press agents trying to impart a favorable spin to a routine release. They'll be the Spin Doctors, senior advisers to the candidates. New York Times, 1984

From the sexual peccadilloes of Tiger Woods, Arnold Schwarzenegger and Anthony Weiner to unflattering diplomatic references generated from the United States government and reports that a British tabloid owned by News Corporation illegally hacked into private communications, negative information is profoundly difficult to keep under wraps and once released seemingly impossible to contain. Even trying to keep consumers from finding cheaper prices from a competitor is no longer possible in today's hyper-connected universe.

Governments can find themselves in a world of hurt where sensitive information finds its way onto the Web, creating diplomatic chaos, as has occurred on several occasions through WikiLeaks[295] or the revelations of a government subcontractor who spills a top secret governmental spy program against mass communications of all types. The Reagan-era term "spin-doctor" was born of politics, but the era of public relations specialist can create and cure damage in reputations of all sorts. And those that are not prepared or respond to all sorts of derogatory or negative information badly can only make matters worse. In a world with too much public information and ubiquitous access to mass communications, damage control become a necessary tool of public life, from politics to personalities to products. Public exposure embraces risks that must be anticipated.

Building and Losing Positive Perception

In a world where headlines scream corporate greed and irresponsibility, where prominent individuals decimate their careers with ethics lapses, the hidden value that may just supersede price sensitivity is *trust*. "'One day, a company might be better off asking not what its margins are, but what its trust factor is,' says Brian Singh, founder of Zinc Research, a social media and marketing research firm in Calgary, Alberta. Singh has begun framing the formation of connections via social networking as a form of 'digital oxytocin' [not the drug, but a trust-generating chemical in the brain].

The idea is that if businesses wish to thrive in our interconnected world, where consumers' opinions spread at the speed of light, they must act as a trusted friend: create quality products, market them honestly, emphasize customer care."[296] Companies that lose trust lose customers even faster. Companies that generate oxytocin responses prosper. The battles that have been fought, even before the digital era, lay the groundwork for understanding this essential marketing ingredient.

While governments can catapult themselves into power by using the above-noted religious beliefs effectively, that route is not available for those seeking to market their products and services. However, the destructive power against an established brand where religion enters the fray can be incalculable. During the 1960s, Procter & Gamble, the world's largest manufacturer of consumer packaged goods, struggled with a rumor that the configuration in the P&G corporate logo – the man in the moon with stars in the background in their corporate logo – was in fact an allusion to Revelation 13:18 in the Bible, a reference to the "number of the beast" … 666, the devil.

A misguided fundamental Christian movement, believing the mega-billion-dollar, publicly-traded company to be managed by a satanic cult of moon worshippers, deluged Procter & Gamble with hundreds of thousands of letters, signed myriad petitions and engaged in a massive boycott of the company's products. Another rumor reverberated that P&G's president had appeared on a popular talk-show to discuss his satanic beliefs (it never happened!).

P&G countered these allegations as best they could and even enlisted established clergy for help to reverse this growing public sentiment. Despite assurances from bona fide Christian leaders like Billy Graham and Jerry Falwell, in 1985, Procter & Gamble abandoned this symbol that it had used since 1882, but it took years to recapture the consumers who had turned away from the company's products based upon this unfounded belief.

What is particularly interesting about the P&G example noted above is how much communication occurred within a core group of Christian believers, how deeply rooted and intransigent those who believed the falsehood had become – enough to stun a Fortune 100 consumer goods company – in an era that *preceded* the connectivity of the Internet. Today's pervasive networks of communications, from simple blogging to acts of criminal sabotage, have multiplied the ability to strike at the heart of any high profile person or company.

Damaging rumors, passed off as emanating from credible and often emotionally "core-belief" sources, have become a daily part of business and government. We have entered the era of constant damage control, spin doctors, and have given rise to a new and extremely important corporate senior executive – the Chief Information Officer (CIO).

Some have looked at this function as the product of required governmental disclosure and reporting obligations, but today, responding to allegations of corporate misfeasance, malfeasance and mistaken rumor have pushed this management competency to the top level of corporate governance. No longer are pro forma statutory compliance reports the driving force behind the information department, and since sales and marketing are definitely in a separate corporate department, this job has "damage control" written all over it.

Whistleblowers can find anonymity on the Web. Disgruntled customers can exact retribution in the ether, charging without having to prove or sustain. Mistakes and apocryphal stories find themselves on the same page as provable facts. And when the facts themselves are devastating, finding a reasonable redirection becomes mission critical.

When Major Disaster Strikes

When a company becomes the symbol of the excess that most people believe was at the heart of the deep recession we have experienced, the questions drive to the very survival of the company itself. Insurance giant, American International Group (AIG) – a recipient of billions of federal bailout dollars and slammed by a badly-handled executive bonus scandal – changed its name to AIU Holdings to sidestep the public relations nightmare that surrounded their brand, figuring that most of their "too big to fail" business isn't consumer-driven anyway.

They may wind up winning by default, because insurance is a necessary component of our economy, and AIG is just too intimately related to too many insurance policies and business credit insurance (even when the issuing insurer may be a different company) to disappear, and ultimately they paid back their government debt.

Todd Akin, the politician whose "legitimate rape" phrase noted above, did not recover. He tried to explain what he meant, but his words were so foolish, his attempts to explain only make matters worse. He lost a coveted U.S. Senate race in Missouri. President Bill Clinton faced major distractions as opponents sought to impeach him over the Monica Lewinsky scandal, but he stayed in office. With the passage of time, most

Americans remember him fondly, and he is a hot ticket for Democratic candidates seeking endorsements these days. In 2009, after lying about "hiking the Appalachian Trail" (while visiting his mistress in Argentina), then South Carolina Governor Mark Sanford, faded out of his state's political scene... until a special election for a House seat in 2013. Humbled and now engaged to his Argentinian lover, Sanford appealed to his Republican Christian constituency, seeking forgiveness. "I am an imperfect man saved by God's grace," he said as a master of damage control.

The Chrysler and General Motors bankruptcies faced during the depth of the great recession brought public relations challenges these carmakers had never encountered or anticipated before: trying to administer damage control from economic failure and dozens of negative disclosures inherent in the process of getting government money to survive bankruptcy while retaining a customer base. First, they had to get "bailed out."

As General Motors and Chrysler executives presented their case for government support in public hearings, they pretty much pointed out all the reasons why consumers should avoid their products like the plague. Their managements and unions were viewed as incompetent, overpaid, and self-indulgent, even though key executives have been fired and replaced. Even after emerging from bankruptcy, these companies faced less-than-steady income, sales rising and falling with every positive and negative statement about the economy. They then had to recapture the confidence of the American public with their laundry list of mismanagement out in the air for all to see.

Trust was long gone. Particularly during the early period of the recession, the public was particularly attuned to wasteful costs, as "no-value-added" mark-ups to the average price of a vehicle. The mere fact that these behemoths, particularly Chrysler, might still go under permanently (beyond the original bankruptcy filings) made consumers worry that warranties would be worthless and that parts for future repairs would not be available – even with government guarantees on warranties, would there be anyone there to perform the work? Further, GM and Chrysler had become associated with the fundamental cause of the financial meltdown, leaving a bitter taste in many consumers' mouths.

The plight of both GM and Chrysler, telegraphed by a series of corporate missteps – ranging from flying in corporate jets to congressional meetings to beg for money to unions' resisting all but the most absurd practices was in the headlines every time they told Washington why they needed money. For example, they finally agreed to stop paying pools of employees who were not working but were literally held in reserve for better times. Beggars have a really tough time inspiring consumer confidence. Poll after poll showed that people just plain didn't think these companies should be saved, that their stupidity should not be rewarded with a bailout. Years after the government rescue, GM appears to be marginally sustainable, but the jury is still very much out with Chrysler's long-term prospects.

Here is how the damage impacted the companies "back then," in 2009: "Since the first congressional hearings on the auto industry in November [of 2008], U.S. sales by GM and Chrysler have fallen a combined 45% compared with the year-earlier period; all other carmakers slid only 33% during that time … By comparison, Ford Motor Co., which has not accepted any government aid, saw its share of the retail car market rise for four consecutive months through January [of 2009], the first time that's happened in 14 years… In the first two months of [2009], the number of buyers considering a GM or Chrysler vehicle fell 12% and 33%, respectively, according to CNW Marketing Research, which specializes in the auto industry. At the same time, Ford saw a 12% increase in consideration."[297]

Consumers at the New York International Auto Show in the spring of 2009 were even less subtle, admonishing the presenters about GM's and Chrysler's impending restructuring. A significant number of attendees indicated no interest whatsoever in buying even the most innovative products of this carmakers. One wag observed that he would not want to buy a car built by autoworkers who were distracted, depressed, terrified and confused.

So what was the remedy for surviving bankruptcy and coming back online? Wait for better times? Unfortunately, that could take years and without serious positive cash flow, the companies faced what Wall Street derisively calls "Chapter 22" bankruptcy – filing Chapter 11 reorganization bankruptcy twice! The federal government tried to jump-start the recovery for its carmakers with a temporary (and moderately successful) "cash for clunkers" program, where old cars were subsidized by the government (and scrapped) if folks would consider buying new, fuel efficient vehicles.

While that helped U.S. post-bankrupt carmakers, it also boosted sales for Japanese imports as well. But even surviving after reorganization with government help doesn't mean that these companies can sell enough cars to remain viable into the distant future. Discounts were pervasive, so offering great deals is not a clear advantage for the GM and Chrysler, even if we assume that credit is reasonably available.

It's all about consumer confidence: (i) consumers needed proof that their rights (like warranties) and values (resale) would survive financial decimation – consumers had to understand why they should still trust these automobile companies as car buyers make the second biggest purchase of their lives, (ii) bankruptcy had to be viewed as a solution to creating a new, reality-based carmakers with innovation as the new priority, (iii) despite massive give-backs, the long-term assumption that union and management excess still needed to be managed – consumers could not accept that they were overpaying for waste or rewarding those whom they believe caused the problem , and (iv) there needed to be a consumer-assisted change in GM's and Chrysler's exceptionally negative image. Unfortunately, this mind-shift required a long-term play, solid and consistent.

The emphasis had to be on dependable value, sensitivity to rising gasoline prices and cutting edge technology. Honesty and instant recognition of problems, open and candid dialog with existing and potential customers, and creating cars that people really wanted. It was buyers who had to define the product now. Consumers were sensitive to watching their taxes rise, aware of the governmental deficit borrowings (used in part to fund these carmakers) threatening the future value of the dollar, and they needed to see once-spoiled managers and workers with cushy benefit packages go lean, roll-up their sleeves and not simply suck down tax dollars because they did not know how to run a company (even after concessions from these participants had been implemented!). This is hardly a "let's reward failure with a purchase" scenario.

So somehow, GM and Chrysler had to destroy the "old versions of themselves" – literally killing the old companies (more than just shutting down a few divisions like Pontiac), old management and old union practices, which were the problem – and sell an entirely new, ground-up reinvented, leaner and meaner, value-oriented set of car companies, run by common-sense managers and consumer-oriented unions, that was clearly be there for the foreseeable future. It does come down to consumer trust and confidence.

How have these two companies fared since their rescue? General Motors went public and stressed engineering, presented a slate of green vehicles at a time of rising energy prices and prioritized reliability, leading to increasingly positive ratings in the relevant trade press. The process has taken and will continue to take time, particularly difficult as economic indicators have been anything but consistent.

Chrysler, having fallen far behind in the engineering from the economic collapse, still struggles to find reasons for consumers to choose their vehicles. Minority shareholder Fiat wants an even bigger stake (perhaps total) in Chrysler and is using Chrysler to bring that Italian carmaker's smaller, more gas efficient vehicles to the American market.

So looking back, how did these carmakers actually do? In 2013, Chrysler almost blew a golden opportunity, based on a government recall of certain Jeep models by reason of a vulnerable gas tank. Chrysler seemed determined to fight the recall, until their marketing executives pointed out how this was quite contrary to the company's overall goals of rebuilding consumer confidence. In June of 2013, Chrysler wisely accepted the recall.

GM did even better in 2013: "When General Motors was given a taxpayer bailout in 2009, many of the criticisms around the deal and around the automaker were about the company's failure to compete on quality with Japanese brands. But those problems are apparently going away: J.D. Power said Wednesday that Chevrolet and GMC both outscored Toyota and Honda in Power's influential Initial Quality Study, which measures customer complaints in the first 90 days of ownership."[298] It took years, patience, consistency and a dedication to excellence, no excuses given

Keeping secrets from customers and hoping the problems will all go away no longer works in an era where information about mistakes spreads like wildfire. Equally destructive, however, is dwelling on past mistakes beyond when the public views a negative incident as old news. But what is particularly galling to consumers is a long period of denial of an obvious issue, and then admitting a mistake and taking corrective measures only when there appears to be no other choice (or when required to do so by government order). Such actions suggest a general policy of not being truthful to consumers that undermines the most basic requirement of maintaining public trust and confidence in a brand.

The rolling recalls of Toyota automobiles in late 2009/early 2010 – mostly for brake and accelerator pedal-related issues – tanked already impaired car sales for the automotive giant by almost 9%, while U.S. American automakers reported sales increases. It wasn't just that defective cars tarnished Toyota's reputation; it was the "lengthy pattern in which [over many years] the automaker has often reacted slowly to safety concerns, in some instances making design changes without telling customers about problems with vehicles already on the road." [299] What could have been routine damage control escalated to the standard mea culpa speech by Toyota's CEO and a costly plan to rebuild the car company's severely damaged reputation. How long will that take? Much longer than an open and candid response when the initial troubles developed.

Toyota must now spread its word far and wide, engage in hundreds of thousands of two-way communications, access social networks, bloggers and newsmakers. It must go to extremes in quality control (and communicate what it is doing), double customer care, incentivize new buyers and reinforce loyalty of older buyers (even if it means exchanging whole cars). And it must let the whole world know convincingly that this "attitude" of battling disclosure and resisting necessary recalls will never ever happen again!

But trust-building (or rebuilding) requires a long-term and consistent commitment that cannot produce change overnight. For companies with limited expertise on or staff for damage control, particularly when defending against falsehoods, there are small company solutions available to just about anyone.[300] And in today's world of open mass communications, one must also track the blogs and tweets that impact consumer perceptions.

The other side of damage control is particularly relevant for corporations who require government approvals or licenses. When outrageous corporate conduct rips across the headlines just as a sensitive government approval is required, damage control can have dire economic consequences. News Corporation literally shut down an entire newspaper over such an occurrence, just as it was seeking approval from the British government for taking complete ownership of the local satellite service, BSkyB: "But it may [have been] too little too late.

The revelations that News of the World [the tabloid that was shuttered], part of News Corp.' s News International unit, was engaged in hacking the voicemail accounts of not only celebrities and members of the Royal Family but also victims of crime and terrorism, has shocked even the United Kingdom, where there has long been a high tolerance for tabloid shenanigans....

"Even if the scandal doesn't kill the BSkyB deal [News Corp pulled their bid, perhaps hoping for better times in the distant future], odds are any agreement will be slow in coming and given intense scrutiny, which will make it even costlier for News Corp. The company had already endured a lengthy review of its intentions to shell out roughly $13 billion for total control of BSkyB. Collins Stewart [financial] analyst Thomas Eagan said News Corp. may have to bid another $1.3 billion.

"Closing News of the World won't even be a blip on the bottom line of News Corp. and its $30 billion in annual revenue. The paper, according to industry analysts, was marginally profitable. However, its value to the company cannot be measured in just dollars and cents." [301] With its stock price crashing combined with arrests of high level employees, News Corp then faced a parallel U.S. criminal investigation by the FBI. Indictments of key News Corp journalists continued well into 2013. Cash settlements to those whose phones were hacked and massive full-page apologies did little to quell a scandal that threatened seismic shifts in the long-term management and control of this media giant. Eventually, News Corp elected to separate out its publishing assets into an entirely separate publicly-traded entity, hoping not to drag down the core values in the balance of the company.

Small signs of trouble had littered the path, occasional publicly-revealed hints of wiretaps and hacking on behalf of the paper, but the players were top honchos in the News Corp newspaper hierarchy so no one bothered to contain the problem. Letting dangerous conduct continue once there are signs of its existence is failed damage control. No one is too important in a company for its executives to look the other way; it only looks that much worse later. Fear of offending most senior management, lacking appropriate checks and balances applicable to everyone, allowed inappropriate conduct at News Corp to continue.

Bloggers and hackers constantly search the Web for misfeasance. Whistleblowers have new avenues of mass expression, often anonymous. News Corp was a sitting duck. So what was once small and containable misconduct became a sea of wrongdoings and management cover-ups that threatened to topple an empire. Paying attention only to stories that become headline-burners is hardly sufficient, since so much muckraking begins in the world of blogs and micro-blogs (e.g., tweets). Keeping track of the little stories before they explode into the mainstream headlines or they spread sufficiently to do real damage is an increasingly necessary task.

The Rise of Grassroots Access to Mass Communication

Blogging is seen by some as simple grassroots journalism posted on designated websites. Others see this form of communication as the unprofessional promulgation of unfounded rumors. Either way, blogging and its very short video/comment-oriented counterpart (so-called "micro-blogging") – tweeting – have become a powerful tools.

Blogging tends to engage older Web users, while Twitter[302] is often domain of choice for younger communicators. Like most fields endeavor, influencers (bloggers and micro-bloggers) that develop consistency and whose critiques resonate with their constituency develop stellar reputations and can often rise into the world of commercial success. But blogs open the world to unfiltered and often unverified comments and tag lines, through links to other blogs. Users hiding behind untraceable user IDs often seem to have the ability to appear and disappear with virtually no trace.

There is an increasing tendency to "do what everyone else is doing" to keep up with generic changes in media patterns. Yet, the choice and timing of the medium of expression can lend itself to reputation damage. For example as useful as Twitter can be to gain recognition, a number of people who have already achieved high profile recognition are backing away from the service, which can become an anonymous, uncensored highway of insults and negativity. Think before you leap. Blogs and micro-blogs often exert influence beyond their apparent reach. Even if the blog is not in itself a uniformly credible source, there is an increasing tendency among mainstream journalists to rely on information that they have discovered in someone else's blog.

According to a survey by advertising agency Omnicom (which has since merged with Publicis Groupe), [303] of the traditional journalists responding, 61.8% indicated that blogging influenced the tone of their reports; 51.1% admitted that blogs actually influenced their editorial and story decisions. Who are these bloggers? In the United States, Web metrics company, Technorati (a company that has, since 2002, tracked and indexed blogs according to reach and authority), examined the specifics:

- "57% of U.S. bloggers are male, 74% are college graduates, 56% work full-time, and 20% are self-employed (vs. 8% of the Internet population for the latter).
- "On average, bloggers use five different techniques to drive traffic to their blog, an average of seven publishing tools on their blog, and four distinct metrics for measuring success.
- "Among those [blogs] with advertising, the mean annual investment in their blog is $1,800, but it's paying off. The mean annual revenue is $6,000 with $75K+ in revenue for those with 100,000 or more unique visitors per month.
- "Four in five bloggers post brand or product reviews. [304].
- "About half of bloggers are professional bloggers — blogging is not necessarily their full-time job, but they blog about their industry or profession

in an unofficial capacity; 12% of bloggers blog in an official capacity for their company.

- "Blogging is having an incredibly positive impact on bloggers' lives, with bloggers receiving speaking or publishing opportunities, career advancement, and personal satisfaction." [305]

Protectors of individual and corporate images once only had to deal with the traditional press. But in today's world where almost anyone has ubiquitous access to mass communications, how do you square the blogging phenomenon with the future of traditional media? Has blogging actually replaced television news or at least achieved a level of success that has elevated some bloggers to broadcast-network levels of credibility gods? At a media conference, Mark Cuban, media mogul and chairman HDNet (since reformatted and rebranded today as AXS-TV) and owner of the Dallas Mavericks basketball team, suggested that the future of traditional paper-based newspapers may be in the bankruptcy courts while AOL Chairman and CEO, Randy Falco, countered that, "The blogosphere is not the most reliable source of news."[306] It was no surprise, in 2011, when AOL bought the successful blog-aggregator, the Huffington Post and merged this acquisition with its AOLNews brands, as part of an AOL-makeover effort.

It must be equally unsurprising, as confirmed in the above-noted Omnicom report, that over three quarters of the surveyed reporters acknowledged that blogs were a consistent source of story ideas and reporting perspectives. For a corporation trying to keep the lid on a damaging story or a celebrity caught in the headlights of a late-night arrest, the sheer number of blogs and tweets suggests that killing a story is close to impossible. Voyeurism and finding dirt appear to be audience-generating efforts that often defy containment.

Bottom line: if something negative surfaces anywhere in the heavily-linked blogosphere, the job of the CIO is both to contain the damage and spin the story in a manner to minimize damage to the company's ability to make money and generate revenues. In the case of the celebrity, it would be to maximize that person's career. That does not always mean suppressing the story – sometime bad is good. Attributions of "edgy and dangerous" have their place in a marketing manager's choice of weapons. Picture a *sweet* gangsta' rapper.

But *bad* can destroy if not countered. For example, political candidates find themselves having interracial babies out of wedlock, divorcing wives, engaging in acts of cowardice when they served in their country's armed forces – all a radical departure from the perception they seek and resulting better fiction-writing than many an amateur novelist. Occasionally snippets of truth emerge. Occasionally scandals are born, but increasingly, total fabrications are disseminated as truth, often by means of random or carefully programmed telephone calls (playing prerecorded falsehoods) or via the Internet.

Rumors are often spread by public relations Web experts with a malicious intent to defeat a rising political star with good, old-fashioned lies. Unscrupulous political action groups, sometimes with their candidate's tacit approval, set out to shred the political chances of an opponent, even if it takes total fiction to accomplish this action. Political candidates spend huge sums creating and placing ad campaigns to present a proper image and often bigger sums to negate the falsehoods that have become "common knowledge" among their possible constituencies.

Modern corporate communications aimed at damage control hardly began with the Internet. However, doing the right thing and quickly, from a corporate perspective anyway, was until relatively recently alien to the typical CEO. When a product failed or created harm, conventional corporate wisdom resulted in pushing the bad press out of public view, exerting pressure on newspapers and other mass media, which cared deeply about not losing corporate advertising dollars, to bury damaging information. Corporations spent billions denying defects or the toxicity of their products, even when it might have been less expensive to remedy the problem. To some, these denials and counter efforts were simply aimed at buying time.

Consider the battle governments have waged against tobacco companies or how Exxon used the courts to delay the payment of damages resulting from the 1989 Exxon Valdez oil spill. These strategies allowed time for litigation reserves to accumulate interest and consumers to spend more money (hence increase the pool of money available to pay judgments and settlements) before the final court order mandating payment is implemented. For a very long time, companies believed that they could deny wrongdoing, suppress the reporting of misfeasance, and still maintain solid consumer brand loyalty. Times have definitely changed.

While one oil company stretched on the process in 1989, more recently, an equally large oil company took the opposite approach. When the largest oil spill in recorded history occurred in the spring and summer of 2010 – from the explosion on the Deepwater Horizon drilling rig in the Gulf of Mexico – petroleum giant BP instantly deployed a massive damage control team, from grassroots operatives at the local level to top-level public relations consultants who filled the airways with advertising showing how BP was responsive to the situation. While BP, its insurance carriers and partner companies incurred some major liabilities from the lax standards suggested by the explosion, a year later the disaster was perceived almost as if it were ancient history.

There were, however, flashes of the future of modern corporate damage control even as far back as 1982, long before the blogging, tweeting, even the Internet and well before the need to hire and staff a large department for the new job of Chief Information Officer became obvious. Take the case of the tainted Tylenol, an analgesic manufactured by Johnson & Johnson. In 1982, a mentally deranged killer (a "terrorist" in today's parlance) planted deadly cyanide into several bottles of these headache capsules, some believe at their point of manufacture. There were seven fatalities in the Chicago area, including a 12-year-old little girl.

The perpetrator has never been caught. Johnson & Johnson reacted instantly, halting the all Tylenol advertising, pulling an estimated 30 million bottles of the product off the shelves and pouring millions into ad campaigns to warn and save the public. It is estimated that J&J spent over $100 million (which would be more than double that number in today's dollars) removing those bottles and dealing with the resulting debacle. In 1982, Tylenol's market share of analgesics was shredded, dropping from 30% to a mere 8%.

Things were bleak at Johnson & Johnson's corporate headquarters. Doing the right thing and placing the public's best interests before their own were unheard of corporate actions at that time, and the loss of market share amplified the financial cost. Many argued that denial and settling in court would have been smarter. One year later, however, Tylenol began moving back towards the top of the list of trusted products in the analgesic category, and today J&J's unprecedented actions (and consistent subsequent philosophy) have solidified that company as one of America's most trusted, recognized and valued brand names.[307]

Today, tamper-resistant bottles have become the norm. However, the company that makes Excedrin was forced to shut down production and revamp their procedures because pills other than Excedrin were found mixed into the Excedrin bottles that had not been tampered. It employed a silent, under the radar damage-control technique that allowed time to pass without much comment. The product was removed from shelves and – almost a year later, the product quietly re-appeared in stores. No big campaign – no mention in the press.

Negative information can burn through the consumers' consciousness – fueled by the Internet, mobile information platforms and instant communications at every level. Johnson &Johnson's once-bold steps are today the only prudent reaction for a corporation placed in the cross-hairs of public scrutiny. Denial creates reactance and resentment; attempting to spin that which cannot be explained easily and quickly creates backlash.

If there is one less obvious lesson for the age of Internet communications from the Johnson & Johnson experience decades ago, it has to be the long-term value of a great reputation as the primary mechanism to defeat mendacious and destructive rumors. But great reputations take years to develop and must be earned.

Managing Scandals

Damage control can get very personal as well. Individual politicians and celebrities have watched their constituent or consumer appeal crash and burn in a scandalous moment. For many the scandal is beyond repair – bribe-taking resulting in arrest and conviction usually (but strangely not always) will destroy a political career – but for many in the media spotlight, the revelation of a sexual indiscretion can result in serious "damage," particularly if "untruth" is at the core of disingenuous denial. Impeachment of offending politicians awaits, not for the indiscretion but for the lies or misuse of government funds, as South Carolina Governor Mark Sanford and former President Bill Clinton can attest.

And then there are the celebrities, particularly athletes, whose strong non-steroid laden bodies are supposed to be the essence of commitment, dedication and hard work – values cherished by all. Pure entertainment celebrities, well, the standard is somewhat lower, and "badness" may actually be a part of their individual persona. Does being depicted as out-of-control and over-the-top really negatively impact actors like Robert Downey, Jr. or Charlie Sheen, who actually like playing roles at the edge? Maybe the negative press is even a career enhancement. Compare that to an actress like Lindsay Lohan, who made her reputation playing innocent teens, yet engages in a series of behaviors that are morally and legally inconsistent with the characters she portrayed.

Perhaps, the denigration of "stars" in the entertainment sector is at least in part attributable to the profound public investigation and reporting of the stars' personal lives and foibles. Athletes face tougher standards of behavior, even when we all know they slip and fall all the time (reflected in the proverbial "professional athlete felon of the week"). Nevertheless, social networking and a wide-open Web have raised the bar on openness and honesty.

Take the case of Tiger Woods and how he handled the press explosion of his purported extra-marital affairs and sexual dalliances in the late fall of 2009. He blogged: "This is a private matter and I want to keep it that way. Although I understand there is curiosity, the many false, unfounded and malicious rumors that are currently circulating about my family and me are irresponsible."

Bad move, Tiger. His best approach would have been an *immediate* "mea culpa" and a humble and sad request for forgiveness. But Tiger held back, slid around the issues, and waited before releasing a very half-hearted and most incomplete admission. [308] While some sponsors terminated their arrangements with the famous golfer most announced a "wait and see" attitude. No matter the formal reaction, there was nary a Tiger Woods commercial anywhere after that nasty story leaked to the media.

Without the slightest doubt, the value of his brand plummeted. The December 11, 2009 FastCompany.com reacted by reminding us that: "Brands exist in the mind of consumers that don't like being lied to." Realizing the gravity of the damage to his reputation and searching for the grand gesture that might generate forgiveness, Woods finally used the word "infidelity" and announced an "indefinite break from professional golf." [309] With new levels of analytics, like the notorious "Q scores" [310] often applied to the commercial evaluation of celebrities, a failure to administer proper damage control (quickly!) can make a bad situation worse and can result in vastly longer (*if ever*) full image recovery.

"Being inappropriate" (both as to theme and timing) can also make a bad situation worse. Woods and his Nike brand sponsor discovered this in April of 2010, just as he returned to play in the famous Masters tournament, when a "rehabilitation" ad actually used the recorded voice of Tiger's deceased father giving him wise words of advice. All the press and blogosphere could see was a manipulative use of a dead father to return the son to commercial value.

To put it mildly, the effort backfired. Bad news continued to mount as his return to golf was underwhelming, his coach resigned in a text message, sponsors continued to withdraw, Tiger's wife seemed to dominate the headlines with her demands and Tiger used a neck injury to pull out of the tour altogether. His advisors, if he were actually listening to them, seemed to misunderstand the full impact of the career crash and by trying to make it all go away quickly actually prolonged the agony.

Many years later, with Nike still by his side, the after-effects of Tiger's scandal and his struggle to recapture the consistency that took him to the top wore off. By 2013, Tiger was older, wiser, but time seemed to heal this wound; he was very much back in the running, although his relationship with videogame maker Electronic Arts ended in the fall of that year. Unless the consequences are immediate, as with running for office to keep your job, a bit of quiet rebuilding and the passage of enough time can help resurrect a career gone awry in public scandal.

Honest, heartfelt reactions, prompt and true, can be used to defeat an issue before it explodes beyond control. Billionaire entrepreneur and outspoken majority owner of the National Basketball Association's Dallas Mavericks, Mark Cuban, had a public relations nightmare in the late summer of 2008 when one of his players, forward Josh Howard, was caught on camera at the beginning of a celebrity flag football game using some pretty strong language about his lack of reverence for The Star-Spangled Banner, just as that American national anthem was being played. The images shot across the Web, telecasts (with the obligatory bleep at the profanity) circulated, and Cuban's email bin (at the Mavericks) began to fill with even more vituperative, racist vinegar. The public reacted horribly against this African-American's athlete's conduct.

Cuban's reaction? He posted some of the most outrageous, barb-infested, racist emails (with the email addresses of the senders in large letters) on his blog, taking them down just a few hours later. Mark's explanation, carried on his blog and entitled, "I Made My Point," is a particularly instructive form of instinctive damage control. In his own words: "I thought it was important to point out the hatred and ignorance of so many who quickly judge people they have never met, based purely on sound bites and headlines. If you think you know any public figure based on what you see on TV or read on the internet or in newspapers, you are sadly mistaken."

In the end, Cuban's efforts hit a balancing point that found favor with most of the fans and press that responded. While his words and efforts showed that his heart was in the right place, they also produced an extremely beneficial marketing result, and his players will never forget how far the boss went to protect one of their own.

In many cases, rebuilding trust and credibility is anything but immediate. For example, in 2007, National Football League quarterback, Michael Vick, was convicted and spent 21 months in prison over professional dog-fighting. He served his time, was consistently contrite, made lots of apologetic public appearances, and slowly began the road back to professional football. In 2009, he signed with a new team, and by 2011 was deemed sufficiently rehabilitated that his old sponsor, Nike, resigned him to a new contract. Patience and persistence take time. Not letting the process unwind and then allowing reputation and credibility to rebuild is painstakingly slow; but rushing the process can actually lengthen the time for any real shot at recovery.

But the above examples involve large, well-capitalized organizations and experienced executives, well-versed in the vagaries of public relations, staffed with experts that deal with the press daily. Yet even they often fail to "fix the broken," as we have seen. Smaller companies, challenged with financing their existence and growing their nascent business, often forget that the mistakes of their early years, etched permanently in cyberspace, can be retrieved as interesting "dirt" years later to knock down an otherwise viable business effort. Lacking resources or experience, smaller companies often let these accusations slide by, only to discover the long-term damage that can be done by ignoring these messages. They may not even have the sophistication to use a tracking service to know if such negative messages even exist.

If one links an indisputable negative fact with a rumor, the credibility of the rumor is enhanced by the existence and statement of the provable negative fact. Past indiscretions are the foodstuff of bloggers, disgruntled competitors, fired employees and dissatisfied customers. Many consumers seek empowerment (and the high that comes with it) by searching for failure, deceit and dirt. They live and breed in the world of viral criticism, smack their lips when high profile people, corporations and governmental agencies deny or conceal, and achieve peer recognition for their efforts.

When the stakes are high enough, a young prosecutor seeking to build a political career might even examine a technical legal violation just as a seven year statute of limitations is about to expire. Neophyte companies have a more difficult time stopping damaging mistruths raging through the Internet, but simple denial doesn't work anymore.

Over-Promising and Under-Delivering

It doesn't help, in a world of hyper-accelerating change, that products, particularly technologically-driven "cutting edge" releases, are often announced with major fanfare and even lots of promises but then significantly "under-deliver" or develop subsequently discovered glitches, even complete shutdowns as experienced by Apple in 2008 as it released its vastly cheaper and more sophisticated iPhone 3G and its "enterprise for the rest of us" MobileMe. The 4G was on the market in July of 2010, more mobile and ever- friendly than ever, but still tied to the less-than-perfect AT&T network in the U.S. [311]

Glitches just flash neon signs of failure to the world. We can laugh at those glitches and the "primitive" technology today, but damage of "once having been cool" and then sequentially being unable to create and sustain astounding new products with compelling new applications, relying on "slight improvements" and nominal upgrades, today threatens to turn Apple from innovator to mature "old world" manufacturer, joining Microsoft that lost its cool a long time ago and has been struggling (including major corporate restructuring) to find explosive innovention in a sea of light "fixes."

The under-delivering and under-whelming assembly line mentality, releasing technology without thorough vetting, has tanked too many companies over time. They die or are compressed as others inflict "creative destruction" on these bureaucratic corpses. Still, riding on the cutting edge into today's complex technologies, is never going to be simple or smooth. We just have to be careful not to make our failures look even worse than they really are. This is particularly difficult in the software universe where ubiquitous new products are released into the market, and corrected with "patches" as the glitches appear. Think of the massive bollix in the fall of 2013 as the implementing software/Website for the Affordable Care Act almost single-handedly derailed this legislation. Imagine if cars were built this way and fixed as the accidents mounted up!

While some of these technical issues are understandable as some software programs consume millions of lines of code (something is bound to come up, and online "fixes" are de rigueur), the hoopla of over-selling can make the subsequent application of damage control even more difficult, particularly when the mistake obviously could have been anticipated. As a result of the above iPhone debacle, Apple was lambasted in the press, a negative message that probably that reached an audience that exceeded the number of eyes and ears targeted by their marketing campaign launching the device in the first place, for simply not having anticipated the server demand created by their product, resulting in a shutdown of their service.

Still, through its consistent release of truly innovative products, Apple easily regained its credibility... until it suffered, once again, from a dearth of releasing the "next new cool"… and its stock began to reek of an old-world dividend-paying company instead of the growth engine it has once been famous for.

Although federal class actions have become much more difficult by reason of recent limiting litigation, automotive manufacturers who resist recalls from the U.S. Department of Transportation, who fight too hard against fairly obvious and legitimate consumer complaints, often find themselves the centerpiece of powerful criticism in the press, in the ether, and most of all, in the showroom.

The Web has made communicating flaws, seeking revenge for bad service and finding defects a virtual national pastime, and the damage from thinking that these matter can be ignore and will go away misses the entire game-change of interactive communicativity. It is easier to stem this tide at the micro-level rather than let the word explode into a tsunami of negativity across the Web. People today seem increasingly justified in taking on the biggies, perhaps lost in the anonymity of the Web. If a company preaches putting the consumer on top, it better act that way! There's nothing like seeing an over-promising ad juxtaposed against a harsh reality of failure… on YouTube, on reviewing websites, and in a massive Twitter campaign to shine a light on harsh practices.

One of the away to avoid these nasties is to allow more involvement from your audience/consumer base in the first place. If expectations are generated because you are *dictating* the expected reactions, perhaps embracing the consumer as a part of the process will allow expectations to settle where they actually belong. With an endless flow of information on the Web, damage to a company's or individual's reputation, even based on complete fabrications, has to be identified before a response can be formed.

There are many programs that simply troll the Web looking for specific references to proper names (Google Alert is one of the most deployed), sending a notification to the subscriber when they find one. The reaction to the alert is obviously up to the user. Expectations, which evolve and change over time, need to be managed; negative reactions need to be addressed.

Every rumor with the ring of truth, however absurd it may be, must be addressed and unless it dies on its own quickly, proactively countered in a manner that will actually reach those who need to be told. If mistakes were made, they should be faced, openly discussed in the relevant forums and steps should be taken and publicized as to how the company or the candidate will insure there is no repetition. The ability to edit news into sound bites does not augur well for the unprepared CIO or celebrity who wants a problem to just vaporize. But even where there are no strong negatives in the immediate environment, communicators have to be aware that if they create expectations that cannot easily be met, there are a horde of critics who will immediately pounce on obvious defects in promised deliverables.

When Facebook went public in May of 2012, its stock took an instant plunge. The excitement of getting in at the ground level pushed a pre-public offering frenzy that fell apart in the harsh light of true revenue growth. When Facebook's management discovered that analysts only seemed to focus on a shortfall in planning for the consumer transition to a mobile, the stock dropped. It took a year for Facebook to begin to solve the "mobile ad revenues" problem and bring the stock price back to its initial offering price.

Twitter, chose November 7, 2013 to go public on the New York Stock Exchange (instead of the more pro-tech NASDAQ) with an aggressive opening price of $23 a share. It had the lessons from the Facebook experience to draw on but opted to go bullish. Within seconds of the opening bell, that share price soared 73%. But analysts will be looking at the revenues picture very carefully as the company moves to fulfill its potential. On the day Twitter hit the public marketplace, The Telegraph (telegraph.co.uk) reminded us:

• *The average Twitter user has 208 followers and spends 170 minutes on the site every month.*
• *About 20 million Twitter accounts are believed to be fake and 40 per cent of active users simply consume content on Twitter, rather than send tweets themselves.*
• *It took three years, two months and one day for the first billion Tweets to be sent on the platform. The same number are now sent every 48 hours.*

Can Twitter live up to expectations? Time will tell.

As we explore the meaning of "prosumer" in Rule Five below, we will address how to access this negative core of relevant consumers and slowly and deliberately turn them around while addressing their very legitimate concerns. With luck and a lot of consistent and persistent effort, these detractors may well become the very supporters we crave. We will also explore how to address the relevant audience, how to reach beyond our own walls for answers, in later chapters, but the basic tenet is that unless harmful statements dissipate on their own and are unlikely to resurface, damage control is real and necessary if there are material economic or social values at stake.

Rule Four – Learn How to Scale Up, Segment Your Audience & *Reach* Them

The Birth of Attitudinal Segmentation Analysis

The notion of mass marketing has been dead for a number of years now, yet we hear those words bandied about as if they continue to have validity. The hard facts are that reaching "everybody" is cost prohibitive. Most American consumers only see a handful of movies (about 8) per year, [312] so *mass* marketing in this arena can cost as much as hundreds of millions of dollars for the production, distribution and marketing of a single title, with cost multiples of four or five times more than what is required for more segment-targeted films (released by the specialty labels of the same major studios, where this even remains a viable business!). Even political candidates cannot afford to reach every voter with their message. Some voters will never vote for candidates who have certain clearly expressed attitudes that contradict their own. Trying to reach them is a total waste of time and money.

As individuals, even in our work or social relationships, we have not communicated, do not and will not communicate everything to everybody – even though it is fairly easy to send information to persons who are in our contact universe. Excluding the delusional and the dysfunctional, people tailor most of their personal communications to their recipients – even those obnoxious mass emailings of bad jokes to our peers. But exactly how do we target the appropriate recipients? What are the variables and how predictive and useful are they?

Advertising agencies looking at attitudes of consumers and building statistically relevant testing formulas to find out where to group them have been with us a very long time, more than half a century. The notion of "non-demographic segmentation," a phrase coined in the 1960s by Daniel Yankelovich [313] – focused on grouping by values, attitudes, and other non-traditional demographic census categories. The Yankelovich surveys gave rise to a generally deeper exploration of attitudinal groupings ever since.

Early experimenters, seeking the holy grail of simplistic consumer predisposition identification, struggled mightily with very little to show for it. Analysts at SRI developed the Value and Lifestyles Program [314] in the 1970s, but they quickly realized that broad-based value and lifestyle segmentations were not useful in determining specific consumer behavior. The categories were just too overwhelming and all-encompassing.

The tried and true formula that the best predictor of future behavior is past behavior increasingly became the new direction for this brand of consumer research.

Yet again, with rapid changes in and new categories of products, this notion became very complicated. Clearly, those consumers who are constantly looking to find the "next new cool thing" are not particularly susceptible to any truly meaningful regression analysis, which tracks past behavior patterns to create future predictors.

Social scientists then began to develop studies of consumer behavior based on complete matrices for different qualities, tangible and intangible variables (including traditional demographic segmentation). They then layer each of these grids over each other to map out intersection points in an effort to predict how to target-market to consumers most likely to respond favorably to the product or service in question.

Governmental applications, many clandestine, also focused on finding such "identifiers" that could help their operatives cull through increasing masses of data and communications to select "persons and groups of interest" for military, terrorist or social dissident purposes. A new field of criminology developed predicated on psychological "profiling" to identify motivation and character types likely to have committed a specific crime, used to narrow the focus of a criminal investigation searching for suspects. "Racial profiling" has been one of the negative off-shoots of this new vector in social analysis.

The general mission of each of these new efforts was the same: to look at a large social grouping and sequentially narrow into more targeted spheres of relevancy. New approaches were developed to track people as they made consumer choices in the field. One interesting example of this type of study attached a scanner to a test subject's head to track eye movement in a retail environment.

They learned that consumers tend to notice shelves immediately below eye level first and that having an attractive display at the end of a clothing store area tended to move consumers in that direction. Color and pattern choices for retail space were analyzed. Air temperature. Background music. Wall coverings. Store layouts. Medically-standard CAT and PET scans were employed to measure how the brains of different categories of consumers differed when they were exposed to different messages or images. Focus groups were able to be assembled online, and Webcams used to track eye movements and facial expressions in response to audio-visual content played on willing subjects' computer screens. [315] Metrics became refined and reasonably predictive – to a point.

What does it all mean? In a world of too much, too fast to the point of overwhelming, sometimes it's about sifting through the piles of too much, drilling down on the most relevant data-kernels and then figuring out to use that information to *interact with* or at least *respond to* the consumer or audience base. This trend is well-described in the following piece from the April 10, 2013 FastCompany.com:

Joe Rospars, co-founder and CEO of <u>Blue State Digital,</u> *the agency behind both of Obama's campaigns, says harnessing the power of big data is not about simply analyzing antiseptic information, it's about using whatever information is at your disposal to understand the people behind it all. 'Big data is about having an understanding of what your relationship is with the people who are most important to you and an awareness of the potential in that relationship,' says Rospars…*

I think the biggest misconception about big data is that volume somehow equals sophistication. It doesn't, necessarily. You can have a ton of data, but If you're not using it intelligently, there's no point. Better to have a program that is ultimately about people and the data is a reflection of your potential relationship with those people. When we speak with companies or organizations, we say it's really about understanding how your organization relates to people.

'There's a tendency with big data to say, 'Mmm… I just want more data.' But basically everyone already has too much data and the question is how to use it and integrate it within your organization. It's about using it intelligently in terms of structuring your conversations with people around the best data you have.'… Smart use of data has the potential to make all of the rest of your decisions smarter. So whether it's buying traditional TV or print or individual direct marketing, and the overall strategy, the smart use of data has the potential to unlock value and insight across everything. It's not a silo; it's a sandbox…

There will be different answers to the questions of what tool or which outreach method to use depending on what your overall strategy and mission might be… When you build a relationship with people, how are you going to serve them, how are you going to interact with them, how are you going to listen to them, and how are you going to give them ownership over your brand? These are the questions a lot of organizations don't want to answer. Learning to ask the right questions is clearly the first step, but knowing who and how to ask is equally critical.

Psychographics

In attitudinal groupings, the basic challenge is simply to find the common message that transcends demographic barriers. Once you identify what it is, you can determine the proper identifying tags to create relevance to one group over another. Denture adhesives and incontinence aids are hardly going to be marketed to adolescents, just as hip hop albums are unlikely to find resonance with the elderly. Selling Christianity in a Muslim country where such efforts are punishable by death and trying to bring Biloxi, Mississippi into Islam's fold may be equally inappropriate. The easy and the obvious don't really concern us, but where the receptive groupings are not so clear, we need to apply an analytical set to the product, service or message we are trying to disseminate.

Simple identifiable groups can fracture into many sub-segments when the matter being communicated crosses various traditional demographics and shatters into small pieces, or when the subject matter becomes religious, political or cultural. *Psychographics* – which address aggregating those with common values, lifestyles and personalities as to a particular subject matter – often are different depending on the subject matters of the "aggregation." Simply put, a psychographic grouping is very message (attitude) specific. By way of example, because a Roman Catholic of almost any age might agree with an Evangelical Christian on the issue of abortion does not mean that such Catholics and Evangelicals would see eye-to-eye on any other comparable politically-charged issues.

Another, more commercially directed, example of how psychographic segmentation works in finding market potential can be illustrated by the Walt Disney Company's struggle to recapture the young male consumer, ages 6 to 14 (while it clearly dominates the parallel marketplace for females). Instead of giving up on this male group as many purveyors of content had done, Disney instead engaged a team of cultural anthropologists and psychologists to discern what makes that male demographic tick. For Disney, this group represents a potential $50 million a year market.

For 18 months, the Disney team engaged in activities such as rummaging through the closets and drawers of test subjects (what's in the front and recent versus what seems to be discarded in the back), tracking (with permission) male activities with video cameras, and even analyzing how boys carry skateboards. Headed by Kelly Peña (who has been described as the "kid whisperer" by some in Hollywood), the team began to tap into that young male mystique.

In an interview, Peña noted that "The guys are trickier to pin down for a host of reasons. They hop more quickly than their female counterparts from sporting activities to television to video games during leisure time. They can also be harder to understand: the cliché that girls are more willing to chitchat about their feelings is often true." [316] Boys like to act older than they are, they found, mimicking the behavior of older teens, but still found a need to cling to a pile of stuffed animals in the corner. Each of these elements is being added to Disney content where a young male seems like an appropriate consumer.

Much of this research is long-term, with many hit-or-miss attempts to generate predictive data. The quality of the selection criteria and the sample base very much impact the overall validity of each study. For example, the young male demographic as presented above is an overly simplistic analysis. The study did not address a boy from an urban ghetto or, alternatively, one who lives in a home where English is not spoken. Add parental income, success in school and athletic ability and the results would probably be significantly different. As variables cross into the entire range of human groupings, the complexity increases exponentially.

Psychographic Tracking and Measurement

The metrics of establishing the relevant psychographic and demographic groupings has created entire industries. Nielsen, a company usually associated with television ratings, has developed or acquired dozens of demographic measuring businesses and offers its on-going accumulated data as well as its research capacity – for a price – to companies trying to minimize marketing waste and maximize the value proposition of their marketing dollars.

An excellent example of how Nielsen addresses segmentation analysis can be seen in the work from one of its subsidiaries (San Diego-based Claritas, Inc. which issues reports under its PRIZMB brand), which has addressed neighborhood types based on information gleaned from data available from the U.S. Census. Nielsen's analysis, often based on statistical sampling techniques, has generated information down to zip codes and, in many cases, even down to significant sub-zip codes. The next two charts are intended to be used together. [317] The first chart looks at what Claritas believes to be meaningful differentiating characteristics, combining age, education, income, household and type of neighborhood, and breaks up the groupings into 66 small, economically complimentary segments:

PRIZM_{NE} TARGET FINDER REPORT RANKED BY SEGMENT

Social Group		PRIZM_{NE} Clusters			Demographic Descriptors		
	#	Nickname	income Level	Cluster Type	HH Composition	Adult Age	Education
S1	01	Upper Crust	Wealthy	Suburban	Couples	Age 45+	College Grad+
S1	02	Blue Blood Estates	Wealthy	Suburban	Families	Age 35—64	College Grad+
S1	03	Movers & Shakers	Wealthy	Suburban	Couples	Age 35—64	College Grad+
U1	04	Young Digerali	Upscale	Urban	Mix	Age 25—44	College Grad+
T1	05	Country Squires	Wealthy	Town	Families	Age 35—64	College Grad+
S1	06	Winner's Circle	Wealthy	Suburban	Families	Age 25—54	College Grad+
U1	07	Money & Brains	Upscale	Urban	Mix	Age 45+	College Grad+
S2	08	Executive Suites	UpperMid	Suburban	Sngl/Cpls	Age 25—44	College Grad+
T1	09	Big Fish, Small Pond	Upscale	Town	Couples	Age 45+	College Grad+
C1	10	Second City Elite	Upscale	2nd City	Couples	Age 45+	College Grad+
T1	11	God's Country	Upscale	Town	Couples	Age 35—64	College Grad+
C1	12	Brite Lites, Li'l City	UpperMid	2nd City	Sngl/Cpls	Age 25—54	College Grad+
C1	13	Upward Bound	Upscale	2nd City	Families	Age 25—54	H.S./College
S2	14	New Empty Nests	UpperMid	Suburban	Couples	Age 65+	College Grad+
S2	15	Pools £t Patios	UpperMid	Suburban	Couples	Age 45+	College Grad+
U1	16	Bohemian Mix	Midscale	Urban	Singles	Age <35	College Grad+
S2	17	Beltway Boomers	UpperMid	Suburban	Families	Age 35—64	H.S./College
S2	18	Kids & Cul-de-Sacs	UpperMid	Suburban	Families	Age 25—54	H.S./College
S2	19	Home Sweet Home	UpperMid	Suburban	Mix	Age 25—44	H.S./College
T1	20	Fast-Track Families	UpperMid	Town	Families	Age 25—54	H.S./College
S3	21	Gray Power	Midscale	Suburban	Sngl/Cpls	Age 65+	H.S./College
S3	22	Young Influentials	Midscale	Suburban	Singles	Age <35	H.S./College
T2	23	Greenbelt Sports	Midscale	Town/Rural	Mix	Age 25—54	H.S./College
C2	24	Up-and-Comers	Midscale	2nd City	Mix	Age <35	H.S./College
T1	25	Country Casuals	UpperMid	Town/Rural	Couples	Age 35—64	H.S./College
U1	26	The Cosmopolitans	Midscale	Urban	Sngl/Cpls	Age 55+	H.S./College
C2	27	Middleburg Managers	Midscale	2nd City	Sngl/Cpls	Age 55+	H.S./College
T2	28	Traditional Times	Midscale	Town/Rural	Sngl/Cpls	Age 55+	H.S./College
U1	29	American Dreams	Midscale	Urban	Mix	Age 25—44	H.S./College
S3	30	Suburban Sprawl	Midscale	Suburban	Sngl/Cpls	Age 25—44	H.S./College
U2	31	Urban Achievers	LowerMid	Urban	Singles	Age <35	H.S./College
T2	32	New Homesteaders	Midscale	Town	Families	Age 25—44	High School
T2	33	Big Sky Families	Midscale	Rural	Families	Age 25—54	High School
C2	34	White Picket Fences	Midscale	2nd City	Families	Age 25—44	High School
C2	35	Boomtown Singles	LowerMid	2nd City	Singles	Age <35	H.S./College
S3	36	Blue-Chip Blues	Midscale	Suburban	Families	Age <45	High School
T2	37	Mayberry-ville	Midscale	Rural	Mix	Age 35—64	High School
T3	38	Simple Pleasures	LowerMid	Town/Rural	Sngl/Cpls	Age 65+	High School
S3	39	Domestic Duos	Midscale	Suburban	Sngl/Cpls	Age 55+	High School
U2	40	Close-In Couples	LowerMid	Urban	Sngl/Cpls	Age 55+	High School
C2	41	Sunset City Blues	LowerMid	2nd City	Sngl/Cpls	Age 65+	High School
T3	42	Red, White Et Blues	LowerMid	Town	Mix	Age 25—44	High School
T3	43	Heartlanders	LowerMid	Rura	Sngl/Cpls	Age 45+	High School
S4	44	New Beginnings	LowerMid	Suburban	Mix	Age <35	High School
T3	45	Blue Highways	LowerMid	Rural	Mix	Age 25—44	High School
S4	46	Old Glories	Downscale	Suburban	Singles	Age 65+	High School
C3	47	City Startups	Poor	2nd City	Singles	Age <35	H.S./College

T4	48 Young £t Rustic	Downscale	Town	Mix	Age <35	High School
S4	49 American Classics	LowerMid	Suburban	Sngl/Cpls	Age 65+	High School
T3	50 Kid Country, USA	LowerMid	Town	Families	Age <45	High School
T3	51 Shotguns & Pickups	LowerMid	Rural	Families	Age 25—44	High School
S4	52 Suburban Pioneers	LowerMid	Suburban	Mix	Age <45	High School
C3	53 Mobility Blues	Downscale	2nd City	Mix	Age <35	High School
U2	54 Multi-Culti Mosaic	LowerMid	Urban	Mix	Age 25—44	High School
T4	55 Golden Ponds	Downscale	Town/Rural	Sngl/Cpls	Age 65+	Some H.S.
T4	56 Crossroads Villagers	Downscale	Rural	Sngl/Cpls	Age <45	High School
T4	57 Old Milltowns	Downscale	Town	Sngl/Cpls	Age 65+	Some H.S.
T4	58 Back Country Folks	Downscale	Rural	Sngl/Cpls	Age 55+	Some H.S.
U3	59 Urban Elders	Poor	Urban	Singles	Age 55+	Some H.S.
C3	60 Park Bench Seniors	Poor	2nd City	Singles	Age 55+	Some H.S.
U3	61 City Roots	Downscale	Urban	Sngl/Cpls	Age 65+	Some H.S.
C3	62 Hometown Retired	Downscale	2nd City	Sngl/Cpls	Age 65+	Some H.S.
C3	63 Family Thrifts	Downscale	2nd City	Families	Age <45	Some H.S.
T4	64 Bedrock America	Downscale	Town/Rural	Families	Age <35	Some H.S.
U3	65 Big City Blues	Downscale	Urban	Mix	Age <45	Some H.S.
U3	66 Low-Rise Living	Poor	Urban	Mix	Age <35	Some H.S.

This segmentation analysis is primarily economically driven and will constantly need to be updated as local living patterns change (gentrification of one neighborhood versus the loss of jobs and industry in another creating decay), general societal forces alter living patterns, weather conditions alter the range of habitability, etc. Further, although there undoubtedly will be significant statistical correlation, this particular delineation would probably be restructured if the grid were to be applied to social, political or religious communications. For example, political segmentation would, most likely, use Congressional voting districts, city and county delineations just as much as zip code analysis.

The second chart takes the group number (from the # column) and social groupings from the above chart and lays this segmentation across a grid where the vertical axis measures affluence and the horizontal access tracks population density:

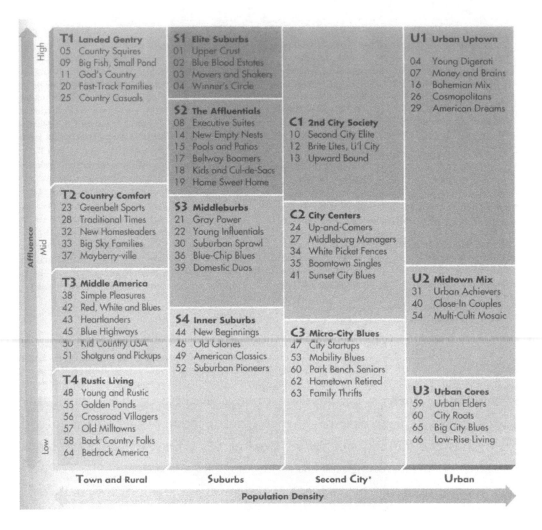

T1 Landed Gentry 05 Country Squires 09 Big Fish, Small Pond 11 God's Country 20 Fast-Track Families 25 Country Casuals	**S1 Elite Suburbs** 01 Upper Crust 02 Blue Blood Estates 03 Movers and Shakers 04 Winner's Circle		**U1 Urban Uptown** 04 Young Digerati 07 Money and Brains 16 Bohemian Mix 26 Cosmopolitans 29 American Dreams

PRIZMB_NEB SOCIAL GROUPINGS BASED ON AFFLUENCE AND POPULATION DENSITY (*non-major urban markets)

By looking at the combined impact of these two charts, on a general and fairly simplistic basis, marketers generate what is referred to as a "cluster" analysis, which allows them to determine customer information that has many varied uses: where to locate a store, how to find new and appropriate customers, how to address appropriate consumers as to personal preferences or what new products or services they might want, which media should be engaged and what kind of advertising or marketing is most appropriate for their particular product or service. [318]

These charts represent the "easy button," but when advertising budgets run into the millions and millions of dollars, the marketing metrics likewise become vastly more focused and based on consumer-specific research by the experts. With technology available to insert advertising into specific programs for targeted consumers, [319] accountability and efficiency are becoming basic requirements for the advertising community. Not only are marketing target segments being narrowed, advertisers are increasingly turning to equally narrow-focused small advertising agencies to address this changed universe.

We can see this segmentation and specialization as large, cumbersome advertising agencies, with high overhead costs and expensive services are beginning to be priced out of the marketplace, undoubtedly accelerated by the economic meltdown that has increased pressure to downsize marketing budgets. A few have even taken to creating side businesses, literally developing their own new brands, to make up for the loss of clients. Using their knowledge of psychographics, they can tailor products for obvious and willing groups of consumers. [320]

Narrowing the focus becomes basic in today's marketing world. As smaller agencies specialize in designated psychographics coupled with providing lower production costs, they deliver the relevant "eyeballs and ears" to the advertisers for a manageable price.

One of these niched companies, Razorfish, began as a small, Seattle-based advertising agency specializing in marketing into the digital world. It – and others like it – have grown into global giants with offices on virtually every continent. Today, this once-small, innovative agency that pioneered interactive marketing has thousands of employees with offices all over the world and is part of that massive marketing conglomerate, Publicis Groupe (which in turn merged with Omnicom in the summer of 2013 to create the largest advertising agency on earth).

But much smaller boutiques are claiming ever-growing numbers of clients, as advertisers seek edgy younger minds, more familiar with the current waves of pop culture and technology. These boutiques are expected to create and implement marketing efforts that even experienced advertising agencies managers may not fully understand.[321] The Web allows such innovators to "show their stuff," to vet their creativity and to justify meeting top level executives at companies seeking innovative marketing solutions.

Further, old concepts are finding new meaning as this stream of inventions ripples through the system. Viral marketing – where consumers spread the intended message directly among and between themselves – is no longer simply an email chain or a mass of widgets and shared links; there are so many other tools. For example, technologies such as RSS feeds (Rich Site Summary or Real Simple Syndication) allow consumers to subscribe to informational sites and receive updates from those sites in the form of email alerts.

Content is often aggregated ("syndicated") in one central location, allowing individual users the flexibility to pick and choose what interests them, ignoring information they might not want at that moment but bringing some other feature to their attention. Popularity can be tracked and measured as well. These emailed updates or alerts often contain metadata (literally "data about data") that provided recipients with enough information to determine if they wish to pursue the story by clicking for more. Consumers often define themselves by such choices – self-segmentation, if you will.

For traditional purveyors of media, who count heavily on advertising for revenues, they are increasingly struggling against a rising tide of sophisticated tracking an ad placement software, employing complex algorithms that factor an aggregated advertiser's demographic and psychographic reach (measured in real time or near real time), and that literally troll mobile, online and even traditional media for spot availability, pricing and effectiveness. It's called "programmatic media buying," and it has those paying big bucks to create content running scared. Appropriate ads are slotted into the correct placement automatically by the programming without the necessity of a human "decider."

While waste for advertisers is eliminated, revenues to these media companies are negatively impacted. Dollars can flee content that doesn't resonate with consumers at light speed. Further, these trends are contracting the use and effectiveness of traditional online display advertising (typically, ads with text, logos, photographs and/or other images, location maps, and similar items) in favor of new mobile apps and richer online media presentations. "New," however, becomes "old" pretty quickly in this rapidly changing universe.

Take for example a system that began in Japan (and grew rapidly in the U.S.) and looks a lot like an updated bar code. It's called a "QR" ("quick response" code) and allows consumers to use their cell phone cameras to photograph magazine ads, billboards and posters – effectively scanning the QR code box somewhere on the image – automatically drawing them to linked Websites. From there, they can shop, load images or simply visit the Website. They can even load an actual functioning video on a printed page to lure consumers to a product or service. [322] It's already an "old" technology!

But what if you didn't even need that mathematically embedded QR code to create the link? What if you simply snapped a photo of a designated image, any image selected by the relevant vendor (in a store window or in an ad somewhere), and produced the same result? Object/image recognition technology can complete the journey, adding sophisticated search software such as "Google Goggles [which] is a downloadable image recognition application created by Google which can be currently found on the Mobile Apps page of Google Mobile. It is used for searches based on pictures taken by handheld devices. For example, taking a picture of a famous landmark would search for information about it, or taking a picture of a product's barcode will search for information on the product."[323]

Eventually, this technology may completely replace credit cards; your face alone might be enough to consummate a transaction. Google is hardly alone in the space, however. For example, a Dutch company (Layar) has offered advertisers the ability to use such images to trigger the transfer of useful information to the consumer that snapped the picture. [324]

The internet has made its mark with plenty of consumer tracking, much of which has generated consternation from privacy advocates. Television, even cable, has done little other than occasional sub-zip code differentiation. Until now. Cablevision Systems has already begun to deliver different commercials into some of its cable households in the New York/New Jersey area based on income, ethnicity, gender or whether the customer has children or pets.

Since Cablevision's system is based on simple metrics, even privacy advocates seem to think that this non-intrusive delivery system passes the smell test. "'We don't have an objection to advertising that is targeted to demographics,' said Marc Rotenberg, the executive director of the Electronic Privacy Information Center, a civil liberties group in Washington. But, he said, there is a need to show 'that they can't be reverse-engineered to find the names of individuals that were watching particular shows.'" [325] Comcast and Verizon are trying similar systems. Tracking consumers is a trend that can only grow in the coming years, particularly as economic pressures make marketing efficiency a primary value to advertisers.

It is also vital to be in touch with your potential consumer/audience base, noting how one communicates can be wasteful or even fatal to an otherwise sound business plan. The greatest error is *assuming* the current communication structures based on what you may think you know. Since, as we have seen, teens don't use email much anymore, it would be a mistake to build a marketing effort to reach them using this method.

Try the texting and social networking universe; it does seem to work for the small businesses that have embraced these new communications techniques. [326] Never assume that anything stays the same! Make sure that the media you plan to use actually reach those you want to address. And when dealing with interactive media, there is another element that can increase effectiveness: personalization.

Personalizing a message for an individual consumer has a disproportionate benefit in getting that consumer to respond positively. "[For example, brands] can increase the number of people who install their Facebook apps by 400% through a combination of private and newsfeed messaging, according to a [2011] MIT study... Researchers found the winning strategy to be up to two times more effective than email, and 10 times more effective than banner ads ... After gaining rare access to an actual business about to launch a Facebook app, Professors Sinan Aral and Dylan Walker were permitted to randomly assign two versions of the product and record user network activity. (The brand, whose name has been anonymized, created an entertainment app where users share information about movies)." [327]

In fact, banner ads are so completely avoided by consumer as to render them virtually useless. "HubSpot's [mid-2013] survey revealed that the average click-through rate of display ads is just 0.1%. In raw numbers, the company estimates that you're 'more likely to complete Navy SEAL training than click on a banner ad or 'more likely to survive a plane crash' than do so."[328] Their experiments tracked how targeted consumers responded, varying the degree of personalization and the degree of activity aimed at engaging the consumer.

The number of consumers who actually adopted the app being offered rose significantly as activity and personalization were increased, a seemingly simple task in today's electronically sophisticated marketing world. [329] It all adds up: appropriate messages for appropriate market segments with personalization and interactivity where possible.

Going through the numerous consumer tracks in the ether and aggregating the metrics into a usable format is now a mainstream focus of marketing consulting and tracking companies (they call it: "Big Data"). Predicting future results and adjusting failing marketing messages mid-stream are the goals. Such systems can track everything from automotive to motion picture marketing campaigns. For example: "Similar to the Zagat restaurant surveys, the system assigns a percentage score to movies based on Fandango's proprietary data collected from its online and mobile traffic, social media sites and advance ticket sales."[330]

The ability to track consumer reactions to audio-visual content across all relevant platforms and screens — thus generating an aggregated analysis of the success of a particular campaign or message — in real or near-real time is becoming a priority for large-scale advertisers and communicators. Fortunately, technology is able to offer reasonable solutions to implement this goal.[331]

Rule Four is simple to state and difficult to implement: Scale Up, Segment Your Audience & *Reach* Them. It requires constant trend analysis, understanding social groupings and how they change as well as their current choice of how to receive and transmit information. Combining all of this information, scaling it up to reach the greatest number of *appropriate* people in the most effective way, requires knowing demographic and psychographic segmentation as it applies to your specific message. One size no longer fits all.

Even when it is the same message that effectively resonates with each segment of your audience; you may have to deliver it through different media. Further, your product, message, service or content may have *different relevance* to different market segments. Through proper target identification and tracking, you should be able to find each separate message that does maximize the value to each *appropriate* segment and deliver it accordingly.

But there is another wonderful side to reaching out to the entire world: embracing resources once available only to mega-corporations, to solve internal issues and generate exciting new marketing and messaging campaigns.

Rule Five – "If you Can't Beat 'Em, Let them Join You!" – *Reach* Beyond Your Own Walls for Answers

There is so much expertise floating beyond the walls of our immediate experience. Today, we have the technological means of reaching out and bringing that competency to ourselves on a cost-effective, as-needed basis. There is also an emerging lexicon used to describe the players and the processes in this outreach program: *prosumers, ideagoras* (also called *crowdsourcing*), *open-source, application programming interfaces (APIs), wikinomics,* [332] *"the world is flat," out-sourcing, global marketplace*, to name a few. This segment of the book examines the evolution of this concept and how to generate the incredible economic values that have resulted.

The above concepts are related: it is increasingly cost-prohibitive to function in a complex and rapidly changing economic and social environment if all of the necessary solutions and relationships must come from within a single company/bureaucracy or within the experience of a single individual. This notion seems so obvious and simple that it is hard to understand why it even has to be written down.

Yet personal and institutional barriers to keep the outside out and the inside safe filter out unacceptable intrusions as well as welcome enhancements and the mechanisms for future growth and prosperity. There are those who believe that if the solutions are not home-grown, they cannot be trusted. That assumption is no longer sustainable.

Looking at the issue from a slightly different perspective, imagine what life was been like in early days of the industrial revolution. Change was so rapid that patent laws were hastily developed and then enhanced to account for the change. Does that sound familiar? In those days, however, significant social change still required decades. Underlying principles for virtually all segments of the new manufacturing processes could still be learned and absorbed – almost in their entirety – by a large segment of educated scientists and engineers of the period; the era of sub-specialization had yet to begin. It was easier to rely on yourself and the resources immediately around you.

Think of the complexity of today's global knowledge base – from robotic engineering and nanotechnology, radiology, computer science and nuclear science to the Internet and ubiquitous access to information replete with interactivity, enterprise resource platforms (software designed to consolidate all corporate operations), online social networking, cell phones, laptop/tablet computers, increasing technical sophistication among younger demographics, video games and all forms of new content expression. With doubling of change occurring within time periods well-short of a year, it is equally obvious that regardless of size or sophistication, unless the issues are profoundly basic, no one organization or individual remotely has enough information or is capable of generating all of the new information necessary to remain at the competitive edge without reaching outside of its own structures to solve problems.

Complexity often dictates that the best solutions for your internal problems may well lie outside your immediate sphere of control. The differences between open sourcing – where no proprietary values are created since the creation is for the good of all – and crowdsourcing (ideagoras) – where groups are invited on a proprietary basis and often economically rewarded, to help an individual or an organization solve a vexing problem – are subtle versions of this same reach to the world for complex, best-in-class answers. This, then, is the story of how to access those external resources.

Open Sourcing

So of course, companies and universities have no problem asking others for their approach to common problems – or do they? If asking a question requires revealing a company's proprietary research, will they ask the question? If what little privacy is left would be further eroded merely in the request for help, will an individual or company allow the intrusion? If an academic's triumphant discovery and research could be co-opted by a competitor far away, is he or she likely to open the door wide enough to share in the spirit of further development? And who owns or controls the new material that was created by the collaboration? In what proportion? How is this applied and enforced? Will a patent, trademark, copyright or other proprietary right be compromised or violated?

Yet open source information sites do exist, from the online encyclopedia Wikipedia, to software technologies such as Linux. Open source obviates notions of "ownership" and proprietary value. For online factual inquiries, many have discovered their answers in a strange online bird called "Wikipedia." Founded in 2001 by Jimmy Wales and Larry Sanger, Wikipedia is, by its own definition, "a free, multilingual, open content encyclopedia project operated by the non-profit Wikimedia Foundation. Its name is a blend of the words *wiki* (a technology for creating collaborative websites) and *encyclopedia*." Although constantly vetted for accuracy by the foundation, information is constantly being added to and new categories submitted simply by the general public.

attempted to prevent such "discoveries" from being used by others without a payment. However, it does seem as if those promulgating open-source solutions may have indeed been prescient.

In 2013, the United States Supreme Court effectively boosted these open-sourced solutions in *Association for Molecular Pathology v. Myriad Genetics*, when it refused to uphold a patent that *discovered* a naturally occurring DNA sequencing necessary to generate values for various new medical tests. Open-source may be the only answer to these complex natural discoveries. Based on this crowd-sourced model, the Obama administration has invited scientists to replicate the above genomic mapping solution to mapping the human brain. Think of the applications that such research could unleash!

Why is this remotely doable? What's in it for the contributors? Is this pure altruism or something more? There's no one answer, but the biggest and most consistent rationale for participating is that the research can lead to a huge number of opportunities that would languish for decades if the necessary underlying solutions were not discovered or created.

These new opportunities, and the economic potential behind them, would be cost-prohibitive otherwise. Further, partial solutions from one source would require blending with the partial solutions of others, generating a complex and very expensive structure for even the most basic applications. And if you are interested, say, in selling pharmaceuticals or running a business on a better operating system, you really aren't facing a competitive threat from your new creations by using a common and accessible platform. In fact, that open platform might be so much better than what you could develop yourself that it allows you to maximize the business that really is your main focus.

Further, a horrible economy has caused once-reluctant companies to participate in open sourcing simply as a survival mechanism. While firms still keep secure their private information, the notion of not reinventing the wheel and accessing/creating generally available data as an industry has become increasingly attractive. According to Ivy Schmerken: "With the financial meltdown eroding IT [information technology] budgets, large investment banks, hedge funds and other financial institutions have been forced to rethink their attitudes toward open source technology. Use of open source technology is quietly booming in the capital markets because of increased cost pressures, and analysts predict the current economic conditions will drive further industry adoption." [335] The recession created hard times and crashing revenues, forcing changes that might have dampened the fall had they been adopted in the first place.

In some arenas, "open source" also allows passionate minds to collaborate in areas where a greater social betterment is at stake. While some school boards with political agendas have slowed the process, the creation of standardized and open-source textbooks has become increasingly common, even overcoming objections from the big textbook roadblock states (Texas and California). Non-profit Currikki (curriki.org) is one of the pioneer sites, leading the way. Their Website boasts a mission statement "to provide free, high-quality curricula and education resources to teachers, students and parents around the world."

Scott McNealy, Sun Microsystems co-founder, and the power behind Curriki "shuns basic math textbooks as bloated monstrosities: their price keeps rising while the core information inside of them stays the same … Mr. McNealy says… 'We are spending $8 billion to $15 billion per year on textbooks' [in the U.S.]… It seems to me we could put that all online for free.'" [336] This may not make textbook companies happy, but as U.S. educational standards continue to drop, the open source effort offers greater quality with the ability to deploy money that would have otherwise been spent replacing aging textbooks.

An additional value to open-sourcing occurs when an individual company cannot scale up, small companies with narrow commercial targets seeking to grow, because of insufficient volume. An aggregation of companies can, however, create the necessary volume and the group can thus effect economic benefits that no individual entity could. The sharing of the Hulu online content platform by several television program suppliers is one such example. The agreement to share the same "test households" and data bases between consumer research rivals, Nielsen Co. and Information Resources Inc. (who will each still process and interpret that data in their own separate and proprietary way), offers another illustration. The efficiencies of scale far outweigh any loss in competitive advantage.

Ideagoras (Crowdsourcing)

A slightly more manageable and less open approach is what some have referred to as "ideagoras" or "crowdsourcing" – meaning nothing more than a company's reach beyond its own walls for solutions to company problems, innovation and new business ideas. Unlike "out-sourcing" (described in the next section) where specific company or personal tasks are relegated to preordained outside vendors, ideagoras represent an open invitation (literally an open "request for proposal") to a wide and unspecified assortment of expertise to pitch the company (or individual) on potential solutions and new business ideas. There are plenty of creative people, experimenters, scientists and thinkers who have a passion for solving problems. In a hyper-accelerating world, it is completely impossible – cost-prohibitive – to hire all of them and pay them full or even part time for possible answers and ideas.

But how do you send an email to "everybody" to ask for ideas or solutions? You don't have to. There are companies out there – such as InnoCentive, NineSigma, Yet2, FreelancerNow, and YourEncore – that that serve as clearinghouses for experts in fields such as business, computer science and systems networking, life sciences, chemistry, physics, most fields of engineering and manufacturing, nanotechnology, pharmaceutical research, design and materials science. [337]

Qualified experts sign up (hundreds of thousands of them!), are vetted by these companies, and if the relevant expert's solutions or new ideas are adopted, the "adopting company" pays a fee that can range into six figures if the suggested alternative is economically viable enough. Companies that have sought such contributions from these experts have included Proctor & Gamble, Dow AgroSciences, Colgate-Palmolive and Lilly, to name a very, very few. Proctor & Gamble has even mandated that its product development corps generate an ever-increasing array of new product ideas from this "idea factory beyond the walls."

What kinds of problems get solved this way? Here's a simple example: "[Colgate-Palmolive] needed a more efficient method for getting its toothpaste into the tube—a seemingly straightforward problem. When [the company's] internal R&D team came up empty-handed, the company posted the specs on InnoCentive, one of many new marketplaces that link problems with problem-solvers. A Canadian engineer named Ed Melcarek proposed putting a positive charge on fluoride powder, then grounding the tube [which effectively sucked the toothpaste into the tube like a magnet]. It was an effective application of elementary physics, but not one that Colgate-Palmolive's team of chemists had ever contemplated. Melcarek was duly rewarded with $25,000 for a few hours' work."[338]

But sometimes, a contest with a hot prize among the customer user base – such as a Netflix award for the best new recommendation model – generates a plethora of creativity such that management just has to pluck the idea from the many submitted solutions. This crowdsourcing approach is nothing more than a "prosumers by invitation" engagement, which has the ancillary benefit of making consumers feel like part of the company.

Outsourcing

Out-sourcing and globalization, dubbed a fomenter of American unemployment because so much of what is out-sourced winds up in distant lands, are more familiar relatives of the ideagora, and we have been using out-sourcing for a very long time. Every time a manufacturer buys a part or raw material to be incorporated into their products, they have out-sourced a portion of their manufacturing process. Think of how many raw materials and parts are supplied by outside vendors to General Motors in the manufacturing of cars and trucks. But the big change in the concept of outsourcing – perceived by many as a threat to American labor – is the economic globalization that is so well depicted in Thomas Friedman's best-selling book *The World Is Flat: A Brief History of the Twenty-First Century.*[339]

Friedman noted that bankruptcies in companies that laid fiber optic cable under the oceans made global interconnectivity cheap. This brought service industries very much into global competition. With falling trade barriers and better transportation capabilities (like containerization in shipping), manufacturing increasingly moved to the least expensive appropriate countries. Even massive infrastructure projects, such as the new Bay Bridge in the San Francisco-Oakland area, could have huge steel subsections constructed in Shanghai, China and then shipped to the United States for installation. It seems that the just about anything could be built and traded in the new flattened global economy.

When you speak to service representative "Bob" to solve a glitch on that new software you bought and cannot figure out, and "Bob" has a funny accent (getting more Americanized all the time) that suggests that he might actually be "Raju," you may well be speaking over a Voice Over Internet Protocol (VOIP) line to a guy on a computer screen in Hyderabad, India. Many companies provide the vast majority of their "tech support" long distance. Computers over ten thousand miles away might be running diagnostics on a file server system located in Los Angeles, California.

Your income tax return may have been anonymously prepared by a data processing clerk in Bengaluru (also India, once known as Bangalore) even if you hired a U.S.-based accounting firm. Your x-rays (taken in New York City) may be screened preliminarily by a radiologist in Chennai, India. Your software designed in part and enhanced by mathematicians and software engineers in Beijing, China and your company's payroll could have been prepared for final payment in a building on the outskirts of Manila in the Philippines.

Finding an outsourcing partner in any particular field can be as simple as using a search engine. Type into the search engine: outsourcing + concrete + accounting – and thousands of possibilities appear on the screen, from huge consulting firms to small vendors situated oceans away. Alternatively, one can join a community, online [340] or even a tangible, physical one – even the local trade association – to help identify the right vendor to get the job done.

There are outsourcing conferences and even mega-consultants who can manage it all for a client. [341] Blogs and online magazines [342] can provide mountains of useful information, paths that can lead to more paths that ultimately can provide an outsourced solution if it exists. The ability to make these connections without the constraint of distance is one of the most profound benefits to local businesses and social organizations.

There is also a balancing act that goes with selecting outsourcing partners – the more capital intensive the project, the more specialized the knowledge and the closer to cutting edge innovation and processing required, the greater the risk of outsourcing failures. This is especially true with long links of specialized technology, where one failure along the chain can send a rather large process into disarray. Boeing Company's more than two-year delay in completing orders for its 787 Dreamliner passenger aircraft can be directly traced to misevaluations of such outside vendors.

Scott Carson, Boeing's former commercial operations head, said, "I think there were places where we went too far … Clearly, we made some poor judgment calls in terms of what people's capabilities were." [343] Since our future is very much going to be built with outsourcing as an ongoing and growing practice, our business education programs are going to need to stress the evaluation and management of outsourcing vendors as one of the dynamic keys to operational success. Boeing's outsource coordination complexities are probably much more complex than average. But even smaller entrepreneurs are now able to grow when they don't require excessive customization and can fit easily into their customers' and vendors' existing designs.

The idea of linking a business application to outside users can sound threatening, but if a design for wonderful new computer program has value only if it works with other computer programs, the inventor is dead in the water without a way to create that connection: an application programming interface (the API). The greater the ability to use an invention, the more valuable it becomes because more people can use it. In fact, great value is created if people are so inspired by the invention that they create new ways to apply the innovation in new applications they have discovered.

Even for stand-alone sites, the way a consumer sees and interacts with that Website – referred to as the user interface (UI) or a graphic user interface (GUI) – is often the difference between success and failure. Thus, one may increase the demand for a new Website with the right GUI or a new core software technology with the correct API. For example, Nike partnered with Apple to link iPods to their running shoes through an API. And going the extra mile to anticipate consumer needs can increase values as well. For example, Websites will often add a "directions" link via MapQuest or Google on their home page to help a consumer find out how to "get there." Posting online answers to FAQs – frequently asked questions – also guides consumers to valuable online economic decisions.

Think of how global shipping companies, with customs clearance expertise and quality control specialists who track software and door-to-door service, have turned small businesses into global niche specialists. They scale up to levels that were once unavailable to a small entrepreneur. Nowhere is this more apparent than in online consumer marketing companies such as eBay and Amazon. Micro-sellers, often just individuals with specialized knowledge of how to provide a plethora of specialized products and services. They now have the ability to access giant virtual store-fronts such as eBay and Amazon and generate hits just from being linked to those sites. eBay and Amazon pay big bucks to the Googles of the world to make sure their vendors get noticed in Web searches [344] and have billing and collection services that used to be available only to big corporate retailers.

A great example of this structure can be found in the music industry. While record companies have found the Internet to be much more of a threat than an opportunity, clever entrepreneurs have discovered a revenue opportunity by helping consumers discover new talent. Artists are able to create and identify fans and sell their music (in hard copy CD form or in downloadable formats) to a vast pool of buyers.

Portland, Oregon-based CD Baby sells millions of CD's based on bands who buy shelf-space on the Website (cdbaby.com). Both "editor's picks" and "new arrivals" drive their marketing efforts, and the company handles the transfer of the digital music supplied by artists to CDs and manages the direct-to-consumer transactions. With per album payments to artists averaging five times what traditional major record labels would pay and *weekly* payments (unheard of in the old world music industry!), CD Baby has paid out well over $80 million in artists royalties since it was founded in 1998.

The CD Baby model is just one example of an outsource aggregator. They perform a marketing function (which the artist can embellish), provide sales and manufacturing capacity, shipping coordination, revenue collection and accounting – all making a recording artist look a whole lot more like a full-blown old world record company. They also give budding artists an entry into a brutally competitive business based that is heavily on "whom you know."

In this over-connected world, small can act big and big can become more efficient. Of all the jobs that were lost to global outsourcing, many new economic opportunities have been created by virtue of the connective tissue and ubiquitous access to expertise can be purchased in tiny "as-needed" lumps or can be bought in stacks and piles big enough to serve a Fortune 500 company's global revenue needs without adding one square foot of building space or one single additional employee.

In a period of staggering unemployment, people who really can't find traditional jobs have been forced to choose between becoming entrepreneurial or becoming homeless. Some have actually become the outsourcing partners to their fellow entrepreneurs. Others have discovered the world of "contract employee" or independent contractor, as corporations staff up with temporary workers who do not accrue fringe benefits. A few of these new micro-efforts will undoubtedly form the basis of some of the mega-companies of the future.

As the recovery progresses, the economic stability required for a vigorous U.S. job market – evidenced by stable consumer demand and confidence – still has not materialized. Instead, we see a reluctance to engage new full-time hires and an increasing reliance on outside contractors and part-time workers, perhaps driven in part by a desire to avoid the healthcare insurance cost-requirements expected under the Affordable Care Act.

Whatever the reason, there is a pool of labor looking for opportunities, and it even seems as if a large segment of Millennials prefer this new job model to notions of lifetime commitments to large bureaucratic companies. This variable pool of workers also can implement entrepreneurial visions on their own without a lot of individuals working in the core "headquarters." With an ability to access expertise only when needed, to assemble task-fulfillment on an ad hoc basis, it does appear that virtual companies can be very competitive. Small may be the new big.

Even before the meltdown, in 2008, according to the Bureau of Labor Statistics there were 3.8 million companies with fewer than 10 employees (providing a total of 12.8 million jobs). But 10 workers can provide the value of a 100 or more if software, sharing common services and outsourcing replace employees. "Economists say there are some peculiarities to this wave of downturn start-ups. Chiefly, the Internet has given people an extraordinary tool not just to market their ideas but also to find business partners and suppliers, and to do all kinds of functions on the cheap: keeping the books, interacting with customers, even turning a small idea into a big idea." [345]

For those entering a perilous job market or those who have lost jobs and are struggling to return to gainful employment, outsourcing and open sourcing may be Godsends. The ability to build a technology or create value may have actually become close-to-free for many applications. Young entrepreneurs who once struggled to put together expensive business plans and documents necessary to raise equity now have the ability to create "something that works" before asking – the lower going-in costs creates an opportunity with a very low cost for failure. In an economy where new businesses and new technology are national, if not global, priorities, these lowered barriers to entry allow solutions never before possible. An example illustrates this amazing alternative business structure.

John Tayman began designing a start-up Website alone, but that solitary effort did not last long. Working off of his laptop and out of his San Francisco apartment, John began formulating a Website (motormouths.com) that would aggregate and summarize car reviews as wells as rank new cars. The industry call this a *LILO* ("a little in, a lot out") start-up. Working at nights and on weekends, he honed his ordinary computer skills with instructional information and open source "freebies" available online. He learned what steps to take, how the pieces fit and how to build the platform he was trying to create.

"On a website called 37signals.com, he learned about the virtues of lightweight programming languages like Ruby on Rails, which are ideal for the project he envisioned. He visited RentACoder.com and Elance.com, sites where one can find software developers. He picked up the jargon he needed to develop his project so he could put it out for bid, and he found his first programmer – in the Ukraine – who agreed to start building the digital scaffolding on the site.

Within months, Tayman had a virtual staff of 20 employees working for him in five different countries. 'In fact, I didn't even meet the guy who built most of the site until the launch party,' he says." [346] The company grew slowly, but for about $10,000 and no outside financiers to please, Tayman was quite content to let the business grow (revenues are based on selling advertising) at its own pace. Will the business survive and expand? The site is still very much around, but if it fails someday, there will be no trail of disappointed investors, and there is nothing stopping John from trying again.

As we've seen above, even at the bigger company level, this strategy of corporate sharing of resources has crept slowly into the entertainment business. Web-portals such as Hulu (which has added a social networking component) have become centralized platforms for many competitors to provide their content to Hulu's aggregate of users. Entertainment is particularly susceptible to such scaled up aggregation platforms since almost no single entertainment conglomerate has sufficient proprietary content to engage consumers with programming only from that company.

Notions of non-exclusivity and working with competitors as opposed to against them represent a new vector in media. The idea of non-exclusive eyeball aggregation to maximize advertisers' reach is a growing field. It's not just using the same platform to deliver content from many suppliers; it's also using different platforms to deliver the same content from a single supplier.

For example, Hutch Media's EGO TV (www.egotvonline.com) has created an 18-30-year-old Internet content network that features "fun and entertaining lifestyle TV shows with a twist on how to become successful." But what this service delivers is viewers, effectively becoming a "portal aggregator" by linking its network (and individual pieces of content) to a host of other online and mobile networks like YouTube, MySpaceTV, Veoh,[347] Joost, and Clearspring, thus multiplying the audience reach well beyond the originating network. This ability to take programming to millions of additional and trackable "eyeballs" creates a targeted volume that is very attractive to advertisers.Kink

Prosumers

The last sub-set in this chapter is the "prosumer," a concept that the youngest "do it my way or not at all" consumer totally understands. It's time for everybody at every level to appreciate what this "customization" and "design from the bottom up" concept means for those seeking prosperity in this new paradigm. Not that what makes someone a prosumer is anything new (just the term, which was coined in the mid-1990s).

Anybody who made an aftermarket modification to a horse-drawn Calistoga wagon was a prosumer, even if they didn't know it at the time. For decades, there's barely a Harley Davidson motorcycle on the road that hasn't been customized in some way by its owner. Whole companies have been created to customize major brands for specific consumer requirements, sometimes being so successful that these aftermarket customizers are absorbed by the brand themselves.

Take for example AMG (Aufrecht Melcher Großaspach, which was founded in 1967 by former Mercedes engineers and Erhard Melcher in a town near Stuttgart called Großaspach), a company totally dedicated to creating consumer-customized, tricked out, super-performing versions of off-the-floor Mercedes Benz automobiles. Consumers used AMG so much, and AMG's engineering was so good, that Mercedes (Daimler) bought out AMG (half in 1991 and the rest in 2005) and now makes AMG versions of just about all of its vehicles.

There is even potential, when the business is right, for the intersection of prosumer and outsourcing. Where outside talent suggests designs, the Web allows consumers to narrow the design choices and the company implements the final product. Try this example: "Threadless is in a pretty old-fashioned business – selling T-shirts (and a few other clothing items). But the company, which has become a full-blown Internet sensation, approaches the business in a completely new-fangled way.

"All of the designs in its online catalog come from its customers, who submit original artwork to the site. Threadless has more than a million registered members and adds more than 20,000 members per month. It receives an average of 150-200 new designs *per day* – that's more than a thousand designs a week. Members rate the submissions on a zero-to-five scale and the most popular submissions, as determined by visitors to the site, become candidates to be made into actual shirts. (A team of Threadless employees makes the final decisions, based on a variety of creative and commercial criteria.) The company selects seven new designs (and reprints two old designs) each week and sells the shirts for $15 to $17 each. The winning designers receive $2,000 in cash and $500 in store credit for their designs, plus an additional fee if their designs get reprinted later.

"This is an organization where, in the words of a headline in *Inc.* magazine, which has spent three decades chronicling how lone-genius entrepreneurs experience the thrill of victory and the agony of defeat, 'The Customer is the Company.' Threadless 'churns out dozens of new items a month – with no advertising, no professional designers, [and] no sales force,' the magazine marveled. 'And it's never produced a flop.' All told, Threadless sells more than 100,00 shirts per month--that's more than a million shirts a year--with just 35 employees … Threadless has attracted nearly 150,000 submissions from 42,000 aspiring designers – with more than *80 million* votes cast by members to express their preferences." [348]

Sure, modification by consumers is a very old practice. What is new, however, is how much today's consumers *expect* to control, influence and modify the products and services they are buying and how much of this bottom-up decision-making is altering the way that companies design and build their wares. To complicate this phenomenon is the fact that not all user-modifications to their purchases are positive. Picture a hit-man adding a custom silencer to a target pistol, a pedophile using an online social network to meet victims, or consumers disabling anti-piracy applications on video game platforms, iPods, tablets and other consumer electronics.

Should manufacturers and product suppliers embrace this consumer trend or fight it? Can they really stop what a customer does once the product has left the showroom floor? What threats and actions can a vendor take when a consumer has twisted a product or altered content in a way that the seller finds objectionable? Void a warranty? Publicly denounce the efforts? Prosecute the violators? Or live and enjoy the proactivity?

The trend is clear and rising, and the value proposition is not just the after-market. Manufacturers have found that letting the consumer speak, customize orders and even participate in the design of the next generation of products and services is an inevitable and useful service to the companies themselves. Moreover, consumers are providing the backbone to marketing efforts, supporting the products and services they like and trust, but decimating companies that they feel have "betrayed" them.

Prosumerism applies not just to the product itself but to issues such as pricing and marketing. There is a fine line in this subcategory that also steps into damage control, Rule 3 above. Consumers are particularly sensitive to "bad" companies with pricing plans that jack up costs to the unwary (particularly when an in-store computer price does not reflect the Website price or the advertised price or the price of goods listed in the store).

Consumers also resent companies that strip necessities out of products to reduce the price and then charge much more for the missing pieces, present misleading advertising, refuse to stand behind their products once sold, deny obvious defects, engage in "bait and switch" tactics, use consumer litigation as a means to delay the implementation of solutions or seek governmental support (by heavy lobbying and significant campaign contributions to friendly politicians) to side-step responsibility.

The bigger the company that perpetrates the "consumer crime," the more likely it is that irate consumers will blog their anger, seek to engage others with similar feelings to aggregate the "bad word of mouth," create negative videos about the company and otherwise pummel the offender. It's much more empowering to "take down" a corporate monolith and be responsible for a viral campaign of negativity against the "big bad company."

Customers also don't like sales people who talk down to them or deal with them as stereotypes. Internal company memos on how to "sell" to a particular stereotype — often created to substitute for training to underpaid sales staff — have a nasty habit of being leaked onto the Web by disgruntled employees. How many whistleblowers have sent incriminating documents to prosecutors, the press or simply and anonymously posted offending internal corporate documents on the Internet?

There is an additive damage-control-cure that involves creating a dialog with those who harbor (and express) negative opinions of the company so as to turn them into marketing prosumers. The issues embraced in these dialogs are, foremost, trust and relevance. If the target consumer is Internet literate and active, the communication takes place in the blogosphere, often with people who have taken a special interest in the company in question or perhaps the particular area of specialization into which the relevant product or service may fall.

Since betrayal means a loss of trust — and since people tend not to buy or deal with people or companies they do not trust — regaining trust can be a long and painful process. But having dedicated negative consumers, especially where these are peer leaders relevant to personal or corporate success, must be dealt with. If the effort is to convert someone whose core beliefs collide with the values being sold, the communication is both unlikely to convince and not particularly relevant. An appropriate mea culpa and apology is almost always the place to start.

Most people are uncomfortable with both the timeline needed to regain trust and the often strong negative reaction that is felt during the initial phase of dialog. Earning trust requires consistency and persistence. To help overcome the notion of a faceless company doing basic damage control, it is not enough simply to admit having erred. The first step requires the patience to follow the core consumer group, their blogs, long enough to understand who they are and what their basic motivations might be.

Diving In without spending some passive time with the communicators is a mistake. Thinking that the company Website is the appropriate dissemination point can even be a bigger mistake. You have to enter the often unfriendly world of the "enemy" and deal with them on their turf. It is equally important to find a company representative who both understands these motivations and is most likely to fit in with each group in question.

And then comes the part most companies miss: whomever the company places into these direct consumer communications must be a specific named person (a real human being – a face for the faceless company), likely to remain with the company for the foreseeable future, powerful enough to make a difference within the company, who can enter, participate and provide longer-term consistency in consumer interaction.

Don't want to keep track of reputational issues yourself? No problem; this task can be out-sourced too. There are companies with tracking software searching the Internet for negative valence descriptions of products, services, brands and political candidates. [349] This is a fact of life even for the company that is not under attack, one that simply wants to embrace its likely consumers into helping it find new designs and products as well as asking them for advice as to how to market and reach appropriate buyers.

For example, to manufacturers, the prosumer has been one of the oldest segments of the Internet. Many car-manufacturers let consumers "build" their dream models, even if they can't afford the vehicle...yet. This gives customers a hands-on familiarity with the product that may lead them to the showroom floor (or the manufacturer can guide the buyer to a dealer or skip the showroom altogether) or might build a desire to buy that brand years later.

Most consumer computer-manufacturers (such as Dell) allow customers to configure their purchases down to the location of the DVD drive, the speed of the graphics card, the processing speed and memory size. Think of the impact on customization as technology for 3-D printing accelerates. Tapscott and Williams see the world of bottom-up design as a seller's opportunity and not as a loss of control. They see smart companies treating their products as beginning stage platforms with well beyond a simple list of custom options available to the consumer. They would like to see more companies supply their customers with user-friendly tool kits to permit and encourage alteration their basic products, making them "modular, reconfigurable, and editable."

They envision more scenarios where consumers become peer creators, alongside the company, to create new product capacities or improve the existing design and functionality. For example, in a virtual world where people are empowered to design characters and environments – as with *Second Life* (an online virtual world) – it is the consumer who makes the experience worth living and playing in. These authors also see a world where companies provide rewards for economically worthwhile values created by their prosumers or enable myriad transactions in exchange for a piece of the revenue stream (like Amazon and eBay). [350]

Or companies can go one giant step sideways and ask the consumers to create the actual marketing campaign for the product. When Doritos brand chips asked consumers to create a 30 second spot with the victor claiming a million dollar prize, the winning entry, created at an actual cost of under $13 (a couple of bags of chips being the high cost budgetary item), found a spot on the 2007 Super Bowl and was voted by consumers one of the five best ads during that massively-viewed sporting event. If you believe you are thinking out of the box, you need to know something: there's really no box to think out of anymore. But there is an ugly battle taking place in a cultural environment where even some of the most resilient prosumer-sensitive companies are having difficulty accepting consumer creativity.

Self-proclaimed digital disc jockeys, video artists, and creative culturalists feel artistically restrained by copyright and patent laws that prevent them from doing what, in their own minds, is nothing more than allowing the existing culture to influence their creativity. To them, it's not about the obvious infringement (particularly when the content that is mashed-up or remixed is itself resold or publicly exhibited), it's about the fact that contemporary technology allows artistic expression in ways that older artists could not envision. They're just reflecting the world around them, as artists have always done. Is this a new market for intellectual property, an arena where a different license can be given or sold to consumers that might permit "artistic play" or is the only path a march to stricter enforcement of copyright laws?

Don Tapscott and Anthony Williams point out one such remix, "bastard pop" as they call it, a hybrid that found popularity on the Web even as it trounced on underlying copyrights: "Want a new twist on your well-worn Beatles collection? Try DJ Danger Mouse's *Grey Album*, which consists entirely of contorted samples from the Beatles' *White Album* mashed together with vocals from Jay-Z's smash hit *The Black Album*." [351]

Content owners need to grapple with a growing trend where consumers want to adapt, change and play with content in their own way. Stephen Colbert's *The Colbert Report* (an on-going fake news television series on the Comedy Central channel) offered video scenes (from the companion online site) with empty backgrounds, showing Colbert in the foreground engaged in some activity (e.g., as a light sword master à la *Star Wars*), asking viewers to submit their own video variations/creations embodying these segments as part of a contest. Winners were announced on the air, and the finalists could see their work incorporated as a part of the broadcast of the program itself. Allowing users access to content, unedited materials that are used in producing news and dramatic television and other "editable" content needs to be a routine part of the relationship between entertainment companies and their customers.

Speaking of *Star Wars*, the clever folks at Lucasfilm took one giant step out into the lives of their consumers by not only inviting their fans to do mash-ups and providing lots of material to them specifically for this purpose, [352] but they created a very successful Website (originally mashup.starwars.com, but with Disney having taken over the company, a more limited interactivity can now be found at starwars.com) where the "producers" of these mini-films could showcase their efforts. Because *Star Wars* is a multi-platformed and repurposed set of intellectual properties, not only did Lucasfilm cater to their fan base, present new "versions" of the brand (*Star Wars* content at virtually no cost to Lucasfilm) that sustained fan loyalty and interest and drew their core demographic to their Website (which is a lean, mean marketing machine), by requiring registration to participate, they also got a whole lot of very relevant consumer contact and tracking information.

Software giant Microsoft found even one more use for allowing consumers on the Web to modify and play with their consumer-provided content, in this case incomplete segments of an online film – using a "finish the film" contest to convince younger techno-sophisticates that Microsoft's new Vista operating system (particularly the enhanced version) could compete with the artist-preferred MAC system. "The contest... is called the Ultimate Video Relay and has its own Web site (ultimatevideorelay.com), a spinoff of the Windows Vista Ultimate Web site (ultimatepc.com).

The relay reference comes from the invitation to computer users to complete a story titled 'The Cube' in several stages. The tale, a humorous cross between 'The Matrix' and 'The Office' (or 'Office Space') begins with a six-minute clip that can be watched on the relay Web site. The clip is directed by Kyle Newman, the director of 'Fanboys,' a coming movie about 'Star Wars' aficionados.

"The online clip is labeled Act I of 'The Cube' and ends abruptly. Contestants are supposed to finish the story by providing first a middle (Act II) and later an end (Act III). The entries are judged by visitors to ultimatevideorelay.com. ... Microsoft is teaming up for the contest with TriggerStreet.com, the Web site of a production company owned by the actor Kevin Spacey that is aimed at aspiring moviemakers and screenwriters. TriggerStreet.com and Microsoft were brought together by Omelet, a company in Los Angeles that works on advertising, entertainment and branding projects with marketers..."[353] But the uses of prosumerism extend well beyond these marketing arenas.

Identifying & Tracking Appropriate Consumers

The essential capture of this "Web 2.0" interactive relationship with consumers does not simply require responding to inquiries. Sometimes the communicating/ marketing party has to reach out and find those who are already talking among themselves – and not with the company itself. Here is one example of a public relations firm that embraces this proactive approach, Virginia-based New Media Strategies: "NMS workers troll blogs that are talking about its clients – and sometimes knocking them. When Burger King recalled 25 million Pokémon toys because they were dangerous, NMS employees (who identify themselves as working for their clients) dug into chat rooms and blogs to tell Burger King's side of the story ... Example: When the SyFy Channel [354] desperately wanted to energize the hard-core audience base for its 'Battlestar Galactica,' NMS found the blogs the audience inhabited and started dishing. Influential bloggers were invited to attend backstage visits, where they were able to meet actors and writers." [355]

Finding authoritative Websites, influential with core consumers and peer leaders, is a big part of finding and using prosumers to defeat negativity and enhance innovation and growth. And the authoritative nature of Websites, especially blogs, is often a function of how many discrete users address the site, how many of those users are relevant to the company, how many other Websites are linked and how "respected" are the key information providers (bloggers) who lead the conversations.

Tracking solutions vary from the obvious blog-tracking solutions [356] to search engine analysis [357] to consultants all over the map (from the obvious to the industry-segmented and specialized). There are even companies dedicated to looking through the vast pools of information available on social networks that can be used to maximize marketing and sales efficiencies. [358]

The essence of this trolling the Web for information is "passive" tracking – simply looking at what consumers are saying without actively "polling" them or creating focus groups to provide answers to specific questions or product tests. This prevents the "test effect" or changing consumer behavior based on the fact that they are being specifically observed and analyzed by the company as to specific presentations. As communications become increasingly effective, the passive consumer can become a marketing prosumer, but knowing how your communications are faring in the ether becomes mission critical in building and maintaining the required trust.

As voluntary ("opt-in") online tracking develops (and is often legally required), understanding consumer (constituent) reactions to communications and how to fine-tune the continuing discussions requires deeper analytical understanding is available through various services that teach company (and individual) users how to maximize their efforts and measure online reactions. [359] One can even see how a brand compares with your competitors, both in how much people are talking and whether this is good or bad news for business. [360]

Our ability to track information passively has its roots in conventional content analysis, in that current search engines (Ask, Google, etc.) [361] rely on correct descriptive words to generate the precise demographic tagging. A "new but old approach" – allowing search-by-texting – even engages human responders who respond to direct questions. [362] More sophisticated browsers can generate fairly rich information based on underlying programmed inferences from even the simplest quest.

For example, people who want to "see it all" at a glance – images, videos and text – could turn to search engines like Kosmix (acquired in 2011 by Wal*Mart, which turned the company into @WalmartLabs, a research division), which provided, in its own words, a "360° view of videos, photos, news, commentary, expert opinions, communities and shopping resources related to any topic—all in one place." The user didn't have to click on "images" to pull them up – everything relevant to the initial query appears in the same place at the same time. But still, inputting key words on most search engines can produce mediocre and frustrating results.

For example, assume a toothpaste company is thinking about co-sponsoring a golf tournament to enhance its brand. Executives want to know exactly who might be impacted by such an effort, their level of sophistication and susceptibility to marketing and whether or not the sponsorship is worth considering. They need word-of-mouth to entice peer leaders (marketing prosumers) to make the effort worthwhile. What do they do? Maybe the marketing department sets up a Google search: they combine "golf" + "intelligent" + "toothpaste."

The result is masses of interesting information (9,960 entries) on arguments for and against the use of fluorides, alternatives to fluorides, biometrics, and a whole lot of cute stories. They then can hire a traditional blog analytical company to track golf blogs, chat rooms and sports pages to see what folks are talking about. What they are going to have trouble finding is any form of psychographic definition of an accessible cohort of bright (or stupid) people who are interested in watching or playing golf that might be willing to try a new toothpaste. In fact, they are not going to discover much in the way of tools to limit their decision criteria.

This key word approach combined with bulletin board/chat room/ blog depends very heavily on the sensibilities and sophistication of the originator of the search, which adds an additional level of subjectivity to the analysis. Moreover, as noted above, search engines may increasingly be relegated to more "research-oriented" tasks with social networking replacing many of the advertiser-related efforts. As we evolve into more sophisticated search structures, with capabilities to identify nuance, emotive characteristics and the ability to track parallel but unarticulated descriptions, the level of psychographic identification and tracking will, of necessity, become more efficient, more accurate and much more cost effective. And a whole lot more complicated, but that future is now.

Even Google, the largest search engine in the world, has added real-time trawling of the Web for the latest Web-postings. Google can also take a user photograph, apply a complex visual algorithm, and research information on the Web about the images in the picture without the user's having to use words to initiate the search. Google is accelerating research to make this an effective tool, and acquired a face and image recognition biometrics company, Neven Vision, for this purpose. Facebook is also moving towards helping its users identify and catalog photographs of "friends" based on such biometric analysis, a capacity that has privacy advocates shaking with fear. [363]

Your entire shopping experience might also be altered by an evolving facing scanning technology developed in a joint venture between Intel and Kraft Foods: [364] a meal planning kiosk can identify age, gender and other telling attributes to make recommendations automatically. Stereotypes anybody? Some advertisers have actually applied this technology to scanning passers-by and adapting an electronic display/billboard to present a message that is perceived as relevant to a potential customer.

Texas-based Mnemotrix Systems, Inc. has developed another and very different nuanced tracking search engine, which has moved away from simply finding key words contained in text into parallel searches that includes finding synonyms for each set of words articulated in the search, idiomatic clusters triggered by combinations of words, verbal equivalents of symbols and numbers (and vice versa), and other "experiences" contained in the company's proprietary database (linking feeling clusters together as well, so that "love" and "enjoy" share the same emotional valence).

As innovations in semiotics and consumer metrics improve, we are going to see an entirely new range of tracking software that will monitor public communications by consumers in many formats. Where people are too young, too old or otherwise unable to establish an online presence, their personality characteristics still find their way onto online sites by academic scholars and journalists writing about them. The wealth of information is obviously infinite, so the task is how to access enough to be statistically meaningful and to find the gold in prosumer marketing potential. The increasing use of "information visualization" – creating visuals from technical information – is a trend that makes trend-spotting or understanding complex analyses vastly easier and most useful to almost any level of user. But even this capacity has elevated to a new level with recent innovations.

Complex mathematical questions can be posed as a basic question in one newly designed software search system introduced in May of 2009. Inventor Stephen Wolfram has created what he describes as an engine to implement "computational knowledge." In English, "[The new Wolfram Alpha engine] doesn't simply return documents that (might) contain the answers, like Google does, and it isn't just a giant database of knowledge, like the Wikipedia. It doesn't simply parse natural language and then use that to retrieve documents ... Instead, Wolfram Alpha actually computes the answers to a wide range of questions – like questions that have factual answers such as 'What is the location of Timbuktu?' or 'How many protons are in a hydrogen atom?' or 'What was the average rainfall in Boston last year?' or 'What is the 307th digit of Pi?' or 'what would 80/20 vision look like?'" The software actually *doesn't find an existing fact*; it *makes its own calculation*, providing diagrams, graphs and links to other questions. [365]

Think of the value in creating market and tracking analysis with this capability! While scientists surely will rejoice, market analysts will also have incredible new powers to analyze complex consumer patterns by simply asking the right question. [366] The search industry, including Google, is also embracing key phrases and idiomatic expressions instead of easily misread keywords with multiple contextual meanings.

Even without the power of engines like Wolfram Alpha, following online consumer behavior has become an essential part of business planning. One of the most interesting new uses of passive tracking can be found, in a primitive state, on YouTube, where a popular video builds viewership virally. News organizations and parallel consumer groups often pick up on videos with big viewer numbers (tracked by the site itself). The value proposition for marketers of content is obvious – where the target is that younger segment of Internet sophisticates that trade communication "moments," sending a few of those video "moments" out into the ether is a means of finding out if the "moment" can find traction and popularity.

What is less obvious, but equally capable of being discovered using the tracking systems described above, is that the actual psychographically appropriate segments of the potential viewership will identify themselves and even tell you what they like or dislike about your "moment." Tracking these reactions with semiotically-sensitive software ("impact" and "sentiment" analysis) can help a marketer (a) figure out if the assumptions for whom the content is targeted are correct, (b) pick up other sub-sets of consumers that might also be attracted to such content, (c) suggest where additional tests might be valuable (it might even define some needed focus group testing) and (d) discover what about such content appeals to these consumers and what turns them off. In short, the relevant consumers will not only tell the marketer who they are but how to market to them! Not sure how to connect with consumers? Again, there are plenty of companies more than happy to help companies find the correct way to engage their client/customer base. [367]

There are obvious places to look, especially when the younger techno-sophisticates are involved. The easiest? Cell phones, personal digital assistants (PDAs) and mobile platforms have an interesting series of side benefits for consumer "trackers." When people sign up for a new cell phone or trade-up to the next generation, they tend to identify themselves, either in-person or online, either through direct personal information, the type of device they select, or even the way they use the phone (texting, surfing versus simple email and phone use).

Further, their actual usage is tracked; numbers called or texted, content purchased or downloaded. The bill often comes from the carrier itself, or even the sites visited. The Web is the next easiest passive tracking system as we have seen, but set-top boxes on television (Nielsen's rating system), folks with clickers counting people as they pass through marked barriers, ticket sales, bar code analysis on products sold, but the situation gets more interesting when the consumer is engaged in an activity that creates relevance for them and information for the tracking Website provider. Getting someone to provide a rating after an online transaction interests a few, but other than revenge or complimenting the extraordinary, most people have better things to do with their time.

Tracking online content consumption and purchases is very simple. [368] For other products and services that cannot be experienced directly in whole or in part on the Web, however, following-up normal old-world hands-on-product consumer testing with after-experience communications from those who were tested can be enlightening. Such passive tracking can refine and enhance both the product/service as well as the relevant marketing. For "what's next" consumers, tracking beta-tests, both actively and passively, becomes yet another path in product development.

Accepting myths about who uses the Internet versus traditional media – without looking at the tracking numbers – can be dangerous. For example, there has been an assumption by many that since video game and Internet usage are "modern, technologically driven," the most likely to use the Internet and engage in gaming are younger techno-sophisticates, skewing towards male. We have already discussed the growth numbers among women in the United States, especially in the over-30 market, in gaming. But the Internet numbers also indicate that the field, particularly when it comes to a "buy" decision, is also strongly grounded in a female demographic.

Analyzing, the scope, breadth and growth of the "woman to woman" communications on the Web have become statistically important trends in marketing. First, there is one hard economic fact, particularly in the United States: "Everybody knows that moms have clout. Marketers will rattle off numbers of percentages of household purchases the Mom-in-Chief makes, the trillion dollar 'mommy market' and the overall power of the purse."[369]

Naturally, this phenomenon has tracked online and grown steadily over the years. "Sites aimed primarily at women, from 'mommy blogs' to makeup and fashion sites, grew 35 percent [2007] — faster than every other category on the Web except politics, according to comScore, an Internet traffic measurement company. Women's sites had 84 million visitors in July [2008], 27 percent more than the same month [2007], comScore said.

"Advertisers are following the crowd, serving up 4.4 billion display ads on women's Web sites in May [2008], comScore said. That is more than for sites aimed at children, teenagers or families. 'Moms are the decision makers of the household as far as purchases are concerned,' said Chris Actis, vice president and digital director at the ad agency MediaVest." [370] By mid-2012, the number of mommy blogs had swelled to over 3.9 million, and of that number there were half a million with measureable reach and impact.[371] Indeed, when it comes to spending consumer dollars, especially in the United States, the female demographic seems to overwhelm male expenditures. [372]

One more path – taking post-transaction surveys – appears to be a consuming passion for many on and off-line businesses these days. These surveys – "Please Rate Your Transaction with _____"' – have provided valuable consumer input, for everyone from small businesses [373] to the mega-eTailers whose products and services seem to envelop the Web. But the plethora of this survey process has led to some pushback from consumers. The volume of requests is substantial: "There is no way to determine exactly how many consumer satisfaction surveys are completed each year, but Mindshare Technologies, a small company that conducts and analyzes on-the-spot electronic surveys, says it completes 175,000 [U.S.] surveys every day, or more than 60 million annually." [374]

To many, survey requests have simply become intrusive: "Many businesses, often against the advice of the experts they have hired to construct their questionnaires, cannot resist the urge to ask, ask and ask yet again. Exasperated consumers, assured that the survey will take only five minutes to complete, often bail out as they approach the 10-minute mark." [375] To entice consumers, discounts and rewards are promised, occasionally entry into a contest with a more substantial reward is the tease. Some show pictures of the business owner with his or her family to make the request more personal, but for many, enough is enough.

Millennials have more patience with this form of feedback: "'Young people send and receive communications at a rate we've never seen before,' said Claes G. Fornell, founder of the American Customer Satisfaction Index and a professor at the Stephen M. Ross School of Business at the University of Michigan. 'They don't seem to mind answering surveys if they're not too long,' he added. 'When you think about it, the whole concept of social media is, I'm going to give my opinion whether I'm asked or not.'" [376] Shorter is better, even if business owners want pages of personal information.

Common sense and an awareness of change frequently elude even seasoned companies, but listening to consumers is an art form with scientific overtones that must be learned. Many managers are not only mired in old assumptions, they are equally intimidated when a consumer elects to modify a product or use it in a way that the company never intended. Perhaps some of these concerns are legitimate (like the aforementioned hit man with his silencer), but controlling consumers seems a lot like herding cats.

This is a particularly sensitive arena for owners of intellectual property (particularly audio-visual entertainment and computer software), where bits and pieces of the whole are taken out of context and mixed and matched, mashed-up and remixed, into new forms.

Pricing and Formatting Consumer Access

One of the most significant challenges of this modern era is the "pricing-monetization" vector. The actual methodology of the pricing model is as important as designing the product in the first place, particularly an issue in selling music and film. For example, in a world where entertainment companies wish to charge consumers on a pay-per-use (or unit) model, there has been great resistance from major content providers against applying a subscription model to hot "new" content (versus older, catalog product).

Mobile phone carriers faced these issues in the mid-1980s as consumers began disconnecting their cell phones because the per-minute charges made cellular communication too expensive. The problem was corrected when phone companies moved to aggregated "lots of minutes" plans. [377] The entertainment industry still believes that copyright laws can force consumers to buy audio and/or visual content as the companies dictate, even as the Netflix subscriptions blow away the downloads.

Employing a variety of techniques aimed at curtailing habitual infringers, U.S. content providers increasingly apply a "graduated response" to such illegal downloaders before mounting a wholesale attack. The Copyright Alert System is one such methodology: "If you use AT&T, Cablevision, Comcast, Time Warner, or Verizon as your Internet service provider, you could receive… one of [a series of these gradually-increasing warning] notes…. The Internet provider is delivering the message, but the legwork is being done by the copyright owners, which will monitor peer-to-peer networks such as BitTorrent… They use a service called MarkMonitor, which uses a combination of people and automated systems to spot illegal downloading. It will collect the IP addresses of offenders, but no personal information. The IP addresses are turned over to the Internet providers, which will match up the address with the right customer and send the notification."[378]

If series of escalating warnings fail to stop the practice, then come the assaults, the cut-off of service and perhaps even an infringement action that could cost the consumer a small fortune. The copyright owners want clear protection and direct paths to monetization "their way." Consumers feel intrusion and over-pricing.

At least the phone companies selling cell-phone minutes recognized quickly that they were fighting a losing battle and changed their pricing structure. But copyright holders have longed, through proposed legislation and through actual litigation, to get the intermediaries to carry to infringement fight to the consumers, try to keep a pricing structure for copyrighted content that seems unsustainable. In today's marketplace, smaller start-ups, which have not developed reliance on expense old-world business plans have a pricing advantage. But in the end, pricing at any level is a balancing act that must take into consideration the global competitive environment, regardless of underlying cost pressures. Proper pricing requires looking at consumer sensitivities and addressing those needs.

It seems that there is a strange consumer conundrum when it comes to buying a product. Several university studies have noted that: "Most of us mentally account for nearly all the money we spend, whether or not we realize it … Usually we won't replace that product until we think we've gotten our money's worth. That explains why some people continue to wear ill-fitting shoes rather than chucking them." [379] The notion of buying, but not getting the full value of what we bought or buying something that disappears or loses its value quickly, is a consumer deterrent. While children may inadvertently run up volume-based cell phone texting charges without parental supervision, adults are more likely to embrace a cell phone plan that offers a bit more than the expected level of service.

The psyche of subscription versus a "pay-per-view" model suggests that the former has vastly more viability in the future of world of direct-to-consumer content distribution. "A subscription moves consumers over the hurdle of mentally depreciating an existing asset. When you go on vacation and don't get any movies from Netflix, it is easier to accept having wasted $30 for your subscription that month than it would be to have bought a $30 DVD and never watched it." [380]

Further complicating matters is the dominance of Netflix in the U.S. consumer subscription model, where pressures are building from competitors like Amazon and Apple who are willing to pay more to studios for content to get earlier windows and premium product. Consumers, accustomed to paying Netflix $7.99 for either a streaming or a DVD delivery system and $9.99 for both, were outraged in July of 2011 when Netflix announced an increase its combined rate to $15.98, a 60% increase. Netflix evolved its consumer model before the above competitive factors entered the marketplace, but its management of consumer expectation was mostly certainly below par. To generate greater fees, such rate increase would seem to need to be combined with perceived increased values.

But the reason behind this seeming price gouge was pretty much a manipulative move to herd consumers into the vastly more profitable electronic-only universe, to discourage consumers from continuing with their hard-copy by mail service in favor of their streaming model.[381] And of course, the Netflix pricing model begged for competition in the U.S. market. Amazon Instant[382] and Redbox Instant by Verizon [383] were some of the earlier entrants. Clearly competition for both content and subscribers is opening up, and a long-term price-war is all but certain. Netflix recovered from this flub and with exciting new and original content (like *House of Cards*) and came back with a vengeance, even as Amazon and Hulu also announced their entre into scripted TV.

The newer subscription models are also beginning to focus on a model that delivers content to subscribers on any platform they choose (cable, Web, mobile, etc.), no matter where located *versus* content delivered only to a residence or a building. [384] After all, consumers are actually buying the content, not the wires. We have lived with the notion of satellite and cable services that are structure based for a long time, but technology shifts suggest that this business structure may soon be rendered obsolete. The notion of platform agnosticism has finally penetrated the thinking of industry leaders looking for a substitute for the contracting DVD market as well. [385]

As consumers migrate away from traditional television sets and DVD players to PCs and mobile devices, the notion of consumers being able to "buy" permanent access to audio-video content – across any playable digital platform and in the most appropriate and best quality available – is at the forefront of new economic models being explored by both Disney, [386] Warner Bros., [387] and the Digital Entertainment Content Ecosystem. [388] The notion of liberating content from a compact device or a limited format or delivery system is a critical step forward in enhancing the home video marketplace. But whether this "pay-per-content" model will sustain (or operate beyond the initial stages when content is "hottest") and supplant a more ubiquitous "all-you-can-eat" subscription model has yet to be established. Whatever the new direction, this represents a huge change from the library/ownership mentality of old.

Perhaps the ultimate structures – assuming they are adopted before the film and television industries make the same mistakes that led to the collapse of the music business – may be a combination of both these models at different stages of the content exploitation continuum. There are still some flies in the ointment that have yet to be fully quantified: (i) the ability to sell a new format (such as the move from VHS tapes to DVDs) disappears as consumers who no longer own the hard copies can pull down their favorites in any format they want and (ii) the impact on granting "exclusivity" in one medium – such a free television – no longer represents exclusivity across all platforms in the system (content still can be accessed by consumers from the clouds).

The issues are also particularly complex for the motion picture industry and in particular to those producers of longer-form content (such as movies) that has had no clear previous life in a theatrical or television medium (where marketing momentum was generated). Except for the television models pioneered by Hulu and Netflix, the future of such longer-form content, even movies, on the Web is anything but clear. Start with the flood of amateur features (which have no serious revenues from any other medium) and then factor in the much higher cost of high production value motion pictures consumers actually want to see. Add in the very high cost that Hollywood spends in marketing to create consumer awareness. Then blend in the expectation of many consumers that online equals "free."

While smaller, Independent fare might find a niche (unlikely to be economically significant anytime soon) in a bigger subscription model (obviously one with a "recommend" feature), the more likely fuel for this content, at least initially, is likely to find traction somewhere in the advertising model, a structure that has so far eluded independent filmmakers, even in advertising revenue-sharing Website such as YouTube. The big bad barrier – creating consumer awareness – is the horrendous cost of marketing.

For example, in the fall of 2009, low budget horror (and other genre) producer Roger Corman created a joint venture with Netflix that provided the latter's customers – for free – an online horror miniseries (*Splatter*), where in part certain plot points were determined through the interactive participation of the online viewers. The event was a marketing tool to draw consumers to Netflix' download business and not an attempt to create a new social network. Netflix vice president of corporate communications Steve Swaysey: "I wouldn't say this would signal anything that's radically different from the Netflix model that we have now. We are a great film distributor. That's what our goal is going to continue to be … There are others that would do social marketing better than we would ever be able to." [389] The field is clearly open to experimentation, but many in the business continue to swim upstream in so-called new media.

Copyright owners have often felt that the legal protection is sufficient to allow them to force consumers to receive content in ways consumers have clearly indicated that they do not want. Unions, guilds and copyright owners have long favored making people pay every time they view/hear content and have not exactly been forthcoming with structures that do not support that model.

The content subscription and advertising-based services that have been attempted in the music industry – from Yahoo, Rhapsody and MTV – have been hampered by a lack of cooperation from the recording industry resulting in a pool of music that was so severely limited so as to make such music services uneconomic. One company that might have the bargaining power to break that restriction, Apple, is exploring the future of their iTunes content delivery platform. Apple has begun subscription service that will open up its vast library of content onto its iPhone and iTunes, a structure that may prove to have greater traction than other services because of Apple's existing contractual relationships with most of the viable music labels in connection with its download/iTunes model.

Amazon and Google are accelerating into this market with new channels and niche targeting, adding potential ad dollars to the mix. If these services break through with enough desirable content, the entire entertainment industry will be forced (sooner or later) to create a ground-up pricing restructuring of its full range of audio and/or visual content directly to consumers.

Reading the tea leaves requires companies to understand that even their pricing policies are not simply a management prerogative based on an old world "supply and demand" set. Where "supply" can be circumvented, even with high demand, the inquiry into consumer behavior becomes essential. The traditional "top-down" determination to control consumer behavior is a model that is fractured if not completely obsolete. Thus we must approach even our most sacred assumptions with an open mind, because resistance to a massive wave of uncontrolled consumer behavior represents a potentially huge economic loss to the stubborn – and a significant new market to those who really understand the potential.

Opportunities, Opportunities, Opportunities

In the end, even in this shredded but reignited universe, we have an incredible set of amazing new opportunities. There is a "next." It is exciting… and bit more unpredictable than we might want. Remember all those younger kids getting cell phones cited above… er smart phones? We can decry giving little kids mobile phones, protest to the government, but if parents wind up giving in to the obvious pressure they will experience from the "children denied," isn't that an opportunity?

Imagine a mobile phone that allows a parent to track numbers called and received in real time, create an "approved list," and even allow only predetermined content to find its way to their children's phone. Problems invite solutions. Finding those solutions creates the opportunity. It just takes a little *reaching.* A successful reach gains economic significance as it gains traction and scales up. It becomes the next.

If we lack the ability to accomplish some major business function because we are too small and lack the resources of a big corporate monolith, we can outsource and get what we need, in precisely the right amount and at a price which represents a tiny fraction of what it would cost to hire staff. If we run out of ideas for how to fix problems or find new products, we have a whole world out there we can access.

We can link to service providers to give us direct access to a buying public, ship virtually anywhere on earth, and we can test our marketing strategy without necessarily having to engage in consumer testing through focus groups. Best of all, when we really don't know how to access or address our customers' needs, we actually can ask them and get their help in finding a path to their doors!

Conclusion

In a world of hyper-connectivity, where the ability to use and understand communications technology has literally become a campaign issue in American politics, truly we live in a new world order. What was it like for President Barack Obama, an admitted "CrackBerry" (someone who cannot let go of his or her tether to an Internet-connected cell phone) of the first degree, when for a moment he thought he might be forced to put his beloved cell phone behind, literally giving up his favorite form of communication. The concern was that many of his electronic messages could become part of his public legacy – under the 1978 Presidential Records Act – or might compromise national security as his phone became a particularly valuable target for foreign intelligence agencies.

A modern leader of our nation forced back in technological times because of a statute that is relevant but also a reflection of times past? "I'm still clinging to my BlackBerry … They're going to pry it out of my hands," the President told CNBC on January 8, 2009, as he searched for a legal opinion in support of his addiction to this device. The only way the President got to keep that device was for the National Security Agency to layer in a "super-encryption" software package to his BlackBerry. [390] Still the President's smart phone (now dubbed the "BarackBerry") will only be used for personal communications that are otherwise exempt from the Presidential Records Act. But the moment was nevertheless historic.

When that administration first stepped into the White House in January of 2008, they were staggered by the lack of sophisticated computers and connectivity as well as the out-of-date software. The new communications era that had begun for many Americans years before was now finding its natural place at the heart of the new government, a seminal and symbolic transition, a social as well as technological trend that motivated my writing this book in the first place.

Pretty much everything in our lives is experiencing a paradigm-shift. What wasn't changed by new inventions and their impact on the surrounding society was slammed into a new reality by the economic collapse. Simple notions, like getting a job and working for an employer, have lost their glitter with job insecurity and layoffs being the new expectation. Outsourcing work to lots of non-permanent independent contractors is likely to gain momentum in the future of American labor.

Fewer workers can do more with technology and the ability to access distant resources. National health insurance options can only increase the viability of new corporate structures based on a flexible outsource/contractor model. We are moving to a work structure where we may soon see a majority of people working for themselves or as smaller contractors, even if they perform services for a huge corporation that used to be fulfilled by its employees.

Does privacy even exist anymore? Is the NSA spying plan – euphemistically labeled "Prism" although for state-secrets-bean-spiller Edward Snowden it may well be eventual "prison" – the quintessential statement about how private even our most personal communications have become? That world leaders screamed like stuck pigs when revelations of U.S. snooping on their personal phones surfaced very publicly?

Within companies, the way bosses communicate to their world must alter forever. Empowerment down the line becomes essential in a universe where interactivity and prosumer input require much faster decisions than can be implemented in old-world decision-tree management styles. Large companies literally require CEOs to blog (via text, tweets and videos) to their mass of employees and customers … and have CEOs read the responses. [391] It's just the way it is.

For those who have found new paths, new choices, through the preceding pages, I am grateful for being the motivator. The best news of all? There's so much change that stepping into the game now means you don't have to learn about all that stuff that is now completely obsolete. For those supplementing much of what they already knew with bits and pieces of new information, I hope that your journey takes you deeper still into the mysteries of modern social communications.

I've used the film and television industry throughout this book for obvious reasons: it is the industry I know best. I have spent over 35 years watching the complete transformation of audio-visual media, making deals for major stars and powerhouse directors along the way, writing and teaching about entertainment and marketing. But commercial entertainment is also the reflector of our culture and the place the world began watching news, sports and entertainment on a screen, long before computers, the Internet or ubiquitous and cheap mobile telephony. Television is the rich media experience that Internet communications are compared to, even as the notion of an electronic input from the "Web" and a television screen blur the meaning of these once-separate universes.

The challenge for the independent creative community is how to mirror the entertainment behemoths' ability to reach massive of consumers — how to scale up — without needing a huge legacy bureaucracy and expensive marketing campaign to break through. And perhaps if that lesson can be learned at the grassroots level, it may also redefine how majors access their commercial audiences in the future — literally doing much more with much less. Change is here and it's accelerating. But how we adapt to that change, even embrace it, will define how we succeed in a globally competitive market.

There are always going to be Luddites who try desperately to stop all this change and push back to a simpler time. But even these souls, who want communications complexity to go away, are ironically a *social network* of sorts. They will still try to filter out what the outside world seems to be forcing upon them and share this resistance with each other.

On the other hand, they might someday understand that — absent cataclysm — change will not stop. If we want hope and the belief in the future, on this planet and in this time, then learning to use the new communications tools to cope and enjoy life seems to be a healthy alternative. It's most certainly not "all good," but there is a whole lot of good, most of it yet to be mined.

If you believe that change will stabilize, take a look at a pre-literate two-year-old with a tablet or a touch-screen smart phone. They may watch you manipulate the screen, but as soon as their hand-eye coordination permits, even before they can read the words they are forming, they will soon fly through the panels on the screen, pulling up images that make them giggle. They are starting out with the very technology that already rocked your world, took strains to learn, changed the way you live and communicate, and perhaps even how you make your living. What is complex for you is pre-kindergarten for them.

It will pay communicators and marketers to watch the evolution of these very young, sense their delights and frustrations, address their focus and attention span, understand their abbreviations and symbols, grasp how they perceive the world around them and most importantly how they *discover* what's next. If you ask them, look at them and listen to them, <u>they will teach you how to communicate with them</u>. But if you assume that your experience with an older child will be mirrored in their actions, if you believe that your own patterns of growing up are still determinative, you will watch a ship leave port, sail into the sunset and disappear over the horizon. They are an entirely new generation in the making. Embrace the next!

I end this journey with a story. A friend of mine in the entertainment industry – a family that is clearly teched-up to the max – was driving with his six-year-old son listening to music on the car radio. When the song ended, the lad asked dad to "replay that." His dad explained that it was a radio that did not have that capability. The boy complained that "mom can do it!" My friend responded that she was probably listening to a CD or her iPod, but radio was different. His son scowled and stated with firmness, "That's just not right!"

Peter J. Dekom

Peter J. Dekom practices law in Los Angeles, California and is also "of counsel" with the Beverly Hills law firm of Weissmann Wolff Bergman Coleman Grodin & Evall. He formerly was a partner in the firm of Bloom, Dekom, Hergott and Cook. Mr. Dekom's clients include or have included such Hollywood notables as George Lucas, Paul Haggis, Keenen Ivory Wayans, John Travolta, Ron Howard, Rob Reiner, Andy Davis, Robert Towne and Larry Gordon among many others, as well as corporate clients such as Sears, Roebuck and Co., Pacific Telesis and Japan Victor Corporation (JVC). He has been listed in Forbes among the top 100 lawyers in the United States and In Premiere Magazine as one of the 50 most powerful people in Hollywood.

Mr. Dekom has been a management/marketing consultant, and entrepreneur in the fields of entertainment, Internet, and telecommunications. As a consultant to the state of New Mexico for almost a decade (2001 - 2011), he was instrumental in creating, writing and implementing legislation to encourage film and television production in the state – since used as a model structure for many state film incentive plans – and supervised the film loan program portion of that incentive structure. He also advised the Governor on film and television-related matters. Mr. Dekom has also provided off-balance sheet, insurance-backed financing for major motion picture studios.

Mr. Dekom served on the board of directors of Imagine Films Entertainment while the company remained publicly traded and was a board member of Will Vinton Studios and Cinebase Software, among others, leaving upon change of ownership. He has also served as a member of the Academy of Television Arts and Sciences and Academy Foundation, Board of Directors, Chairman (now Emeritus) of the American Cinematheque, and on the Advisory Board of the Shanghai International Film Festival. He serves on the Board of Governors for the America Bar Assn.'s Sports and Entertainment Law Section, where he has often authored articles and delivered lectures.

The Beverly Hills Bar Association honored Mr. Dekom as Entertainment Lawyer of the Year in 1994, the Century City Bar Association accorded him the same honor in 2004, and the Family Assistance Program named him Man of the Year in 1992 for his work with the homeless. Author of dozens of scholarly articles, Mr. Dekom also is the co-author of the book Not on My Watch; Hollywood vs. the Future (New Millennium Publishing, 2003) with Peter Sealey. He has served as an adjunct professor in the UCLA Film School, a lecturer (entertainment marketing) at the University of California, Berkeley Haas School of Business as well as being a featured speaker at film festivals, corporations, universities and bar associations all over the world.

Mr. Dekom graduated from Yale in 1968 (BA), and graduated first in his class in 1973 from the UCLA School of Law (JD). He is married to former art gallery owner, Kelley Choate, and has a son, Christopher (b. 1983), who is a 2006 graduate of Duke University, a 2013 MBA grad from Darden (University of Virginia) and an associate with Macquarie Capital Partners in Los Angeles. Chris's wife, Stephanie, is a physician-resident in pediatrics at UCLA.

Follow Peter on his daily socioeconomic-political blog: unshred.blogspot.com

ENDNOTES

[1] On the other hand, Reed Hastings might also be the poster boy for moving *too* quickly without fully thinking out the impact of a decision or, more importantly, asking his consumer base for their opinion before implementing a massive change in consumer pricing. In the fall of 2011, Netflix separated streaming from hard copy home entertainment subscription services, effectively raising the price for both services by 60%, costing themselves almost a million customers and seriously tanking their stock price.

[22] FastCompany.com, March 18, 2013.

[3] "For the first time, a majority of American adults are now smartphone owners, according to a study released [June 5, 2013]. The Pew Center for Internet and American Life found that 56 percent of all American adults now use mobile phones that run an operating system such as Apple's iOS, Google's Android or Microsoft's Windows Phone. That's up from 46 percent in 2012 and 35 percent in 2011." WashingtonPost.com, June 5, 2013. What do Americans do on their smartphones? "According to Nielsen's ... Q1 2013 Cross-Platform Report, smartphone users spent 87% of their 'app/mobile web' time on mobile apps, and the other 13% surfing the mobile web. Both men and women spend more than four hours per month on the mobile web." CynopsisDigital.com, June 11, 2013

[4] One would suspect that as societies become more connected, consumers would slowly accept that their behavior is being tracked at every turn. Yet even in the United States, online and mobile users are 90% concerned about this tracking behavior, and many simply believe that current and proposed "do not track" legislation offers clear protections for their digital connection at a significantly higher level than actually specified. For a more detailed discussion of these expectations, see: *Privacy and Modern Advertising: Most US Internet Users Want "Do Not Track" to Stop Collection of Data About their Online Activities* by Chris Jay Hoofnagle (University of California, Berkeley - School of Law, Berkeley Center for Law & Technology), Jennifer M. Urban (University of California, Berkeley - School of Law) and Su Li (University of California, Berkely - Center for the Study of Law and Society) presented at the *Amsterdam Privacy Conference 2012,* October 8, 2012.

[5] "Google Glass (styled 'GLASS') is a wearable computer with an optical head-mounted display (OHMD) ... developed by Google in the Project Glass research and development project, with the mission of producing a mass-market ubiquitous computer. Google Glass displays information in a smartphone-like hands-free format, that can interact with the Internet via natural language voice commands." Wikipedia

[6] On October 11, 2012, the United Nations' International Telecom Union reported that by the end of 2011, there were 2.3 billion Internet users out of a global population of approximated 7 billion (approximately one out of every three inhabitants on the planet) connected to the Web. This statistic favored wealthier developed countries (70%) over poorer, developing nations (24%). Cell phone penetration reached 6 billion (India is almost a billion, and China is over a billion) in the same period.

[7] "[S]martphone users have developed what they call 'checking habits' -- repetitive checks of e-mail and other applications such as Facebook. The checks typically lasted less than 30 seconds and were often done within 10 minutes of each other... On average, the study subjects checked their phones 34 times a day, not necessarily because they really needed to check them that many times, but because it had become a habit or compulsion." CNN.com, July 28, 2011 summarizing a study in Personal and Ubiquitous Computing, Journal 779, May 2011.

[8] The June 16, 2010 FastCompany.com provides this insight into lies ahead for this particular communications method: "'If you want to know what people like us will do tomorrow, you look at what teenagers are doing today,' Facebook COO Sheryl Sandberg told the audience at Nielsen's conference [on June 15, 2010]. And according to Sandberg, only 11% of teens email daily--clearly, a huge generational drop. Instead, they are increasingly turning to SMS [texting] (or Twitter) and social networks for communication... 'E-mail--I can't imagine life without it--is probably going away,' she said... But this transition will be good for businesses and brand marketers. Why? Because while it's very difficult to gain access to a consumer's email address, connecting with them via social networks is quite simple. Indeed, with Facebook's 400 million [now over 1.1 billion] members and 100 million daily mobile users [try 751 million in 2013!], the network enables brands to connect with more customers than ever before--or, as Sandberg explains, 'On any given day, you can reach twice as many people in the U.S. as watch *American Idol*--and that only makes up 30% of our global audience.'" But when ages are averaged, email still holds its own, although trending and effectiveness point clearly to the ever-growing impact of social networks: "According to a new report by marketing firm SocialTwist, Internet sharing trends have shifted heavily shifted toward social networking, but other platforms still have a strong presence for word-of-mouth advertising. SocialTwist analyzed more than a million referral messages sent using the company's Tell-a-Friend tool, a widget that lets users share sites through social media... In the last year, social networking sites saw a 10% increase in usage, and a 16% bump in click-throughs. Overall though, email still accounts for 55% of referrals...However, when it comes to click-throughs, social networking sites are far more effective, accounting for more than 60% of the market share...Among social networking sites, Facebook is by far the most preferred service for sharing, making up more than 78% of usage. Yet other sites are gaining: Twitter maintains 5% of referrals, and MySpace, surprisingly, comes in at second with 14.5% share...Yet Twitter has become the most effective tool for click-throughs. Twitter yielded a whopping average of 19.04 clicks, whereas Facebook only produced 2.87 clicks." FastCompany.com, October 11, 2010. But how about this stunning and counterintuitive statistic: "[T]he fastest growth on social networking sites like Facebook has come from internet users 74 and older. Usage quadrupled since 2008... fully 16% [socially network] now." FastCompany.com, December 16, 2010, citing a report from Pew Internet & American Life Project. Still, Twitter followed in Facebook's footsteps, becoming a public company in late 2013, but choosing instead a listing on the New York Stock Exchange.

[9] "Almost half (49.7%) of U.S. mobile subscribers now own smartphones, as of February 2012. According to Nielsen, this marks an increase of 38 percent over ... February 2011, only 36 percent of mobile subscribers owned smartphones. This growth is driven by

increasing smartphone adoption, as more than two-thirds of those who acquired a new mobile device in the last three months [of 2012] chose a smartphone over a feature phone." Nielsen.com, March 29, 2012

[10] NYTimes.com, October 22, 2012.

[11] "Google's Android is poised to overtake Windows to become the dominant operating system/software by the end of 2016, according to a new forecast from Gartner, per a report from Reuters. The research firm projects that by the end of 2016, 2.3 billion computers, smartphones, and tablets will be powered by Android, versus 2.27 billion devices running on Windows." CynopsisDigital.com, October 25, 2012.

[12] Ibid

[13] " [T]he number of mobile broadband connections worldwide will rise to 2.1 billion [by the end of 2013], nearly three times the total of fixed-line subscriptions." NYTimes.com, September 26, 2013"The amount of time people spend on their phones surfing the Web, using apps, playing games and listening to music has more than doubled in the last two years, to 82 minutes a day, according to eMarketer; the time spent online on computers [grew] just 3.6 percent [in 2012]." CynopsisDigital.com, October 25, 2012.

[14] Ibid

[15] The music business was reduced in half by a combination of the destruction of the "album only" economic model into almost all singles structure and by massive file-sharing which continues heavily into the present day, despite lots of inexpensive subscription services and cheap singles downloads. "Americans downloaded nearly 760 million songs using the BitTorrent file-sharing network in the first six months of [2012] -- surpassing the number of digital tracks purchased over that same period, according to [London-based MusicMetric)." Los Angeles Times, October 2, 2012.

[16] Which include everything from polling and taking surveys, conducting focus groups and interviews, objective experiments to isolate the relevant variable in consumer behavior to professional observation and content analysis, data-base marketing, panels of consumers engaged to assess product viability, to name but a few.

[17] The Media Behavior Institute has released the latest data from its USA TouchPoints Nearly a quarter (22%) of adults now own some kind of tablet computer, double the number a year ago (11%), and smartphone ownership is up nine points, from 35% to 44%. As a result, half of all Americans (50%) now have mobile internet access through either a tablet or a smartphone... Fully 64% of tablets owners and 62% of smartphone owners say they use the devices for news at least weekly, according to the survey. And a third of all U.S. adults now get news on a mobile device at least once a week. And Americans are doing more than just clicking headlines on their mobile devices: 73% of adults who consume news on their tablet read in-depth articles at least sometimes, including 19% who do so daily...Among other findings:.. Just over half, 52%, of tablet owners report owning an iPad, compared with 81% a year ago. Fully 48% now own an Android-based device, including two in ten, 21%, who own a Kindle Fire... Rather than replacing old technology, the introduction of new devices and formats is creating a new kind of 'multi-platform' news consumer. More than half, 54%, of tablet news users also get news on a smartphone; 77% also get news on a desktop/laptop and 50% get news in print. What's more, 25% of get news on all four platforms." Results from a detailed survey of news use on mobile devices conducted by the Pew Research Center's Project for Excellence in Journalism (PEJ) in collaboration with The Economist Group released on October 1, 2012. But with new mobile devices falling into the market rapidly, these statistics were dated almost as they were published.

 The second wave of data to come from [The Media Behavior Institute in its USA TouchPoints reporting service as of September 2012]... finds that weekly tablet usage now reaches 19.3% of adults 18-64, and daily reach among this group is up 15% when compared to the data from the previous report. In addition, among tablet users, the top three activities on the device in terms of weekly usage are the internet (excluding email) at 54%, apps (excluding email) at 44%, and email at 37%. Watching videos on a tablet on a weekly basis now encompasses 20% of tablet owners 18-64. Other data from the service, which is used by the likes of Optimedia, Starcom, MediaVest, Mindshare, ESPN, and Turner Broadcasting, include:

- Watching programming on a DVR now stands at 40% weekly reach and 18% daily reach. This is much higher than VOD, which reaches 13% and 3% of adults 18-64 on a weekly and daily basis, respectively.

- 8% and 6% of the US adult population watch TV episodes via a streaming service on a weekly and daily basis, respectively. While the Media Behavior Institute agrees that this is still relatively small, it notes that it's still an increase of over 40% when compared to data from February.

- Social networking grew 6% to reach 37% of adults 18-64 in the past week." CynopsisDigital.com, September 6, 2012.

[18] The March 27, 2009 ShowBizData.com: "Younger baby boomers between the ages of 45 and 54 are the biggest consumers of video media, averaging over nine-and-a-half hours daily, according to a $3.5-million study by the Council for Research Excellence. Live TV dominated the viewing habits of the young boomers, accounting for more than five-and-a-half hours. The Internet accounted for 46 minutes; DVR playback, 17 minutes; and email, 51 minutes. [T]the study itself observed, 'TV users were exposed to, on average, 72 minutes per day of TV ads and promos -- again dispelling a commonly held belief that modern consumers are channel-hopping or otherwise avoiding most of the advertising in the programming they view.'"

[19] Quoted in the New York Times, March 17, 2009. Note that after the January 12, 2010 earthquake in Haiti, the American Red Cross raised $22 million in just the first week via texting (1/5 of the total they raised that week), where contributions were simply added to the donor's monthly cell phone bill in $10 increments; the previous texting record had been $400,000.

[20] According to the February 4, 2008 Daily Variety (at page 6), Google's income from searches pushed its revenues sky-rocketing by 51% in 2006, numbers and growth well above the competition; Google accounts for 7.7% of all U.S. Web traffic. According to The Wall Street Journal (at page 1), February 2-3, 2008, as of December, 2007, Google controlled 62.4% of the U.S. search market – generating $11.6 billion/year, out of a total of $16.6 billion, from online ad sales; MSN and Yahoo combined control only 15.7%. But the numbers online are accelerating once again; it is interesting to note which categories of U.S. Web ad sales are the most productive: "2010's rebound saw $26 billion spent, with Search (46%) continuing to lead the way, followed by banner/display ads (24%), Classifieds (10%) and Rich Media (6%)." Cynopsis Digital, April 14, 2011.

[21] While feature films are finding difficulty as original online programming, if you need evidence of the slow but steady merger between traditional and Web-based television: "Netflix [followed] up on the $100 million drama 'House of Cards' with four more series [in 2013]. Microsoft is producing programming for the Xbox video game console with the help of a former CBS president. Other companies, from AOL to Sony to Twitter, are likely to follow... The companies are, in effect, creating new networks for television through broadband pipes and also giving rise to new rivalries — among one another, as between Amazon and Netflix, and with the big but vulnerable broadcast networks as well...Unlike the early stabs at Internet television, these shows look and feel like traditional TV. That is partly because more viewers are watching Internet content on big-screen TV sets, but it is mostly because the companies involved are throwing money at the screens: each of the Amazon comedy pilots cost the company upward of $1 million, according to people involved in their production, which is less than the $2 million invested in a broadcast comedy pilot, but more than is typically invested in cable pilots...Not only are the budgets comparable, so are the perks for actors and creators — like trailers and car-service pickups. The writers are guild members. The actors have what the people involved say are standard television contracts, with options for several seasons if shows succeed." NYTimes.com, March 4, 2013.

[22] [On September 25, 2012, Yahoo premiered] CSI Creator Anthony Zuiker's new digital film, Cybergeddon. Starring Olivier Martinez and Missy Peregrym, the film follows two special agents and an incarcerated hacker as they try to save the world from a series of cyber-attacks launched by a group of e-terrorists. The film ... debut[ed] exclusively on Yahoo in over 25 countries and 10 languages. Adapted to the digital platform, Cybergeddon [was] broken down into nine chapters, three of which [were] released every day over ... three days. The launch includ[ed] a custom site that features a series of short films that offer[ed] a deeper glimpse into the characters, along with other complementary content like on-set photos, behind-the-scenes clips, and interviews with the cast and crew." CynopsisDigital.com, September 25, 2012.

[23] Variety.com, June 12, 2013.

[24] As well as a group of television stations with coverage that extends to more than half the U.S. market and infamous Chicago Cubs. While some point to the extreme levels of acquisition debt that plagued the Tribune and could not be applied to other papers, serious reductions in the subscriber base during the financial crisis, the erosion of ad revenues and the hemorrhaging of the classified sections from Internet competition clearly was pushing other print media players into fire sales and considering Chapter 11 reorganization filings under U.S. bankruptcy laws.

[25] Washington Post, May 11, 2009. The June 2, 2009 TechCrunch.com reported that 2009 newspaper business started out with a 28% first quarter decline in advertising and a 42% decline in classified advertising (compared to the first quarter of 2008). This trend of falling advertising revenues antedated the big meltdown, beginning in 2006.

[26] The Pew Project for Excellence in Journalism, The State of the News Media (2011 Annual Report) stated: "Among the major sectors, only newspapers suffered continued revenue declines [in 2010]—an unmistakable sign that the structural economic problems facing newspapers are more severe than those of other media. When the final tallies are in, we estimate 1,000 to 1,500 more newsroom jobs will have been lost—meaning newspaper newsrooms are 30% smaller than in 2000... Beneath all this, however, a more fundamental challenge to journalism became clearer in [2010]. The biggest issue ahead may not be lack of audience or even lack of new revenue experiments. It may be that in the digital realm the news industry is no longer in control of its own future... News organizations—old and new—still produce most of the content audiences consume. But each technological advance has added a new layer of complexity—and a new set of players—in connecting that content to consumers and advertisers."

[27] "[T]he abundance of free content online has shrunk newspapers' print audience, in some cases cutting it in half during the past decade... But the sharp decline in print advertising has been far more damaging. Advertisers can better target their messages online, for a fraction of the cost. That's why revenue from print advertising, traditionally a newspaper's financial backbone, has declined by more than 50 percent [between 2006 and 2011]. Attempts to increase online advertising revenue so far have done little to inspire confidence that newspapers can evolve into big moneymakers on digital devices." Washington Post, March 23, 2011.

[28] NYTimes.com, June 9, 2011

[29] New York Times, March 11, 2009: "'[By] 2010, all the two-newspaper markets will become one-newspaper markets, and you will start to see one-newspaper markets become no-newspaper markets,' said Mike Simonton, a senior director at Fitch Ratings, who analyzes the industry." Need more proof? Some states' entire newspaper industry has already been decimated. Economically hard-hit Michigan, reeling from cutbacks in the automotive sector, is a prime example. The Ann Arbor News ceased publication as a daily in July of 2009, after 174 years, switching into an online community, and with a ground up new staff, went to a semi-weekly print edition. In June of 2009, The Flint Journal, The Bay City Times and The Saginaw News cut their print editions from seven to three days a week. In April of 2009, even the larger Michigan dailies were hit; the Detroit Free Press and The Detroit News cut home delivery to three days a week, opting instead for printing small editions on other days and asking their customers to get information online.

[30] News Corp.'s publishing business kept the name News Corp., while its entertainment business is known as 21st Century Fox.

[31] Google and several other industry players are among those proposing this alternative.

[32] The New York Times is experimenting with a model where consumers would have free access to a limited number of articles and views per month (which sustains their advertising rates), but excess usage would require payments for either for a larger subscription or for the specific additional content.

[33] Not if Long Island's NewsDay.com is any example. According to the February 8, 2010 Time Magazine (at page 12), The "[n]umber of new subscribers to Newsday.com since the Long Island paper began charging $5 per week for its website [since October 2009 is 35]."

[34] The first periodical to become strictly Web-based was a local Ann Arbor, Michigan paper, which pared their staff to the bone.

[35] With Google's various Android platforms and Apple's service launching their own subscription portals, the amount of the cost add-on for existing aggregators to participate threatened the latter's revenue model (fixed with each periodical). The good news was that when Google and Apple began their subscription services in early 2011, they immediately engaged in a price-cutting battle to solidify the consumer value of their particular tablet-enabled platforms.

[36] Often an emailed alert or simple update of an ongoing blog. RSS stands for Rich Site Summary or Really Simple Syndication.

[37] Paper and periodicals are no longer necessarily linked, and the trend lines with some of America's staple publications is very clear: "[In August of 2011,] Time Inc. announced that the remaining 17 of its 21 U.S. magazines will be available in iPad, Android, HP and Next Issue Media tablet editions by year-end. The publisher also reached a deal with Barnes & Noble to sell digital subscriptions and single copy issues for the Nook Color starting later this month. As with *Time*, *SI [Sports Illustrated]*, *People* and *Fortune*, which each already have tablet versions, print subscribers will be offered the digital editions at no extra charge (the only way to buy an iPad subscription at present). Time says it has sold more than 600k single digital copies of the above books." Cynopsis Digital, August 4, 2011. However, today, many critics do not see Nook with a sustainable going-forward market share or business plan.

[38] PCmag.com, December 1, 2009. Emphasis in the original.

[39] Ibid.

[40] In March of 2011, the New York Times moved into an Apple-iTunes-powered subscription model for people who read more than 20 articles per month electronically, offering differing levels of consumer platform access ranging from $15 to $35 per month.

[41] Bloomberg.com, December 20, 2012.

[42] Newspaper owners have fought "for free" online aggregators by denying access to their content, but several others have argued for a shared monetization model. Consumers seem to persist in the belief that online equals free. Will consumers change that habit if presented with a better choice? " The (TCP) Content Project may change that. Developed by WPP, the world's largest advertising firm, TCP is a scalable platform that will help content-providers share revenue from a pool of consumer payments. Rather than doling out $10/month to, say, the *Wall Street Journal*, users will be able to pay a single fee to TCP to gain access to a network of sites. Revenue will be shared among this network depending on usage." FastCompany.com, September 14, 2010. Also: "[Yahoo's] Livestand, deliver[s] continually refreshed content based on users' interests. The platform... [is trying] to entice publishers to distribute content supported by sophisticated advertising that relies on data targeting, actionable ads and location-based marketing." Cynopsis Digital, February 11, 2011.

[43] Deadline.com, September 9, 2010. In March of 2011, the New York Times moved into an Apple-iTunes-powered subscription model for people who read more than 20 articles per month electronically, offering differing levels of consumer platform access ranging from $15 to $35 per month.

[44] Jeff Jarvis, author of "What Would Google Do?," teaches journalism at the City University of New York and writes about news and media, writing for the Opinion Section of the March 20, 2009 Los Angeles Times.

[45] Alan D. Mutter is a former newspaper editor turned businessman turned independent media analyst, writing for the same Los Angeles Times piece.

[46] Newspaper and magazine subscriptions have been available on eBooks such as Amazon's very portable Kindle for some time. The May 4, 2009 New York Times describes technologies, like the one being released in 2010 by a German company, Plastic Logic, as a potential re-invigorator of this medium: "[N]ew gadgets, with screens roughly the size of a standard sheet of paper, could present much of the editorial and advertising content of traditional periodicals in generally the same format as they appear in print. And they might be a way to get readers to pay for those periodicals — something they have been reluctant to do on the Web."

[47] Howard Kurtz, writing for the May 11, 2009 Washington Post: "A survey by the University of Southern California's Annenberg Center found that Net users are spending 53 minutes per week reading online newspapers, up from 41 minutes in 2007. The problem, as you've undoubtedly heard, is that the print advertising that has supported sizable newsrooms is plunging, while online ads bring in just a fraction of the revenue. Combine that with an Internet culture built on free content, and newspapers suddenly find themselves on a starvation diet."

[48] 2011 seems to have been the big turning point in the consumption of eBooks. "Sales of e-readers have been rising quickly in the United States. A recent survey from the Pew Internet and American Life Project found that one-fifth of all American adults have read an electronic version of a book [in twelve months spanning 2011/12]...E-reader ownership jumped from 17 percent to 21 percent between December [2011] and February [2012]..." WashingtonPost.com, April 11, 2012.

[49] Although the seemingly uniform pricing policies have drawn the ire of the U.S. government: "The Justice Department announced [on April 11, 2012] that it was suing Apple and five major publishers, charging that the companies had colluded to keep the price of e-books artificially high to kill the competition... The antitrust suit names Apple, HarperCollins, Simon and Schuster, Hachette Book Group, Penguin Group and MacMillan. The Justice Department alleges that the chief executives of these firms worked together to control the price of e-books, overcharging consumers an average of $2 or $3 per book. Sharis Pozen, the agency's acting antitrust chief, said that the alleged price-fixing cost consumers millions of dollars... The Justice Department's inquiry focused on how Apple transformed the way publishers charge for e-books. The tech giant allowed the publishers to set the prices of books on Apple's online store. In exchange, Apple got 30 percent of the proceeds... The publishers say that the deals gave them the opportunity to break e-book giant Amazon's hold on the market. The Apple pricing model gave publishers leverage over Amazon, which tried to set book sales at $9.99 when it debuted its Kindle e-reader in 2007." Ibid. The European Commission was exploring similar charges. On the other hand, this challenge might just put eTailer Amazon in the catbird seat, creating even greater monopolistic issues: "The government's decision to pursue major publishers on antitrust charges has put the Internet retailer Amazon in a powerful position: the nation's largest bookseller may now get to decide how much an e-book will cost, and the book world is quaking over the potential consequences." Ibid.

[50] "'We've reached a tipping point with the new price of Kindle,' [Amazon CEO Jeff] Bezos said in the statement. 'Amazon.com customers now purchase more Kindle books than hardcover books -- astonishing when you consider that we've been selling hardcover books for 15 years, and Kindle books for 33 months.'... In [the spring of 2010], Amazon has sold 143 Kindle books for every 100 hardcover books, the company said. In July [2010], sales of e-books accelerated to 180 sold for every 100 hardcover versions. Kindle book sales this year have also exceeded broader e-book sales growth, pegged by the Association of American Publishers at 207 percent through May, Amazon said." Washington Post, July 20, 2010.

[51] According to a Pew Research Center's Internet & American Life Project report (dated June 27, 2011), the number of American adults owning eReaders doubled from 6% of the total market in November of 2010 to 12% in May of 2011, far out-stripping any growth in tablet computing (tablets reached 8% of the U.S. adult market as of May 2011)

[52] In the spring of 2011, Amazon reported selling more eBooks than hard covers. This trend permeated the U.S. book market. "According to a report made by Publishers Weekly, for the first quarter of 2011, e-book sales were up 159.8%; netting sales of $233.1 million. Although adult hard-cover and mass market paperback hard-copies had continued to sell, posting gains in March, all the print segments had declined for the first quarter with the nine mass market houses that report sales. Their findings revealed a 23.4% sales decline, and that children's paper-back publishers had also declined by 24.1%.E-book sales easily out-distanced mass market paperback sales in the first quarter of 2011 with mass market sales of hard-copy books falling to $123.3 million compared to e-books' $233.1 million in sales... According to .net sales report by the March Association of American Publishers (AAP) which collected data and statistics from 1,189 publishers, the adult e-Book sales were $282.3 million in comparison to adult hard-cover book sales which counted $229.6 million during the first quarter of 2012. During the same period in 2011, eBooks revenues were $220.4 million. These reports indicate a disconcerting diminishing demand for hard-copy books." HartmannSoftware.com, August 10, 2012

[53] The fly in even this ointment may be the revenue split between Kindle and the newspaper publishers, which as of this writing heavily favored Kindle (making the numbers of questionable value to the print media); one may expect this model to change to a more balanced split as negotiations become more intense.

[54] eReaders face anti-discrimination statutes and policies governing schools, colleges and universities in many jurisdictions where the text is inaccessible to those who are legally blind (or have other visual impairments), but this should be a relatively easy hurdle to overcome. The November 11, 2009 Washington Post: "According to the National Federation for the Blind, there are about 1.3 million legally blind people in the U.S. Many more people have other disabilities such as dyslexia that make it difficult to read.... The Kindle could be promising for the visually impaired because of its read-aloud feature, which utters text in a robotic-sounding voice. For blind students in particular, the Kindle could be an improvement over existing studying techniques - such as using audio books or scanning books page by page into a computer so character-recognition software can translate it for a text-to-speech program. The University of Wisconsin-Madison and Syracuse University are two institutions who have made clear that electronic platforms must address these issues.

[55] Amazon is reporting a staggering rise in online download book sales to its Kindle, rivaling or on occasion surpassing hard copy sales. While Amazon steadfastly maintained a $9.99 retail cap on most books up through the spring of 2010, a stance fought by publishers wanting a higher and more flexible pricing structure, when the iPad format offered publishers the desired flexibility in March of 2010, Amazon relented on its price cap.

[56] The May 11, 2009 New York Times: "[S]ome publishers say the [piracy] problem has ballooned ... as an expanding appetite for e-books has spawned a bumper crop of pirated editions on Web sites like Scribd and Wattpad, and on file-sharing services like RapidShare and MediaFire." The October 3rd New York Times expands on this topic: "Free file-sharing of e-books will most likely come to be associated with RapidShare, a file-hosting company based in Switzerland. It says its customers have uploaded onto its servers more than 10 petabytes of files — that's more than 10 million gigabytes — and can handle up to three million users simultaneously. Anyone can upload, and anyone can download; for light users, the service is free. RapidShare does not list the files — a user must know the impossible-to-guess U.R.L. in order to download one... But anyone who wants to make a file widely available simply publishes the U.R.L. and a description somewhere online, like a blog or a discussion forum, and Google and other search engines notice. No passwords protect the files." While RapidShare reacts quickly to take-down notices, unfortunately, the damage is often undetected and without the specific U.R.L., the notice to RapidShare has no effect.

[57] While growth in eBooks and eReaders is, according to the November 5, 2009 Washington Post, somewhere between a staggering annualized 150-200%, eBooks still account for less than 2% of book sales in the U.S. Clearly, we are in the earliest phases of the adoption cycle, and it seems that the macro-socioeconomic changes suggested by this technology shift are very likely to track, at least in part, the issue-laden music business...sometime in the future.

[58] Google's use of excerpts and fingernail photos of books within its browser has drawn the ire of the publishing world. While Google settled a class action with major publishers to define, limit but ultimately permit such activities, the settlement was rejected by the court in March of 2011, forcing the parties back to the bargaining table.

[59] The November 22, 2009 Washington Post: "[In November 2009], 1,365 library branches in the nation participated in [the second annual 'National Gaming Day,' sponsored by the American Library Association], giving students an opportunity to play video games while also, hopefully, encouraging them to check out a few books. The organization said it has heard anecdotally that libraries in Canada and Japan participated as well... According to a recent study conducted by a university in Wisconsin, [ALA President Camila] Alire said, video-game fans spend four times as much time reading reviews, blogs and strategy guides as they spend with a game controller in their hands. In other words, if you're going to beat a video game, literacy helps."

[60] Most public libraries are reacting surprisingly well to the tsunami of change in communications technology: "The latest national data from the Institute of Museum and Library Services show that library visits and circulation climbed nearly 20 percent from 1999 to 2008... Since libraries started rebranding themselves for the iPod generation, thousands of music geeks have downloaded free songs from library websites. And with many more bookworms waiting months to check out wireless reading devices [like Kindles], libraries are shrugging off the notion that the Internet shelved them alongside dusty books... Now, the digital sphere is expanding: 82 percent of the nation's more than 16,000 public libraries have Wi-Fi - up from 37 percent four years ago, according to the American Library Association... Since the recession hit, more people are turning to libraries to surf the Web and try out digital gadgets...Public library systems have provided free Internet access [including functioning computers] and lent movies and music for years. They have a good track record of syncing up with past technological advances, from vinyl to VHS." Washington Post, October 4, 2010. Of course, as libraries embrace increasing technology, the question of whether or not any of such uses violate copyrights becomes infinitely more important.

[61] In the spring of 2011, eTailer Amazon announced it was selling more electronic than hard copy books on its site.

[62] NYTimes.com, October 15, 2009

[63] NYTimes.com, November 22, 2011.

[64] For example, Borders was forced to reorganize under U.S. bankruptcy laws, filing for Chapter 11 protection in February of 2011. The filing left a number of publishers, who had provided books to the retailer, with a serious revenue shortfall.

[65] Created by San Mateo, California software company, CourseSmart, which has offered the same capacity for personal computers since 2007.

[66] Since textbooks often have color photographs and charts, the eReaders that basically provide only large caches of black and white text would seem to create a barrier to become mainstream vessels for many students. A slightly pricier "hybrid" two screen eReader (with one side being a traditional black and white provider of electronic text and the other an LCD where colored pictures and charts can be displayed) – a device called the eDGe ($490 initial price) released by enTourage Systems – seems to be one solution. The December 6, 2009 New York Times: "The dual screens of the eDGe open like a book with facing pages. The e-reader screen is 9.7 inches diagonally; the color touch screen on the liquid-crystal display is 10.1 inches. The two screens interact in many ways. For instance, if the textbook on the black-and-white e-reader displays an illustration from a file that is in color, 'the machine can move the illustration over to the LCD and run it there in color'… The e-reader screen is used with a stylus that can underline or highlight text, take notes in the margin, pull up a blank piece of e-paper for solving math problems, or touch a link for a video of a chemical interaction that is then displayed on the LCD screen… [another, less sophisticated hybrid is] Barnes & Noble's new Nook e-book reader ($259) [that] has a small LCD touch screen beneath the reading display to be used primarily for navigation." The more advanced Nook Color ($249) debuted in the first quarter of 2011 as full tablet-like product, competitive with other tablet fare across the board, despite its primary function as an e-reader. Clearly Kindle faces stiff competition. The attractiveness of the Nook was not lost on entertainment giant Liberty Media, which offered a 20% premium over the market stock price to acquire all of Barnes & Noble in May of 2011. Generally, analysts believed the play was Liberty's way of entering the consumer tablet world. The March 15, 2010 FastCompany.com showed 120,000 *pre-orders* had been made for iPads on the first day of availability. The first day of sales (April 3, 2010) produced 300,000 sales (including the pre-orders), and while lines were long, inventory was sufficient. Companies were stumbling all over each other to provide new apps – 1 million were downloaded on that first day alone. The new platform appealed to users wanting movies (NetFlix was one app), books (Apple reported that 250,000 eBooks were downloaded the first day) and iPad-specific video games.

[67] The February 23, 2010 FastCompany.com notes the heavily discounted electronic textbook offering of academic giant Macmillan Publishers: "Macmillan's newly announced DynamicBooks textbooks are a huge change for the stodgy, ultra-conservative world of academic writing. The digital textbooks give professors the power to reorder chapters, insert extra reading, delete irrelevant passages, rewrite individual sentences, and scribble in the margins. Oh, and they'll cost half the price of physical textbooks…The inherent question here is whether professors should actually have the right to alter textbooks as they see fit – but he fact of the matter is, they'll do that anyway. Today's college classes often require a textbook, of which only half the content is relevant and which costs over a hundred dollars, as well as a coursepack or smattering of disorganized articles to supplement it. These DynamicBooks would allow profs to simply streamline their existing syllabus into a single digital file – essentially, allowing them to do what they already do, and better."

[68] WashingtonPost.com, July 20, 2011.

[69] NYTimes.com, August, 8, 2009.

[70] "The television is the most popular screen for watching paid and free streaming video content. According to data from The NPD Group's Digital Video Outlook report, in the past year the number of consumers reporting that the TV is their primary screen for watching web videos has jumped from 33% to 45%. Conversely, those reporting that the PC (laptops and desktops) is their primary screen have dropped from 48% to 31%. To NPD, some of this has to do with the growth in connected TV adoption in the US… [NPD] has also conducted research over the past year, finding that 43% of connected TV users accessed online entertainment (video, music, and cloud services) directly from their TVs… Among the other data from the report, 40% of consumers use their connected TVs to stream video from Netflix, making it the top web-to-TV video app. 12% access Hulu Plus and 4% use Vudu." CynopsisDigital.com, September 27, 2012. Nielsen tells us that "16 percent of [U.S.] households have Internet-enabled televisions…" CynopsisDigital.com, December 16, 2013.

[71] "Video viewing on non-PC/Mac devices such as smartphones, tablets, game consoles, and other portable connected devices tripled between Q3 2011 and Q3 2012, reaching 1.3 billion total video views. This is according to FreeWheel's Q3 2012 Video Monetization Report, for which the company analyzed over 14 billion video views and 10.7 billion video ad views (both of which were new records) from its roster of media clients. Apple' iPad maintained its dominance as it accounted for over 60% of all non-PC/Mac video viewing." CynopsisDigital.com, November 14, 2012.

[72] Hollywood Reporter, February 8, 2013, page 36.

[73] Cynopsis.com, July 30, 2013

[74] LATimes.com, June 14, 2011.

[75] Time Warner Cable CEO, Glenn Britt said it very well: "There clearly is a growing underclass of people who can't afford the services they want. It would behoove all of us to work together to meet the needs of that population.. Most of the people want everything but not everyone can afford it. The economics of all of us [programmers and operators] make that difficult, and it would serve us well to worry about that group of people." Ibid.

[76] CynopsisDigital.com, August 16, 2013.

[77] CynopsisDigital.com, January 14, 2013

[78] Los Angeles Times, July 19, 2013, at page B-1.

[79] Ibid. Analyst Laura Martin also predicts debundling would eliminate 124 channels with a la carte costs kicking consumer bills up by 75%. Deadline.com, December 4, 2013.

[80] Deadline.com, July 26, 2013.

[81] On June 19, 2013, Apple announced that U.S. "customers were downloading 800,000 television episodes and 350,000 movies a day… In a recent study, the NPD Group, a research firm, said Apple was by and large the leader for home video downloads. For television shows, iTunes accounted for 67 percent of this market in 2012, and Microsoft's Xbox video service was a distant second with 14 percent of the market, NPD said. For movies, iTunes had a 65 percent share of the market, with Amazon and Microsoft far behind at 10 percent each, it said." New York Times, June 19, 2013.

[82] "In the [U.S.] subscriptions-based video streaming market, Netflix is dominant, with a 90 percent share, and Hulu Plus and Amazon are still hardly relevant." Ibid

[83] "To put things in perspective, subscription-based streaming is the most popular method for watching online video. For all the movies watched at home in the first quarter of 2013, 19 percent of consumers watched a movie using a subscription-based service like Netflix, and 5 percent downloaded a movie rental from an on-demand service like iTunes… About 74 percent of consumers watched a movie on a DVD or Blu-ray disc they bought or rented… (The numbers are not mutually exclusive; some people watch movies on Blu-ray, Netflix and iTunes.)." Ibid.

[84] Citing data from research firm GfK, CynopsisDigital.com (July 19, 2013) observed the following trends:

- "21% of Netflix viewers reported watching less programming on cable channels and 58% reported lower viewership of video on-demand services from pay-TV operators
- For Hulu viewers, 72% report lower viewership of video-on-demand services from pay-TV operators.
- More than half of the respondents view streaming video through their TV instead of on other devices.
- Streaming video viewing on tablets took place just 8% of the time, even though tablets can be found in a third of U.S. households."

[85] Deadline.com, February 25, 2013.

[86] "Netflix users now watch as much video per month as they do on the largest cable nets, including Disney Channel, according to one Wall Street analyst — although the comparison is somewhat bogus, given that Netflix is not an ad-supported 'network.'" Variety.com, April 12, 2013

[87] CynopisDigital.com, April 23, 2013.

[88] Variety.com, April 26, 2013.

[89] One example: "Redux's system seems a little like Apple's Genius music recommendation service in iTunes in that it suggests content you'd like to experience--but unlike Genius, or YouTube's recommendations based on your viewing history, Redux blends in experiences your friends, 'interesting curators' and other 'influencers.'.. The goal is to 'help you discover video you'll love,' and it works almost like a traditional TV system with content spooling automatically. Instead of coming from the minds of channel programmers, however, it's based on algorithms--and if you don't like what you're watching, you can use the typical up/down remote controls to surf to something new. Over three million users arrive at Redux's website every month, so it's certainly offering something desirable from your friends, 'interesting curators' and other 'influencers.'" FastCompany.com, June 14, 2011. With Facebook adding a music component to its available applications, this paradigm of linking choices/recommendations to track your "friends" should grow rapidly. New substitutes for surfing are evolving all the time to the extent that some believe channel surfing will soon be a thing of the past: "'[T]he channel-surfing paradigm will die,' says Thiru Arunachalam. 'The only paradigm that will work is discovery: I've just come home from work, I want to be entertained, tell me exactly what you think I'd like.'… That's the promise of Peel, his startup that's helping viewers navigate the fractured world of home entertainment by turning their iPhones and iPads into ultra-intuitive remote controls. Its free app, which has racked up more than half a million downloads since its October debut, offers users a sleek, visual programming guide…updated in real time. Then, with help from a new infrared-enabled plastic device called "the fruit" (sold separately for $99), the app syncs wirelessly with almost any TV set or cable box, and gets smarter over time. Because the … platform remembers you tapped to turn on Mad Men, for example, it'll automatically recommend other stylish period dramas, such as Boardwalk Empire, that are on air whenever you open it." FastCompany.com, June 22, 2011.

[90] As of the fall of 2012, for example, YouTube's foray into a online television programming substitute continues steadily building: "According to some numbers released by the company: The top 25 original channels average over a million views a week; 800 million viewers are watching 4 billion hours every month; the number of subscribers has doubled year-over-year; and channel partners are reaching the 100,000 subscriber milestone five times faster than they did two years ago (this presumably includes partner channels before the initiative officially launched last year). The video company now plans to expand the program globally by launching 60 new channels from media companies in France, Germany, the UK, and yes also the US. These new channels, which add to the approximately 100 that are already available, span categories from local cuisine to sports, animation, comedy, and news." CynopsisDigital.com, October 9, 2012.

[91] By way of example, "[t]he percentage of viewers watching live TV from 8-9 p.m. has plummeted from 83% in 2008 to 64% in 2012… Meanwhile, those watching a recorded program (DVR or DVD) in that hour jumped from 16% to 26% over the same period. Streaming video options like Netflix, which weren't even measured in the 2008 survey, registered 7% in 2012… The trend away from live only gets more pronounced among younger viewers. The segment of audience ages 13 to 32 made only 57% of their 8 p.m. viewing live, while streaming accounted for 12… The 13-32 demo[graphic]'s live viewing in [that] hour dropped 30% from 2008 levels." Daily Variety, October 17, 2012, at page 12.

[92] "According to Nielsen's Advertising & Audiences Report, US television advertising expenditures grew by +4.5% in 2011. The report reveals television continues to dominate ad dollars spent as well as consumers' media time. The total TV advertising expenditure is $72 billion, more than all other ad platforms combined. Other key findings in Nielsen's reports shows TV has increased at a steady rate the last several years and is up by +42% since 2007; the average TV commercial in 2001 was 28.4 seconds; Spanish-language cable and network TV saw double digit growth in ad spend, up 24% and 16% respectively from 2010; AT&T and Verizon were the top TV spenders in 2011 for their brands AT&T Wireless Web Access at $1.1 billion and Verizon Wireless Web Access at $702.2 million;

and automotive was the largest category for advertising spend in 2011 across all media at $10.2 billion spent by various automotive brands." Cynopsis.com, May 9, 2012.

[93] In the United States, "Baby Boomers are one of television's top viewing groups and on average they spend 174 hours a month watching television just behind the 65+ crowd that watches 205 hours of television per month... Today, Baby Boomers consist of 80 million Americans and the 50+ segment totals close to 100 million consumers." Cynopsis.com, October 17, 2012.

[94] "[N]ot only is the original A18-49 demo shifting older, they are taking with them $2.5 trillion in spending power. That is $2.5 trillion." Ibid.

[95]"Overall, [American] women spend 15 hours more than men watching TV each month and spend 35 more minutes per month watching on mobile phones... [W]omen also comprise more of the online video audience and spend more time with iPad apps than men. ...WE tv conducted with Nielsen an online and in-home survey of more than 5,000 women in [2011] that revealed that 75% to 85% of consumer purchases are driven by women and that women are the breadwinners in 45% of dual-income homes. In addition, the network learned that 87% of women are responsible for managing the household budget and 95% of women pay the bills, said Carole Smith, VP of research for WE tv." Cynopsis.com, October 10, 2012.

[96] NYTimes.com, July 22, 2013. Also: "Nielsen's quarterly Global AdView Plus report says TV is still the place to be for advertising investment, with 59% media share and 3.5% global growth, and continued slow decline in print. Where did digital fit in? 'We see less-steep ad spend increases in TV and very slight declines in print, making way for growth in the digital space,' said Randall Beard, global head, Advertiser Solutions for Nielsen. 'Although these changes in traditional media are slight, it's worth noting how the placement of ad dollars is shifting over time.'" CynopsisDigital.com, July 26, 2013.

[97] "Traditional TV programmers should feel uneasy about some of the findings out today from consulting firm Deloitte's seventh annual *State Of The Media Democracy* study. Only 64% of U.S. consumers ranked TV watching as one of their three favorite media activities, down from 69% in 2011 and 71% in 2010, the firm found in a November online survey of 2,129 people." DeadLine.com, March 20, 2013.

[98] Deadline.com, February 25, 2013.

[99] According Deloitte's *State Of The Media Democracy* study noted above: "Just 40% of 14-to-23-year-olds put TV among the Top Three [preferred media activities]. About 51% of TV viewers have connected their sets to the Internet — and another 16% have the equipment to do so. And there's a sharp increase in the number of people who frequently watch shows on platforms where ratings aren't measured, or where ads can be avoided. Some 21% (up from 11% in 2011) watch free online video services while 14% (vs. 9%) watch discs of previous seasons and 13% (vs. 4%) watch on a smartphone or mobile device. The number of people viewing shows from an online peer-to-peer network was up to 8% from 3% in 2011, and includes 16% of Millennials. Viewers also are distracted: Just 19% said that they always or almost always just watch TV when they tune in. But 27% said that they browse and surf the Web, 26% read email, and 23% either send text messages or use a social network. Here, too, the numbers are much higher among viewers under 30. The changing behavior 'impacts both the entertainment and advertising industries, and highlights the continued importance of using multiple platforms and devices to build brands and engage consumers,' says Deloitte Consulting Director Alma Derricks." DeadLine.com, March 20, 2013. The pervasiveness of YouTube videos, for example, which are particularly attractive to younger viewers, reached a billion users a month in March of 2013, in significant part to availability of Smart Phones capable of showing them. BBC radio broadcast, March 21, 2013.

[100] Daily Variety, October 2, 2012, at page 1.

[101] "According to Nielsen, 50.3 million of the [America's] 114.2 million homes with a television have a digital video recorder — nearly half of all homes with a television. Although DVR penetration is starting to slow, people are using the devices more. CBS research indicates that DVR usage has grown 6% so far this [2012] television season compared with the same period last season. DVRs are also getting more sophisticated and can record multiple shows at the same time." LATimes.com, October 29, 2012. Viewership can rise by 30-50% when DVR usage is factored into ratings analyses, but the option of skipping commercials still looms large. "Network executives and Nielsen contend that not everyone using a DVR is skipping commercials. In May 2010, a Nielsen analysis showed that in homes with DVRs, average prime-time commercial viewership among adults 18 to 49 — the demographic most popular with advertisers — jumped 44% from the time ads first aired to three days later." Ibid.

[102] Disney joined as an owner in April of 2009. Providence Equity Partners has been a non-strategic financier in this mix as well.

[103] By mid-2009, MGM began to teeter as a viable operating company as it faced severe capital shortages as well as possible reorganization because of significant debt restructuring issues. By the end of 2009, MGM and its subsidiary UA were placed on the auction block to satisfy the requirements of its debt holders and ceased operations as independent companies. The fall of 2010 saw MGM file Chapter 11 bankruptcy, emerging from that condition in early December of 2010 in a vastly contracted condition, with debt-holders as shareholders and an entirely new management team at the top.

[104104] "Dedicated gaming sales — including living-room consoles and handhelds — are in the midst of a four-year tailspin. You might say that's because of a bad economy, but then you'd have to explain why movie revenue and cable TV subscriptions have largely stayed the same... The problem seems to be isolated to dedicated video games. Video game industry sales in the United States, including game discs, consoles and accessories, were down 24% in September [of 2012] when compared with the same period [in 2011]. Many experts believe these decreases in profits, the rise of casual and social gaming and waning consumer interest are affecting makers of the three big living-room consoles: Microsoft's Xbox 360, Sony's PlayStation 3 and Nintendo's Wii.." CNN.com, November 9, 2012 But note the record-breaking $800 million in first day sales for Grand Theft Auto V in September 2013, a console game.

[105] The experience of the largest casual game company, Zynga, is quite illustrative: "While Zynga once had a 'mobile division,' that mostly handled its 'with friends' games, now, said [CEO Mark] Pincus, every division is a mobile division. No games have been greenlit this quarter without some mobile component." FastCompany.com, November 13, 2012.

[106] Ibid.

[107] "Since the '80s, console makers have dreamed of using their 'dedicated gaming machines' as Trojan horses to further control the living room with a single, proprietary device... That time has come. Gaming consoles have transformed into entertainment hubs for people to stream movies or YouTube videos. So much, in fact, that gaming consoles no longer are being used primarily for gaming. In fact, '40% of all Xbox activity now is non-game,' Microsoft boasts. Amazon and Netflix streaming accounts for most of that, as they do for Wii and PS3." Ibid.

[108] As of March 2009, according to the May 11, 2009 Los Angeles Times. As of May 2010, YouTube generated north of 2 billion views per day.

[109] "The data comes from *Silicon Alley Insider*, and partly from, ComScore, and it's pretty clear actually...Hulu was watched at least once by 38 million people in July [2009], whereas Time Warner Cable was viewed by some 34 million souls. Hulu was only beaten by satellite broadcaster DirecTV's 47 million viewers and Comcast's 62 million, when you look at the raw viewer statistics." FastCompany.com, August 31, 2009. In the fall of 2011, Hulu moved overseas with a parallel operation in Japan.

[110] "Hulu, which ranks second only to Google's YouTube in terms of monthly video streams in the U.S., said it turned an operating profit in its [first] two most quarters in [2010]. The ... service... generated more than $100 million in revenue from advertising." Los Angeles Times, April 22, 2010. In 2010, revenues approached double the 2009 numbers. The November 10, 2010 Los Angeles Times reported an internal Hulu projection of $240 million in revenues for 2010, more than doubling the 2009 revenues of $108 million.

[111] Variety.com, April 30, 2013.

[112] A proliferation of similar platforms is clearly on the horizon, with many delivery systems already creeping online. For example, AT&T has launched an Internet portal featuring television content that the September 10, 2009 HollywoodReporter.com com referred to as *Hulu 2*: "The site, at www.entertainment.att.net, features ad-supported movies and TV shows from ABC, CBS, NBC, Bravo, Oxygen, Syfy, the CW, USA Network and others... 'The site will grow and evolve to make more content available to consumers in new and better ways,' said Dan York, executive VP content programming at AT&T... York said the creation of AT&T Entertainment advances the telco's strategy of making premier content available to consumers across three screens: PC, mobile phone and TVs."

[113] LATimes.com, May 11, 2009. Having left the U.S. television episode rental market in 2011 (consumers found the price difference between buying and renting an episode marginally different and generally opted to buy), according to the November 3, 2009 FastCompany.com, Apple was rumored to be exploring the ability to sell subscriptions to network programming through iTunes, making television content available instantly online or on mobile devices and reaching over 65 million users. But like the challenge mounted against Hulu, the advertisers and cable companies are not lying down: "[T]here's going to be one big roadblock in Apple's way: The cable companies. They're fiercely defending their current role as the channel for delivering TV to your home, because there're billions of dollars of revenue involved." Fast Company.

[114] "While a one-hour [broadcast] network show typically has sixteen minutes of commercials, shows streamed online run only two to three minutes of ads. If online streaming cannibalizes on-air broadcasts, the TV business model could suffer a collapse like the newspaper industry." Emmy Magazine, Issue No. 3 (June 2009, at page 125). However, with fewer ads (less clutter) and more targeted demographics, these online content providers are sometimes able to charge premium advertising placement rates (even 50-100% higher than comparable television rates based on a cost-per-thousand-viewers calculation). Hulu's management has introduced an under $10/month subscription component, either as an alternative or supplement to the ad-supported model (clearly with fewer ads, also featuring movies), that will also work on several video game console platforms. It was far from clear that consumers would accept this modification when (i) Hulu cannot provide an overall "all you can eat" content base and (ii) most of what Hulu provides can be found, legally and/or illegally, elsewhere for free. "Under [a] proposal [announced in late April 2010], Hulu would continue to provide for free the five most recent episodes of [certain current hit] shows[, but] viewers who want to see additional episodes would pay $9.95 a month to access a more comprehensive selection, called Hulu Plus..." Los Angeles Times, April 22, 1010. By the fall of 2010, however, Hulu's sign-up subscriber rate was so low – signaling the obvious consumer reluctance to pay for Web-sourced content and competition from companies like Netflix (which was also offering an online streaming service at $7.99/month) – that Hulu slashed the subscription rate by 20% (to $7.99) with media industry speculation that this rate would eventually be cut substantially more to stimulate consumer interest. By the summer of 2011, Hulu still had only about one million paid subscribers, a number that, according to LATimes.com (January 12, 2012), reached 1.5 million by the end of 2011.

[115] The numbers in the "old world" still dwarf any semblance of revenue generation from Web-based distribution. Just looking at the U.S. cable industry, the May 20, 2009 Hollywood Reporter, in an interview with Cablevision's Rainbow Media CEO, Josh Sapan, shows that there is approximately $50 billion being paid annually to the channels (half from advertising, and half from the cable distributors as affiliate fees), which obviously funds programming acquisition and creation in a huge way. In July of 2011, Netflix angered consumers with a 60% increase in its all-you-can-eat model by charging $7.99 for *each* of its DVD and streaming service. The 2011 significant price increase in the cost of the combined streaming and hard copy delivery services cost the company both subscribers and stock value. The company did not reduce prices but moved to separate its hard copy service under a new name (Qwikster). Going forward, they said, there would be two different accounts, billed separately, and Netflix would be the streaming component. By early October, Qwikster was dead, the separation DVD vs. streaming was over, as the company apologized and returned to their older model. But with almost one million angry subscribers gone, Netflix's stock value plunged in the fall of 2011.

[116] One suggested solution, announced on June 24, 2009 and rolled out on a test basis in July by cable-providers Time Warner and Comcast, is to offer original, first-run programming (in this case from the TBS and TNT networks) on broadband to subscribers who have already paid for the program on pay cable. This "free" additional service would use an authentication technology to verify that those seeking broadband versions of the programs were bona fide cable subscribers. Former Disney CEO, Michael Eisner's 2006 Web launch of his Vuguru set about to produce and release online a series of original productions like "Prom Queen," a series of 80 young demographic-targets 90 second shorts, expanding to longer productions shortly thereafter. Will Ferrell and Adam McKay launched their Funny or Die Website in 2007 with a short, "The Landlord," with cable programmer HBO buying a piece of the company for $10 million in June of 2010, adding a "Funny or Die Presents" program to their cable television schedule.

[117] Turner Broadcasting conducted a field study (which paralleled a similar study by the CW television network that reached similar findings), reported in the November 22, 2010 New York Times, concerning the willingness of American consumers to tolerate a commercial load, comparable or greater than that of normal television viewing, in watching programming through Web-based streaming sites. "[T]he answer is yes. Research conducted by Turner suggested that programmers could surround the online streams of shows with even more ads than TV broadcasts have… To conduct the test of online viewers' behavior, Turner randomly assigned three sets of anonymous visitors to tnt.tv and tbs.com to a specially built video player. There, the first set was shown about a minute of ads an episode; the second was shown 8 to 10 minutes of ads; and the third was shown 16 to 20 minutes… Viewers of 30-minute TBS sitcoms like 'Meet the Browns' watched, on average, 40 percent of the episode, including the ads, if there was one minute of ads and 37 percent of the episode if there were 16 minutes of ads. Viewers of hour long TNT shows like 'Memphis Beat' watched 59 percent of the episode if there were one minute 15 seconds of ads, and 49 percent of the episode if there was 20 minutes of ads… [V]iewers watched, on average, for the same number of minutes no matter how many ads were embedded within. Indeed, the Turner research highlighted one of the oddities of online TV viewing: viewers often do not watch an entire episode, just as they channel-surf while on the couch… Turner also found that the commercial retention rate for online video was higher than for traditional television."

[118] Viacom, Comedy Central's parent, relented in February of 2011, and the programming was restored to Hulu along with several additional popular series.

[119] FastCompany.com (March 3, 2010) reported: "This is a serious problem for Hulu. Two of its most popular shows removed because it couldn't show enough profit? That doesn't spell much confidence for the third-party streaming site, which has sat in the red since its unveiling. Hulu's response, in the form of a blog post, is more sad yet hopeful than upset, voicing 'confidence' that a future relationship between itself and Viacom isn't out of the question. If Hulu does move to a pay model, as has been rumored, the company might be able to pay Viacom enough to re-secure the shows." The problem is not that Hulu cannot generate profits – it can as reports noted later in 2010 proved – but that it cannibalizes media that produce far greater revenues. Further, with NetFlix in direct competition, a price war, noted in the subscription price reduction above, is clearly on the horizon.

[120] "[Hulu's] owners—industry powerhouses NBC Universal, News Corp. and Walt Disney Co.—are increasingly at odds over Hulu's business model. Worried that free Web versions of their biggest TV shows are eating into their traditional business, the owners disagree among themselves, and with Hulu management, on how much of their content should be free… Fox Broadcasting owner News Corp. and ABC owner Disney are contemplating pulling some free content from Hulu, say people familiar with the matter. The media companies are also moving to sell more programs to Hulu competitors that deliver television over the Internet, including Netflix Inc., Microsoft Corp. and Apple Inc… And in what would be a major shift in direction, Hulu management has discussed recasting Hulu as an online cable operator that would use the Web to send live TV channels and video-on-demand content to subscribers, say people familiar with the talks. The new service, which is still under discussion, would mimic the bundles of channels now sold by cable and satellite operators, the people said." WSJ.com, January 27, 2011.

[121] "Hulu's free lunch may be over. Its new purported deal with media giants to extend access to TV shows could delay the site's ability to air episodes for free if other streaming sites are willing to pay for the privilege, per the WSJ. The deal could delay access to network shows for as long as a week if cable providers, who are looking to build out their TV Everywhere services, are willing to pay." Cynopsis: Digital, May 19, 2011.

[122] According to the December 16, 2009 Cynopsis Digital: [Comcast's] TV Everywhere 'Fancast Xfinity TV' service [is] now being promoted on [its] Fancast.com online video portal. Comcast cable and internet customers in good standing (you must subscribe to both) can use the site's authentication service to view full-length episodes of shows they receive through their cable subscriptions. The interface includes access to some 2,000 hours of programming from a total of 30 networks, including uncut movies and [even premium cable] shows. Comcast customers who don't subscribe to the cable modem service will be able access the shows in the near future, according the company. A Fancast Xfinity mobile service and parental controls enabling blocking of forthcoming adult-oriented Cinemax content is also on the way." And when the FCC approved the Comcast/NBC-Universal merger on January 18, 2011, they expressly limited the ability of the newly merged giant to exercise "corporate control" over the Hulu joint venture.

[123] The March 5, 2009 Cynopsis Digital provides this example: "A start-up called Zillion.tv has lined up agreements with Disney, 20th Century Fox Television, NBC Universal, Sony Pictures and Warner Bros. Digital Distribution to offer 1,500 on-demand movies and shows delivered directly to the television set via a broadband-connected box build using Hillcrest Labs technology. (Hillcrest built the user interface and the system's Wii-like motion sensor remote that allows users to access bugs across the entire screen.) Zillion will partner directly with [Internet Service Providers] and content providers to offer a triple threat model, allowing viewers to choose between free addressable ad-supported content, rentals, or download-to-own titles depending upon what options are offered by each content owner tied to each specific program." The Hulu model was economically impressive enough to encourage telecasters in other nations to follow suit. For example, Cynopsis Digital (August 9, 2010) noted: "RTL and ProSieben, Germany's two largest commercial broadcasters, said Friday they have submitted plans for a new Hulu-style ad supported platform of catch-up TV services across Germany and Austria to the European Commission antitrust committee. The platform would be open to all broadcasters, including private competitors and public TV stations…"

[124] Which has since emerged from reorganization under American bankruptcy laws.

[125] Search-based marketing plays off of consumers' use of key words to find goods and services as they browse online. Search engines (like Google or Bing!) sell ads that link to such searches and appear on the consumer's search pages as well as priorities to place the links for some companies ahead of those who have paid less or nothing at all. Finally, the data generated from such searches, where privacy laws permit, can also prove useful to advertisers looking for consumers who have evidenced interest in the companies' own sites as well as "in category" searches for comparable products or services.

[126] "Google is putting up more than $100 million to become the cable provider of the future with 100 online video channels for YouTube… [I]t it looks as though Google is relying on YouTube as an anchor for its television strategy. YouTube plans to encourage users to subscribe to the channels, each of which will contain hours of programming… The partnerships that YouTube announced

[October 28, 2011] with dozens of media companies, production companies and online-video creators will generate about 25 hours of new programming each day for YouTube." LATimes.com, October 28, 2011.

[127] Forbes.com, May 21,2012

[128] "Want to up your chances of getting your video shared? Research from video-tech company Unruly Media says that posting it on a Wednesday can help. Unruly studied 12 commercials from Super Bowl XLVII and how they were shared. Almost half of the shares 48.3% - took place between Wednesday and Friday. However, the study also showed that share totals usually topped out a couple of days after the video was posted, and about 25% took place in the first days after being posted... Online video advertising's effectiveness is on the rise. A recent survey from research company eMarketer says that 75% of U.S. advertising agency executives think online video ads are equally or more effective than traditional TV advertising. One of the biggest draws of online video advertising, the survey concludes, is the ability to target consumers whether by demographics or behavior" CynopsisDigital,com, July 12, 2013.

[129] The August 6, 2010 Cynopsis Digital summarized a Nielsen report on Internet how video consumption patterns are holding globally: "Europe and North America lag behind Asia, Latin America and the Middle East in terms of Online Video usage, according to a new Nielsen global *How People Watch* survey reaching over 27k users. Online video usage was strongest in China, Indonesia, the Philippines, India and Mexico, while consumers in Germany, France and Denmark - who are just beginning to get access to premium content online - were at least 50% less likely to watch it. Other trends included:

- Globally, 57% of respondents report having watched online video on their PC at work
- Consumers in North America and Europe, where content blocking filters have been installed, were 40% and 33% less likely to consume video in the workplace, respectively
- Europe and North America also lag in mobile video adoption, with Asia-Pacific online consumers 45% more likely to use mobile video
- 22% of global online consumers owns or has a definite interest in purchasing an internet-connected TV with Latin Americans and Middle Easterners expressing the most interest
- Only 11% of global consumers already own or expressed interest in buying a tablet PC

[130] Which reflect the frequency that consumers actually respond to the ads by clicking on the advertising link to go to the advertiser's homepage.

[131] FastCompany.com, December 2, 2010.

[132] Ibid.

[133] "The social economy: Unlocking value and productivity through social technologies," July 2012

[134] Ibid.

[135] FastCompany.com, August, 30, 2012.

[136] As of late August, 2012: "The site's 955 million users spend an average of six hours and 35 minutes per month on Facebook's desktop site, posting 3.2 billion likes and comments every day... Facebook posted a 67 percent year-over-year mobile growth rate (543 million monthly active users on mobile)... 58 percent of users return to the site daily." AllFaceBook.com, August 27, 2012. The billion user mark was crossed almost immediately after this posting. With almost 165 thousand users at about the same, Facebook's U.S.-based market penetration level hit 52.65%. SocialBaker.com, September 13, 2012.

[137] According to a July 2012 report from ComScore Inc.

[138] Facebook's Instagram launched this video-sharing capacity to boost the underlying share price: "Hot on the heels of Twitter-owned video app Vine's phenomenal success comes Instagram's latest announcement that video is being introduced to their platform. Instagram is already hugely popular, with more than 130 million users, but Vine is currently more popular than Instagram for media sharing on Twitter... although all that is about to change...

"Now that Instagram has added the ability to record and share video directly from the platform to social media, the feature is already beating Vine in the battle to attract the biggest brands. The fact that Instagram is already heavily used by brands will help the new video feature's quick adoption by companies looking for new ways to market products and connect with their followers. According to Mashable, videos shared by brands on Instagram have twice the level of engagement as Instagram photos and significantly higher engagement than videos on Vine...

"The brands that are already using Instagram have been quick to test out the new video function. The 15-second recording facility will be a relief to companies who have struggled with Vine's 6-second time limit, and it opens up greater possibilities for marketing ideas that need a little more space than Vine currently provides. Of course, having the mighty weight of Facebook's billion users behind the sharing potential of Instagram will help to persuade brands new to Instagram to explore it.

"The filtering capacity which has made its photos so instantly recognizable will be of great interest to brands wishing to use the video feature for creative marketing. Its users have already been delighted with how easy the photo filters are to use, so the potential for producing artistic video clips and then uploading them straight to followers will surely be hugely popular." FastCompany.com, July 2, 2013

[139] "[T]he site ... bills itself as 'the front page of the Internet.' What started out as a single collection of user-submitted links created by two University of Virginia undergrads in three weeks has spawned thousands of sub-communities (or subreddits, in the site's parlance), each with its own topic of obsession--from corgis to college football. Each subreddit is combination of links out to other sites and text fields for original reader content... It's a potent mix, and Reddit now has over 43 million unique viewers a month." FastCompany.com, September12, 2012.

[140] FastCompany.com, March 4, 2013

[141] Ibid.

[142] NYTimes.com, July 24, 2013.

[143] Ibid.

[144] CNET.com, March 2, 2013.

[145] "Facebook: The age group of 45 – to 54-year-old has been growing since the end of 2012 by 45%, 73% of users have an income of about U.S. $ 75,000." Ethority.net, October 14, 2013. This analysis naturally leads to a shift in the relative value proposition in various social media sites: "Facebook does have a slightly older user base than Twitter and Pinterest which may be of relevance to you if your target is between 35 and 54 years of age, however Twitter or Pinterest may be a better fit if your audience is between 18 and 35 years of age." Jobstock.com, December 24, 2012

[146] Here are some sample statistics on social media networks that can help determine appropriate and targeted reach from Hypebot.com, May 26, 2013: "City dwellers are more likely than those in rural areas to be on Twitter... Women are 5X more likely as men to use Pinterest... Blacks and Hispanics are heavier users than whites of Instagram."

[147] These time-spent numbers are already becoming quite apparent. "When it comes to time spent online in 2013 across social networks, it's quite astounding to note that Pinterest users spend over an hour on average which is almost unheard of. When compared with Twitter's 36 minutes and Facebook's 12 minutes, this is unusually high, and presents an unparalleled opportunity for those looking to sell, especially in the home and entertainment industries. Although Pinterest's time on site is very high, it should be noted that both Twitter and Facebook users' time on site is excellent and not to be discounted." Jobstock.com, December 24, 2012.

[148] CNET.com, March 2, 2013.

[149] FastCompany.com, May 24, 2013

[150] Amy Jo Martin *is the founder and CEO of* Digital Royalty, *a social media and education company based in Las Vegas, Nevada, and of* Digital Royalty University. *In 2012 her book* Renegades Write the Rules *made the New York Times Best Seller list.*

[151] FastCompany.com, May 24, 2013

[152] CNET.com, March 2, 2013.

[153] NYTimes.com, August 17, 2013

[154] A study from researchers from Harvard, Carnegie Mellon, Stanford and the University of Pittsburgh, cited in the June 2008 Spirit Magazine (at page 48), found that test subjects who watched a sad movie "clip" were willing to spend four times more on a sporty-looking water bottle than subjects who watched a more emotionally neutral excerpt. The authors theorized that sadness and depression cause people to be more self-centered and devalue what they have, and then overspend in order to compensate for their feeling of loss.

[155] "A study taking place in [the Baylor College of Medicine's Human Neuroimaging Laboratory], the results of which were published in the journal *Neuron* in 2004, reported that subjects' preference for a popular soft drink increased when drunk from cups bearing the drink's logo, and that brain regions involved in decision-making and memory were more stimulated when sips of the drink [measured using the medical school's functional MRI facility scanner] were accompanied by a visual presentation of the drink's brand." Medicine@Yale, Volume 5, Issue 2 (March/April 2009, page one)."

[156] Statistics reported in BMO Capital Markets, *Perspectives on the filmed Entertainment Industry 2012*

[157] Is the revenue stream going to rise, as competition gives Netflix a run for its money, or will the digital competition fractionalize the marketplace and turn off consumers as buyers might have fewer funds to buy product? Amazon's massive economic power is now dedicated to this new space. "Amazon has secured a multiyear licensing agreement with EPIX to add 'thousands of films and original programs to Prime Instant Video for subscribers in the US. Programming covered by the agreement includes movies from EPIX studio partners such as Paramount Pictures, MGM Pictures, and Lionsgate." CynopsisDigital.com, September 5, 2012. In late October 2012, kiosk-DVD rental firm Redbox added Warner Bros. as the first major studio to its new Redbox Instant by Verizon streaming subscription service, adding yet another competitor to the mix. CynopsisDigital.com, October 29, 2012. But despite the competition, Netflix is still riding high... at least for now: "[H]ere's a study from broadband network solutions provider Sandvine that offers some good news if you're Netflix: In its latest internet traffic trends report, Sandvine finds that when it comes to data usage, Netflix accounted for 33% of peak period (9pm to 12am) downstream traffic among fixed networks in North America in September 2012. 'Audio and video streaming account for 65% of all downstream traffic from 9pm to 12am and half of that is Netflix traffic [on North America fixed networks],' said Dave Caputo, CEO of Sandvine. Netflix's competitors, on the other hand, didn't even come close, according to the study. Amazon's share of peak internet viewing traffic last month stood at 1.8%, while Hulu and HBO Go accounted for 1.4% and 0.5%, respectively. Overall, Sandvine reports that mean monthly data usage has increased by 120% from 23GB to 51GB in the past year on North American fixed line networks. This is the equivalent of 81 hours of video." CynopsisDigital.com, November 8, 2012.

[158] In the March of 2010, Google and Sony announced a new hardware product – Google TV, which could either be added as a set-top unit or integrated in new televisions – to allow a user to bring whatever is available on the Web (like television programs and movies for example) onto the user's main television screen (a "search" function, but with a home screen, lots of grids, icons, etc.). This technology, which joins other systems that combine television and Web usage like Slingbox, the Boxee Box, TiVo, HTPCs, Roku, etc., is built on Google's Android mobile phone platform, but it can be controlled by virtually any smart phone, tablet or, obviously, a full on computer. Google is opening the platform for outside developers to add new applications to the system, but does not feature a recording device. Will Google extend its power outside of the cell phone/computer universe and into your home television set? Google TV, NetFlix, Apple TV and their ilk are not the only players in the consumer content aggregation business. More elegant solutions are deploying all the time. FastCompany.com (December 22, 2010) describes one such newcomer: "[T]op executives from Disney and Electronic Arts left to start Qvivo, a media center app that manages your videos and mynd all in one place, streams files over the cloud on any number devices (TVs, smartphones, tablets), and integrates with all your social media. After months of development, Qvivo has blossomed into a gorgeous app with a sleek interface, which will launch in beta after the holidays. It serves as a stark reminder that Google TV is far from the only major player in this space.. When installing the app on your computer, Qvivo will scan all your files for media content--photos, MP3s, TV shows, movies--and build a library of your collection. The files are displayed in Cover Flow-like fashion, and can be streamed from anywhere. Though still in development, Qvivo will enable users to stream their media on HDTVs, iPads, and other mobile devices from Androids to iPhones."

[159] FastCompany.com, June 28, 2011. Aside from Sony's crackle.com, sites like Vimeo.com, blip.tv, DailyMotion.com and YouTube.com provide venues for series programming.

[160] According to a report prepared by Internet Evolution and cited in the April 15, 2009 ShowBizData.com, which also noted that YouTube's annual revenue was estimated to be $90 million by Bear Stearns and $240 million by Credit Suisse. The numbers appear to have doubled into 2011.

[161] CynposisDigital, April 29, 2013 citing an April 2013 comScore survey.

[162] Second only to parent Google's search capacity, although those who believe that since Twitter electronically responds to inquiries, it has to take its place on the list of search engines – in second place behind Google and ahead of YouTube! "On the online video front, comScore finds that 180 million US internet users watched 33 billion pieces of online video content in June 2012. When compared to data from May of [2012], the number of US internet users watching videos online remained the same at 180 million; however, there was a drop in the number of videos watched – in May, comScore reported that Americans watched 36.6 billion pieces of video content on the web. There were also some changes among the top five online video content properties (in terms of unique viewers): Google and Yahoo held their top spots with 154.5 million and 51.5 million unique viewers, respectively. Those two were followed by Facebook (49 million, up from #5), VEVO (46.2 million, down from #3), and Viacom Digital (38.9 million, new). Microsoft, which was at #4 last month dropped to #6 in June 2012, allowing for Viacom Digital to shoot up into the top five." CynopsisDigital, July 19, 2012

[163] "Though Google does not report YouTube's earnings, it has hinted that it is hovering near profitability. Analysts say YouTube will bring in around $450 million in revenue this year and earn a profit. Revenue at YouTube has more than doubled each year for the last three years, according to the company." New York Times, September 2, 2010.

[164] Under the Digital Millennium Copyright Act, American law allows copyright holders to demand (via a "take down notice") that open content platforms and Internet service providers remove unauthorized consumer uploads of copyrighted material, and requires compliance with such demands in order that such platforms and providers themselves avoid liability for copyright infringement.

[165] Los Angeles Times, May 17, 2010.

[166] AdWeek.com, June 7, 2011. According to the November 16, 2011 Hollywood Reporter (at page 3), GBTV had 230,000 subscribers at launch.

[167] Built around a Newtek Hardware Video Mixer, which allows images from various computers, the Web, Skype, etc. to be used for on-air source material.

[168] The ability to allow replays seems to be an interactive enhancement that makes the Internet as natural for sport fans. The following baseball service is jointly offered at a discount with the NHL service described above. The February 9, 2009 New York Times: "Fans with fast connections to the Internet can now see the sweat pour from players' faces. MLB.com [Major League Baseball] is introducing an enhanced MLB.TV video player with high-definition video. Technology by Swarmcast, a content delivery network with headquarters in Minneapolis and Tokyo, will help the league determine the speed of a fan's Internet connection and adjust the quality of the video accordingly." This addiction to sports will also migrate baseball to other platforms: "Bob Bowman, chief executive of MLB.com, said the company was also adding to its offerings for mobile phones, including bringing radio broadcasts to its applications for Apple's iPhone and Research in Motion's Blackberry. That will let iPhone and BlackBerry users who buy the At Bat application, which MLB.com says will cost less than $10, to listen to any game, anywhere they get cellphone coverage." The same Times article. The scared "blackout" of home games is also giving way to economic reality: "Yes Network, Cablevision and MLB Advanced Media officially announced their agreement to allow YES Network cable subscribers to watch Yankees Games online via Cablevision's Optimum Online internet service. It is the first time a MLB team has streamed games within its home market. Online telecasts ... cost $49.95 for the rest of the season and $19.95 for any 30-day period." June 24, 2009, Cynopsis.com. Baseball appears to be the sports industry leader in the streaming-for-the-Web space and mobile delivery as well: "Being an early mover in the live video space has made Major League Baseball an expert in all things streaming and the league is now branching out to offer its services to others. ESPN's soon-to-be-renamed web video portal ESPN3.com is changing web video service providers from April, turning to Major League Baseball Advanced Media (MLBAM) to handle support of its more than 3,500 live streaming events. ESPN360.com previously utilized Move Network's platform, which requires users to download Microsoft's Flash player." March 9, 2010 Cynopis.com. By 2011, the digital revenues to major league sports had become monumental: "Digital viewing for sports can increase overall watching and loyalty, said a new eMarketer study. 'Content owners that take a proactive approach in reaching audiences on as many devices and platforms as possible are often rewarded with long-term gains in viewership and loyalty,' eMarketer said, adding that the NFL, MLB, NBA and NHL are generating hundreds of millions in digital revenue. The NFL tops the list at about $500 million in digital revenue from paid content, ads and other revenue streams, with MLB at $450 million, the NBA at $225 million and the NHL at $120 million. Events like the Olympics, World Cup Soccer and college basketball have helped grow audiences and demand for streaming sports." Cynopsis Digital, September 16, 2011.

[169] The Open Mobile Video Coalition (whose members include NBC Universal, Gannett and PBS) commissioned Frank N. Magid Associates (Magid Media Labs) to conduct a survey among Web-users to assess whether enough consumers would actually watch television on their mobile devices. In November of 2009, Magid polled over a thousand Americans, ages 18-59, on this issue. 88% of those surveyed expressed interest, and 46% actually found the prospect of watching mobile television "appealing." Not surprisingly, the strongest showings appeared among 18-29 year-olds and so-called "early adopters." WSJ.com, December 9, 2009. Mobile television is certainly a reality today, and it can only expand as demand for the service expands. According to the National Association of Broadcasters November 13, 2009 SmartBrief.com, one such product introduced to the market at that time: "FLO TV, a mobile-television service that has been sold as an add-on to voice or data service in the past, now is being offered as a stand-alone product at a variety of consumer-electronics stores. The FLO TV Personal Television serves up 10 to 15 channels from cable and broadcast networks for $15 a month." But consumers have been fickle, turning the service on and off based on special programming: "Qualcomm [suspended] the direct-to-consumer portion of its Flo TV mobile television service and says it may do

away with Flo TV subscriptions altogether... [T]he bottom line is that the company is beginning to think there has to be a more profitable way to monetize the bandwidth it acquired for the service... Company executives have been forthcoming in recent months about the challenge of selling subscriptions of linear mobile TV feeds of networks that users only tend to drop in on when breaking news happens. The growth of Netflix on platforms such as the iPhone and iPad hasn't helped either - consumers will only shell out for so many monthly services." Cynopsis Digital, October 6, 2010. By the end of March, 2011, consumers were so distracted by more elegant mobile television offerings that Qualcomm just turned FLO off, leaving the space open to the flood of competitors. In an interview with Charlie Nooney, CEO of MobiTV - which provides a television platform for RIM, BREW, Java, Android, iPhone, WebOS, WinMo – the March 28, 2011 Forbes.com com reported: "[Mobile TV is] definitely a dynamic and growing space to be a part of, especially with Nielsen numbers showing mobile TV viewership up 44 percent [in 2010]. Nearly every major media provider, content holder and cable operator has entered the mobile space in the past year...The biggest drivers of viewership are breaking news and sporting events, both which are driven by immediacy and ease of access."

Fox Mobile Group also has a new wireless video subscription service called Bitbop, which offers on-demand access to cable and broadcast TV shows from Fox's cable networks and NBC Universal for a $9.99 monthly fee. The March 24, 2010 Los Angeles Times reports mobile streaming isn't catching on significantly – yet – with the smart phone users: "One survey of 15,000 American consumers conducted by Yankee Group found that fewer than 10% of mobile phone owners subscribe to a streaming video service. Independent ventures, like Qualcomm's MediaFlo service, haven't overcome the hurdle of the $15-a-month subscription fee, said Carl D. Howe, Yankee Group's director of consumer research.... The bigger challenge for pay services like Bitbop may be increased competition from local TV broadcasters. A new mobile DTV standard clears the way for local stations to inexpensively modify their broadcast equipment and begin beaming live local news and other shows for free to mobile phones." Perhaps as access to television programming begins to mirror the greater array of choice available on cable, public acceptance will accelerate, but as the above data suggests, there will probably be a big shakeout with only a few survivors.

[170] Jennifer Gillan, *Television and New Media: Must-Click TV.* New York: Routledge, 2010, cited in the Journal.Transformativenetworks.org, Vol 9, 2012.

[171] Product placement into television productions, video games and motion pictures has become commonplace – examples include cars in the James Bond franchise, company coverage in *The Apprentice* as would-be executives competed for jobs, big box companies in programs for do-it-yourselfers or a cereal box on a countertop of a popular dramatic series. The more an advertiser becomes a part of the storyline, the notion of "product placement" becomes the more encompassing "product integration." This trend has writers and actors concerned as commerce further intrudes into their "art." Since the product is part of the main storyline, however, skipping past the "ad" with a DVR is no longer an issue. But today's digital product placement goes one giant step farther – literally putting a product into a scene where it was not originally filmed or taped – offering advertisers placement opportunities after a production has been completed or the opportunity to replace competing brands with their product. Companies like British-based MirriAd offer advertisers the ability to "embed" such placements electronically, opening up another potential advertising revenue stream.

[172] The ability to track consumer television viewing habits and commoditize ad sales on television has become extremely detailed: "TiVo has joined forces with Google to provide second-by-second viewership data to advertisers using the Google TV Ads platform. Launched [in 2007] with some 3.6 million Dish Network set-tops, Google TV Ads allows advertisers to bid on available commercial time using auction-style software. Providing second-by-second measurement gives even more granular data to participating clients. The pact could also help open up a vibrant market for pods placed just before the end of commercial breaks, which tend to have higher viewership numbers. Google TV Ads has served some 100 billion television ad impressions on its partner cable channels to date... Google says about 30% of those purchasing inventory are advertisers buying TV ad time for the first time." Cynopsis: Digital, November 25, 2009

[173] "TV viewing in the home [in the U.S.] is at an all-time high, averaging 5.13 hours per viewer per day during the fourth-quarter 2009 and more than eight hours a day for the entire household, according to Nielsen tracking. During the fourth-quarter 2007, TV viewing in the home was 4.86 hours per viewer per day." The Hollywood Reporter, May 3, 2010.

[174] According to the Hollywood Reporter, June 20, 2008, Page 11.

[175] The 2010 Supreme Court decision, *Citizens United vs. Federal Elections Commission*, essentially removed the spending cap on political action committees (a "PAC") that were not directed by the candidates themselves. 2012 saw literally hundreds of millions of dollars flow into both the presidential and congressional races, substantially motivated by this ruling.

[176] Not only do viewer often fast-forward through commercials when they have recorded programs, but many viewers aggregate episodes of a particular drama or comedy series to watch a group of such show at the same time. This latter trend further negatively impacts advertisers who have a time-sensitive product (e.g., a film opening).

[177] "The U.S. online advertising market is expected to reach $31.3 billion [by the end of 2011], according to... market researcher eMarketer. Spending is projected to grow by 20% from 2010 when advertisers invested about $26 million in online marketing... The increase is fueled primarily by significant gains in spending on display advertising, a category that includes banners, online video and sponsorships. U.S. advertisers are expected to spend $12.33 billion on online display ads [in calendar 2011] -- a gain of nearly 25% from a year earlier. Video advertising is the fastest growing online ad format." LATimes.com, June 8, 2011.

[178] As noted in the September 26, 2008 online ShowBIZ Data Daily Wire: " 'The financial implosion occurring on Wall Street will hit Madison Avenue ... with a force that will take down some media companies and prompt many to seek financial relief in digital interactive solutions,' MediaPost.com editor-at-large Diane Mermigas predicted [September 24]. She cited respected RGE Monitor economist Nouriel Roubini who recently warned of an 18-month recession in which stocks and housing will fall 40 percent even as corporate debt climbs, banks fail, and the FDIC goes bust trying to cover insured accounts. 'This will inevitably lead to companies reducing expenses, including their advertising and marketing budgets,' Mermigas predicted. She cited a study by TNS Media Intelligence that spending by advertisers in the second quarter, even before the current financial crisis hit, was down 3.7 percent from last year, the steepest quarterly drop since 2001."

[179] Cynopisis.com, June 10, 2011.

[180] Before every broadcast season, networks typically sell 70-80% of their ad spot inventory to advertisers wanting to assure themselves of sufficient access to that medium. The 20-30% reserved by the networks is used to provide the auction for possible make-good commitments when certain programs do not deliver the necessary CPMs, and balance of unused inventory is usually sold at a premium.

[181] Deadline.com, July 11, 2013.

[182] "Only three of the 38 new programs introduced by ABC, CBS, Fox, NBC and the small CW network [for the fall of 2010 were] unscripted, the industry term for contest and so-called reality shows. That signals a sharp retrenchment from [2009], when the networks introduced eight unscripted shows, expanding the genre to fully one-third of prime-time programming, excluding football." Ibid.

[183] "A relatively tame and mildly upbeat industry luncheon discussion about the television industry's future came to a grinding halt when a senior advertising executive threw cold water on everyone's optimism about where the business is headed… 'There is not more money coming into national advertising' declared Tim Spengler, president of the big media buying firm Initiative [Media Worldwide, Inc.]. 'The business will have to figure out where new money is coming from because advertising is flattening out.'" Los Angeles Times, June 23, 2010.

[184] According to the January 12, 2010 Hollywood Reporter, the cost of an average 30 second spot on the 2010 Super Bowl (on CBS) dropped to between $2.5 and $2.8 million, down from $3 million the year before on NBC.

[185] FastCompany.com, January 5, 2009

[186] April 2010, Issue 2, page 42.

[187] "Ad exchanges are technology platforms that facilitate [and often automate] the bidding, buying and selling of online media advertising inventory from multiple ad networks. The approach is technology-driven as opposed to the historical approach of negotiating price on media inventory." Wikipedia. New York and Chicago based IIN Networks, Inc. has assembled a vast array of telecasters and digital media, allowing advertising placement to be determined by such psychographic variables in lieu of traditional media buying and placement. Additionally, aspects of Internet advertising look very much like the trading floor of a virtual national stock exchange. According to NetLingo.com, an *ad exchange* is "a company that brokers online advertising by bringing Web publishers and advertising buyers together on a website where they can participate in auctions for ad space. Set up in a Nasdaq-like exchange for the buying and selling of digital advertisements, an ad exchange is a marketplace where publishers and advertisers can find and execute advertising transactions (similar to what happens on a stock exchange)… An *ad network* also extends to text link ads where participating sites display text ads in exchange for credits which are then converted (using a predetermined exchange rate) into ads to be displayed on other sites." Google has dominated the small text ad business – where small ads appear on search results – while Yahoo has been a driver in the larger graphic display ad world. Google, not often an Internet underdog, is challenging Yahoo display ad dominance with its enhanced DoubleClick Ad Exchange model that will automatically enable hundreds of thousands of publishers and advertisers who currently use Google's AdWords and AdSense systems to run their ads and ad space through the exchange. The sheer volume of sites has created another type of aggregating exchange to take advantage of many sites with too much available time and space inventory: "Online video ad network BrightRoll is launching its own video ad exchange to automate the process of placing unsold ad inventory across its network of sites. Similar to the OneSource platform introduced by Adap.tv earlier this year, the system will allow advertisers to insert pre-rolls across hundreds of sites, targeted by audience segment. As fast growing as the online video ad medium is, publishers are still having trouble unloading all of their inventory, with nearly half having at least 20% unsold at the end of each month, according BrightRoll research." CynopsisDigital, August 5, 2010

[188] Communications Daily, February 21, 2008, Volume 28; Issue 35. In April of 2008, Warner Television announced one step towards that disintermediation: TheWB.com, "a new Web-based, advertiser supported, programming platform aimed at adults 16–34 demographic (with an emphasis on women), featuring original programming created or acquired specifically for TheWB.com as well mining the re-release The WB Network's most popular series and other successful programming." The WB Network had been earlier blended with Paramount's UPN to form The CW Television Network, not a particularly successful effort. By the middle of 2009, reeling from the economic meltdown, The CW had returned both Saturday and Sunday night programming responsibility to its local affiliated stations, providing network fare only on weekdays.

[189] While the CBS recovered from its low of below $5/share (from approximately $25), the stock has fallen well below the relative value of entertainment shares in general; CBS' credit rating was downgraded in the spring of 2009.

[190] According to the October 23, 2008 The Hollywood Reporter (pages 28-29), CBS won the fall premiere major broadcast network race, but with average prime ratings representing 3.1 of those watch television and a median-age for viewers of 53, even that wasn't great news. ABC had a very slightly lower average rating with a median viewer age of 51, NBC earned a 2.9 rating with the median age of viewers at 46, Fox at 2.7 rating and a median age of 45, and CW – which has eliminated weekend programming entirely (announced in May of 2009) – at a network-killing 1.1 rating even with a median age of 33. Not exactly spectacular viewership, is it? But the trend line for the traditional networks is reflecting the drop-off of younger viewers. According to an August 28, 2009 Daily Variety report, 10 months later, the median age of every one of the above networks got older: CBS – 55, ABC – 51, NBC – 49, Fox – 46 and The CW – 34. What's worse, revenues are falling; according to the June 16, 2009 theDeal.com, GE's media unit, NBC Universal, posted a decline of 45% in the first quarter of 2009, and by 2011, NBC's failed ratings, now under Comcast's reign, had become an industry-wide joke! Also by 2011, the numbers aged further: "CBS's audience is 60 to 40 female to male with an average age of almost 56, ABC's is 64 to 36 with an average age of just under 54, and Fox's is 55 to 45 and 43.5 years of age." NYMag.com, December 7, 2011.

[191] Leno's ratings opened strong in September of 2009 but soon plunged to mirror the ratings of his form late-night program (a sizeable decrease in the ratings of the dramatic programming that preceded it), leading NBC to a lackluster fall season. Critics assailed the negative impact of Leno's low ratings on lead-in and following programming, which they claimed decimated the value of the overall network and the local affiliates. Analysts correctly predicted that this negative impact of these ratings on local affiliate

programs that followed Leno (which generated a large outcry from those local stations against Leno) would eventually kill this "experiment."

[192] As a sign of waning enthusiasm for this sector, General Electric – NBC-Universal's parent (Vivendi owned 20% as well) – was in the midst of entertaining a buyout of minority owner Vivendi and taking on cable giant, Comcast, as a 51% majority partner in this entertainment subsidiary, just as Leno's ratings plummeted. The FCC approved the mega-merger on January 18, 2011.

[193] The February 28, 2009 New York Times: "Financially, the networks are on shaky ground, partly because they rely almost solely on advertising. CBS reported that for the fourth quarter of [2008], as the recession deepened, operating income in its television segment declined 40 percent, even though it was by far the most-watched network. In the second week of February, CBS had 12 of the top 20 shows, according to Nielsen Media Research… News Corporation, which owns Fox, reported operating income of $18 million in broadcast television, compared with $245 million [in 2007]. And Disney's broadcasting business [which includes assets like ABC and ESPN] had a 60 percent drop in operating income." The September 2, 2009 Cynopsis.com: "Indicative of the times, Nielsen reports advertising revenue in the US declined by -15.4% during the first half of 2009 compared to the same period in 2008. The total ad dollars spent in the first two quarters of 2009 equals $56.9 billion, a figure that is down by more than $10.3 billion versus last year. There were a couple of bright spots as overall Cable TV increased by +1.5% during the first half of 2009 and Spanish Language Cable TV also saw a slight bump of +0.6%. All other broadcast categories saw decreases: Network TV -7%; Network Radio -9%; Spot Radio -9.1%; Spanish Language TV -10.1%; Syndication TV -11.6%; Spot TV Top 100 DMAs ["designated marketing areas" – basically regional markets built around urban centers] -17.4%; and Spot TV 101-210 DMAs -32.1%. Additionally, internet advertising also declined by -1.0% during the same period." It is interesting to note the heavier decline in traditional advertising approaches when compared to newer and more targeted media.

[194] Time Magazine, April 6, 2009. Clearly an industry that needs "ratings" to justify ad rates is struggling with consumer measurement services – like Nielsen – that suggest continued erosion in media advertising reach. A number of companies, whose self-measurement may be deemed suspect, have developed a new approach: "A coalition of 14 media giants including Time Warner, News Corp., Walt Disney and NBC Universal calling itself the Coalition for Innovative Media Measurement (CIMM) - announced plans to team up to develop new methods to measure TV viewing across multiple platforms. The group plans to mine set top box data, measure internet video consumption and analyze cross-platform usage to gain a more accurate picture of how audiences now consume premium content. The companies have agreed to make contributions of at least $1 million combined to build new research apparatus." Cynopsis: Digital, September 14, 2009.

[195] NYTimes.com, November 20, 2009.

[196] The December 30, 2009 Hollywood Reporter illustrates the advantage that cable networks have over the traditional, advertising-only-driven broadcast network model: "Cable channels make most of their money by charging pay-TV providers a monthly fee per subscriber for their programming. On average, the pay-TV providers pay about 26 cents for each channel they carry… A channel as highly rated as ESPN can get close to $4, while some, such as MTV2, go for just a few pennies… With both advertising and fees, ESPN has seen its revenue grow to $6.3 billion this year from $1.8 billion a decade ago… It has been able to bid for premium events that networks had traditionally aired, such as football games. Cable channels also have been able to fund high-quality shows, such as AMC's "Mad Men," rather than recycling movies and TV series…. That, plus a growing number of channels, has given cable a bigger share of the ad pie. In 1998, cable channels drew roughly $9.1 billion, or 24% of total TV ad spending, according to the Television Bureau of Advertising. By 2008, they were getting $21.6 billion, or 39%." Broadcast networks have demanded that, despite their unique "free access" over government-provided digital airways (which cable does not have), they too should be accorded a reasonable share of subscriber revenues when their signals are retransmitted over cable or satellite. An eleventh hour agreement between Time Warner Cable and Fox Broadcasting, reached in the early hours of January 1, 2010, set the tone for the expected levels of revenue-sharing that cable operators are willing to pay broadcast networks for retransmission – in the range of 50-60 cents per month per subscriber. In early March of 2010, Disney pulled its New York television station, WABC, off of Cablevision's cable system over a similar carriage fee dispute, resolving the conflict hours before the scheduled March 7 Academy Awards ceremony, telecast on that station. In October of 2010, a similar dispute pulled Fox Broadcasting off Cablevision during baseball's World Series. With the acceleration of carriage disputes, cable operators are asking for government help to resolve these issues: "In a petition filed with the FCC, Time Warner Cable, Verizon Communications, Cablevision and advocacy group Public Knowledge said that regulations governing transmissions from broadcasters to subscription-television providers are outdated and warned that [the March 6-7, 2010] standoff between Cablevision and Walt Disney Co. [over carriage of WABC] will be repeated unless the FCC issues new rules. They also called on regulators to assign an arbitrator during stalled negotiations and to require broadcasters to maintain their signals if talks break down." Washington Post, March 10, 2010.

[197] WSJ.com, June 27, 2009.

[198] But the U.S. Federal Communications Commission is exploring requirements to "standardize set-top box technology across the industry to allow third party connected box devices to work as cable and satellite set-tops across the country" (Cynopsis.com, November 12, 2010), to increase consumer choice and access to content. Nevertheless, streaming U.S. television network transmissions without telecaster permission, even with embedded advertising, still seems to cross the line. In November, a federal district court in New York issued a temporary restraining order against such a streaming site, FilmOn. "The temporary restraining order was put into effect as the court deliberates on a final decision on the [plaintiffs/broadcast] networks' plea for the Web site to be shut down. The controversy surrounding FilmOn and a similar streaming site, iviTV, highlights a scramble by broadcasters to control the distribution of their content as a plethora of new distributors such as Google TV, Apple TV, and streaming sites try to bring shows and film to Internet users." Washington Post, November 23, 2010.

[199] Dealine.com, November 12, 2012.

[200] Ibid.

[201] "[In the fall of 2012, Google] released some internal data on its TrueView video ad units (the ones on YouTube that let you skip the ads after five seconds). Looking at sales impact during and two weeks after 92 different ad campaigns, Google says it found that

on average every $1 invested in YouTube delivered a $1.70 return in sales. It also found that ads on YouTube and the Google Display Network drive a 36% increase in website visits and a 36% increase in search queries." CynopsisDigital, October 3, 2012.

[202] "According to a Turner research report, the average person watched 32.2 hours of TV per week [in the summer of 2009]. In 2004, the average number of TV hours viewed during the summer was 29.8…. The gains were driven by cable TV programming, which continues to erode the traditional advantage of the Big Four networks." The August 26, 2009 HollywoodReporter.com

[203] "In terms of breaking down Q4 2010 [U.S.] TV viewing habits by age, Nielsen data shows that average monthly minutes spent watching traditional TV is significantly higher among older viewers. The highest monthly average recorded in Q4 2010 was by viewers 65 and up (210 hours and 34 minutes), while the lowest monthly average was recorded by viewers 12-17 (105 hours and seven minutes)." MarketingCharts.com, March 2011.

[204] "The Open Mobile Video Coalition (OMVC), a voluntary association of more than 800 broadcast stations, announced [on October 16, 2009] it is 'All Systems Go' for a new era of television service on mobile devices. With [the] adoption of a final mobile digital television (Mobile DTV) broadcast standard by the Advanced Television Systems Committee (ATSC) on [October 15, 2009], U.S. broadcasters are poised to roll out an array of digital program services that will be available to consumers on devices ranging from in-car screens to portable DVD players and mobile phones… Mobile DTV technology uses existing 6MHz channels [a sliver of the new frequencies that Congress allocated for high-definition broadcasts for broadcasts to wireless devices] from broadcasters to transmit a mobile stream of programming services that will not interfere with existing high-definition and multicast services." BusinessWire.com, October 16, 2009

[205] February 8, 2009 New York Times. As noted above, tracking showed average daily television consumption per American viewer rose from 4.86 hours in 2007 to 5.13 hours in 2009. The Hollywood Reporter, May 3, 2010. But on May 3, 2011 Nielsen also released its estimates as to the going forward reduction in the percentage of U.S. households with televisions from 98.9% to 96.7%.

[206] MarketingCharts.com, March 2011.

[207] CynopsisMedia.com, October 4, 2012, which also notes: ""African-Americans watch 6.5 hours of TV a day, more than any other single demographic according to a report Nielsen released [in September 2012] in conjunction with the National Newspaper Publishers Assn. As the largest racial minority group in the United States, African-Americans wield a collective buying power estimated to reach $1.1 trillion by 2015, according to the study. That number should and is--raising eyebrows."

[208] Ibid.

[209] "A New York Times/CBS News poll [in August of 2010] found that 88 percent of respondents paid for traditional TV service. Just 15 percent of those subscribers had considered replacing it with Internet video services like Hulu and YouTube…Younger people, though, are more intrigued by the possibility: respondents under the age of 45 were significantly more likely than older ones to say they had considered replacing their pay TV service. The poll was conducted Aug. 3-5 [2010] with 847 respondents and has a margin of sampling error of plus or minus three percentage points… Even through the downturn, the number of people subscribing to pay TV continued to grow. Cable, satellite and fiber-optic providers added 677,000 customers in the first quarter of this year, according to the investment firm Sanford C. Bernstein." New York Times, August 23, 2010.

[210] "Netflix traffic, be it movies or TV shows streamed over the wires, now accounts for close to 30% of Net activity in U.S. homes in peak evening hours, according to a study by hardware/software net traffic experts Sandvine Inc… In total, the 'real time entertainment' share of Net traffic, which includes Netflix, takes up 49.2%--basically half of data flowing into homes. Web activity, presumably covering all other use cases including reading digital news sources or accessing social network resources, takes up less than 17%... Around 25% of homes with a broadband connection subscribe to Netflix, but the traffic-heavy nature of the service explains its larger share of the Net traffic compared to low-data-burden uses like email." FastCompany.com, May 17, 2011. While the service does experience an occasional glitch, such as a contractual issue with Sony product when Netflix' streaming subscriber base topped 23.5 million in June of 2011, the service has experienced exponential growth and consumer acceptance, passing 25 million consumers by August of 2011. A summer 2011 significant price increase in the cost of the combined streaming and hard copy delivery services cost the company both subscribers and stock value. Notwithstanding a hefty retail price increase to consumers effective September 1, 2011, the entry of new "bidders" for digital content prompted one of Netflix' largest product suppliers, premium cable channel giant Starz, to discontinue its output agreement with Netflix. Starz issued this explanation on September 1, 2011: "This decision is a result of our strategy to protect the premium nature of our brand by preserving the appropriate pricing and packaging of our exclusive and highly valuable content. With our current studio rights and growing original programming presence, the network is in an excellent position to evaluate new opportunities and expand its overall business." By October 2012, Netflix announced 30 million subscribers worldwide (25 million in the United States). Deadline.com, October 25, 2012. But growth had clearly slowed. Netflix continued to eye the international market for its next phase.

[211] In September of 2010, Time-Warner Cable refused to add Epix as a channel, citing the prior exploitation on Netflix Web service as the reason. Effectively, Time-Warner appears to be equating Webcasts and television, a very interesting philosophical change. With Netflix' stock soaring from this new business model, Web-retailing giant, Amazon, and telephone carrier Verizon each began building its own online subscription service in 2011 to provide a commercial alternative. Netflix' July 2011 attempt to charge $7.99 for *each* of DVD-driven and streaming service, representing a 60% increase over then-existing rates, generated strong consumer backlash. Still, the industry was squeezing Netflix on the other side demanding higher prices for premium content. The price increase in the cost of the combined streaming and hard copy delivery services cost the company both subscribers and stock value.

[212] Weekly Variety, August 23-29, 2010 at page 1. In July of 2011, Netflix announced another such transaction with DreamWorks Animation.

[213] CynopsisDigital.com, April 9, 2013. The issue is now headed to the United States Supreme Court for a final decision.

[214] "34% of American adults ages 18 and older now own a tablet, up from 18% a year ago, according to the Pew Internet & American Life Project. The demographics most likely to own a tablet include: Those living in households with an income of at least $75,000 a year (56%); adults 35-44 (49%), and college graduates (also 49%)… In other words: Tablets carry a higher premium (aka: $$) than smartphones, which skew more toward younger (though still decently affluent) people. What's more interesting is the staggering

year-over-year increase in ownership, which signals that as tablet prices begin to drop (as a result of more lower-cost alternatives rolling out in the market), tablet sales should continue to rise." CynopsisDigital.com, June 11, 2013.

[215] "Warner Bros. announced that it is using Facebook to offer pay-per-view movies for 48 hours in exchange for 30 Facebook Credits ($3) to its network of more than 500 million users." Deadline.com, March 8, 2011. Their first film? *The Dark Knight.* Other studios suggested that exploring these new constructs would soon become industry standard: "Comcast cable [owner of 51% of NBC/Universal] president Neil Smit said [March 7, 2011] during a Deutsche Bank investors conference in Florida that he is confident his company can compete in the sector via video-on-demand offerings and new content, compared with Netflix's emphasis on library titles." Ibid.

[216] For example: *Arrested Development*, an American broadcast television comedy series that aired from 2003 to 2006 and developed a cult following, but one insufficient to sustain its presence on Fox Broadcasting, was resurrected for new and additional original episodes to be streamed on Netflix in 2013.

[217] "Application software, also known as an application or an 'app,' is computer software designed to help the user to perform singular or multiple related specific tasks." Wikipedia. On tablets or mobile phones, an app allows the user to engage in some particular activity enabled by the downloaded software.

[218] What Cablevision released in April of 2011: "...[I]ts new in-home Optimum live TV app for the iPad claiming that it has the right to distribute programming over iPads because it is distributing the content over its digital cable network rather than the internet. The app provides access to some *300* live channels and 2,000 selections from [Cablevision's] extensive [video-on-demand] library, acts as a channel guide and enables users to program their [digital video recorders] remotely. Like TWC, Cablevision argues that the iPad is basically just another screen within the home and that it plans to deploy additional apps that deliver the same experience to other tablets and display devices in the coming months." Cynopsis Digital, April 4, 2011.

[219] Indeed, for well-positioned companies, such vendors provide unique benefits that once belonged only to enterprises that could afford their own ad sales staffs. One such company which provides both ad sales capacities with targeted ad placement, Alloy Media + Marketing, explains their appeal on their Website as follows: "Alloy Media + Marketing is one of the country's largest providers of targeted media programs. Within the Alloy Media + Marketing group of companies, marketers and their agencies can access the depth of expertise and breadth of programming needed to meet their specific goals. Long-standing, quality relationships and proprietary partnerships enable us to provide unique access to consumers nationwide."

[220] The March 3, 2009 Cynopsis: Digital: "Time Warner CEO Jeff Bewkes provided *Ad Age* with a bit more insight into Time Warner's multiplatform content strategy. He described the company's "TV Everywhere" initiative as an industry wide effort to find a way to place cable programming on all of the web's popular portals by extending today's subscription model (i.e. limiting access to the content only to paying cable or satellite subscribers.) The need to preserve the subscription model is obvious, given that Turner Networks and HBO accounted for a third of Time Warner's revenue in 2008 along with nearly 50% of the company's operating profit."

[221] fuzzster.com

[222] .modelmayhem.com

[223] muxlim.com

[224] vox.com

[225] blackplanet.com

[226] yub.com

[227] The August 16, 2009 DailyTrojan.com (University of Southern California)

[228] Maybe "not-so-giant." In the late spring of 2009, a very frustrated Time-Warner spun AOL off into a separate publicly-traded company (effective in the third quarter of 2009), an ignominious end for what was supposed to be the game-changing media 2001 merger. In November 2009, the spin-off took place; the new company rebranded itself as "Aol." and promptly reduced its workforce by a third. But revenues continued to decline, and many wondered whether the new "Aol" would be merged into another service… or even survive at all. The February 3, 2011 Cynopsis Digital explained: "Work-in-progress AOL reported a 26% decline in earnings and a 29% decline in ad revenue during Q4 2010. Domestic display advertising declined by 14% while subscription revenue dropped by another 23%. Aggressive cost cutting and asset sales helped the company increase profits to $66 million for the quarter, but it still posted losses of $782 million for the year. A leaked copy of a future business plan, dubbed 'The AOL Way'… highlighted plans to chase search traffic by increasing the sheer volume of blog posts, stories and videos…" In February of 2011, in an effort to remake itself as a "go-to" news portal, AOL purchased blog-aggregator and Internet news purveyor, The Huffington Post, for $315 million in cash and stock. "Arianna Huffington, the cable talk show pundit, author and doyenne of the political left, [was given] control of all of AOL's editorial content as president and editor in chief of a newly created Huffington Post Media Group. The arrangement [gave] her oversight not only of AOL's national, local and financial news operations, but also of the company's other media enterprises like MapQuest and Moviefone." New York Times, February 7, 2011. AOL's existing AOL News and Daily Finance were absorbed by this new operating group.

[229] An Associated Press report on AOL.com, May 16, 2008.

[230] FastCompany.com (September 1, 2010)

[231] Ibid. Note that Microsoft has let its Zune platform die a slow, natural death, simply by not updating it. As the March 14, 2011 Washington Post noted: "Leaving a device in the electronics market for one and a half years unaltered, with only a price cut and a storage increase to distinguish it from newer competitors, invites its irrelevance."

[232] Cynopsis Digital, August 31, 2011.

[233] Wikipedia: "The form is defined by intense player involvement with a story that takes place in real-time and evolves according to participants' responses, and characters that are actively controlled by the game's designers, as opposed to being controlled by artificial intelligence as in a computer or console video game. Players interact directly with characters in the game, solve plot-based

challenges and puzzles, and often work together with a community to analyze the story and coordinate real-life and online activities. ARGs generally use multimedia, such as telephones, email and mail but rely on the Internet as the central binding medium."

[234] FastCompany.com, September 10, 2008.

[235] Whether it is a sign of a slowly improving economy or a continuation of a shift from bricks and mortar stores, this little statistic is a pretty strong indicator of the importance of eCommerce: on the Monday following the 2012 U.S. (late November) Thanksgiving weekend – so-called "Cyber Monday – U.S. online consumer sales reached $1.98 billion, a whopping 17% increase over the previous year. Adobe.com, Digital Index, November 26, 2012. U.S. Commerce Department statistics show that not only has online retailing in the U.S. surpassed pre-recession numbers, annual growth beginning in 2013 has accelerated into solid double digits. InternetRetailer.com, August 15, 2013

[236] FastCompnay.com, November 20, 2012.

[237] While the online video numbers aren't yet staggering, growth was clearly present in this sector as well. "Digital video saw an increase of 18% year-over-year, generating a little over $1 billion in revenue during the first half of 2012." CynopsisDigital.com, October 12, 2012.

[238] Deadline.com, October 11, 2012

[239] The March 14, 2007 BusinessWeek.com, March 14, 2007.

[240] The IAB's Internet Advertising Revenue Report, a survey conducted independently by PricewaterhouseCoopers, June 3, 2013.

[241] "Google earns 56 percent of all mobile ad dollars and 96 percent of mobile search ad dollars, according to eMarketer." NYTimes.com, October 28, 2012

[242] As of the fall of 2012, advertisers were still spending only 2% of their ad budgets on mobile. Ibid.

[243] "In addition, Google has benefited from the fact that one main way people use Google on phones is to search for nearby businesses, a prime source of advertising. Thirty percent of restaurant searches and 25 percent of movie searches are done on mobile devices, according to Google... One of Google's most successful mobile ad types is the click-to-call ad. After running these ads, Starwood Hotels' mobile bookings grew 20 percent in a month." Ibid.

[244] Mobile trends show parallel consumer expectations with television websites as well: "For consumers, usefulness is the top-most priority for TV websites and mobile apps, according to a new study from Frank N. Magid Associates, commissioned by TV Guide.com and TV Guide Mobile. In fact, 86% of the 1,000 study participants surveyed in the study indicated as such. The next-most important attributes for consumers were trustworthiness and high quality, with each tied at 83% of survey respondents. Interestingly enough, and this might say something about the rise of social TV and second-screen services, only 47% of consumers cited 'a good way to connect with others' as being an important attribute of TV websites and mobile apps." CynopsisDigital.com, November 1, 2012

[245] FastCompany.com, November 20, 2012.

[246] "Internet advertising hit $99 billion in 2012, representing a 16.2 percent increase over the previous year and accounting for 19.5 percent of all global measured advertising expenditures, according to a new report from GroupM [GroupM is the leading global media investment management operation. It serves as the parent company to WPP media agencies including Maxus, MEC, MediaCom, and Mindshare].... North America led the world in overall digital advertising investment with an estimated $38.3 billion; Asia-Pacific came in second with $30.6 billion followed by Western Europe with $24.1 billion, according to the study, entitled This Year, Next Year: Interaction 2013. .. The study is part of GroupM's media and marketing forecasting series drawn from data supplied by parent company WPP's worldwide resources in advertising, public relations, market research, and specialist communications. It was released today by London-based GroupM Futures Director Adam Smith and New York-based Global Chief Digital Officer Rob Norman... The study also predicted that in 2013 digital advertising spending will reach $113.5 billion globally, 14.6 percent more than 2012. The figure represents more than 21 percent of all measured advertising investment. In the 2013 forecast, North America once again ranks first with an estimated $42.8 billion in digital ad spend; Asia-Pacific follows with $36.8 billion, followed by Western Europe with $26.6 billion." WPP.com, March 27, 2013

[247] *Cloud computing* allows users to access information and computing power stored and operating on some outside server – they don't have to download the capacity into their own computer, but they can use their computer, cell phone or other device (like a controller) to engage this "computing power in the clouds." This concept is often confused with *grid computing* where a group of computers are networked together to provide the functionality of a much larger mainframe computer.

[248] LBNelert.com, April 16, 2012.

[249] As noted in a report issued by the Pew Internet & American Life Project November 25, 2012.

[250] NeilsenWire.com, March 29, 2012

[251] The above-noted report issued by the Pew Internet & American Life Project November 25, 2012.

[252] "While 25% of [U.S.] teens say they access the Internet mostly through mobile devices like smartphones and tablets, females are more likely than males to do so, at 29% compared to 20%. Girls between the age of 14-17 accessed the web via mobile the most at 34% compared to 24% for boys... Usage was also high among black teens, with 33% using mobile devices to surf the web versus 24% of white teens." Variety.com, March 27, 2013.

[253] According to onlinemarketing-trends.com, June 13, 2011, the number of U.S. smart phones with access to the Web will eclipse the number of computers (desktop and laptop) in 2012.

[254] WiMax, which has been called "WiFi on wheels," is beginning to open up the next generation of cell phone bandwidth (also available for laptops equipped with the right card); some call it "4G," which truly expands mobile capabilities almost exponentially. Network infrastructure supplier, Cisco Systems, is joining to help Clearwire Corp.'s efforts to roll WiMax into 80 U.S. markets by the end of 2010. Cisco's May 13, 2009 announcement: "A single high-end data phone today generates more data traffic than 30 basic-feature cell phones, while a single laptop air card generates more data traffic than 450 basic-feature cell phones. Cisco projects that mobile data traffic will increase 1,000-fold over the seven years from 2005 through 2012, with video being a significant component. This growth is the primary reason why Clearwire, enabled by Cisco, is building a data-centric 4G network across the U.S."s AT&T and Verizon also are implementing similar 4G networks.

[255] Using data publicly available data from comScore.com and Alexa.com for Internet tracking and Flurry Analytics data for mobile applications, the June 20, 2011 BusinessInsider.com reached the following conclusions: "Today, however, a new platform shift is taking place. In 2011, for the first time, smartphone and tablet shipments exceed those of desktop and notebook shipments... This move means a new generation of consumers expects their smartphones and tablets to come with instant broadband connectively so they, too, can connect to the Internet.... Our analysis shows that, for the first time ever, daily time spent in mobile apps surpasses desktop and mobile web consumption."

[256] Myxer's Boombox Report (*Girl Power*), April 2010.

[257] "Six out of 10 African Americans and Hispanics use their cellphones to get onto the Internet, a greater portion than for the overall adult population, according to a report by the Pew Research Center released this week...And although wireless Internet connections have their limitations, cellphones and laptops are recasting the access issue for minority and low-income communities that have been disproportionately left behind as Facebook, Wikipedia and Skype become fixtures in homes and at businesses." Washington Post, July 10, 2010.

[258] The November 23, 2010 FastCompany.com examines the findings of a Pew Internet study on American Internet usage based on income, community type--urban, rural, suburban--educational attainment, race, ethnicity, gender, and age. "None was nearly so strongly correlated as income... The report, an umbrella analysis of three Pew surveys conducted in 2009 and 2010, compares Internet use among American households in four different income brackets: less than $30,000 a year; $30,000-50,000; $50,000-75,000; and greater than $75,000. Respondents--more than 3,000 people participated--were asked a variety of questions about how often they used the Internet, and what sorts of services they took advantage of (such as email, online news, booking travel online, or health research)... As might be expected, the wealthier used the Internet more. But the degree of the spread was a surprise... Almost 90% of the wealthiest respondents reported broadband access at home. Of those in the under-$30,000 households, that figure was only 40%... [T]here appeared to be a tipping point somewhere in the $30,000-$50,000 range. Consider, for instance, the data on those who researched products online. Only 67% of lowest-income Internet users research products online. Make it over the hump into the $30,000-$50,000 bracket, though, and all of a sudden 81% of internet users do so--a jump of 14 points."

[259] The reference to a "smart phone" or "smartphone" is a category of mobile phones that have content-viewable screens, some minimal internal processing power and memory, are data entry-capable and offer at least some access to the Web.

[260] "Schlage, a major lock maker, markets a system that lets homeowners use their mobile phones to unlock their doors from miles away, and manage their home heating and air-conditioning, lights and security cameras. Customers buy locks that are controlled by wireless radio signals sent from an Internet-connected box in their home... In October [2010], General Motors introduced an app that lets owners of most 2011 G.M. models lock and unlock the doors and start the engine remotely. It allows car owners to warm up the engine on a frigid day or fire up the air-conditioning on a hot one from the comfort of their office cubicle..." NYTimes.com, July 4, 2011.

[261] The February 20, 2009 RSS feed from Cynopsis Digital (a Horowitz Associates company) noted: "Mobile ads served on the iPhone platform have been extremely effective in terms of response rates - particularly those that take advantage of the device's GPS capabilities, according to research from Limbo and GfK NOP quoted by *eMarketer*. About one half of iPhone users who were served ads responded to them compared to a 33% non-iPhone response rate. Recall among iPhone users came it at 41% compared to 33% for other users. iPhone users are more than twice as likely as non-iPhone users to browse the mobile Web on their phone and more than three times as likely to use location-based services, including maps, restaurant locators and friend finders." The ability to point a phone (not just an iPhone) at a billboard or even a store window display and trigger a "buy" command is being tested now, and if you have an iPhone and download the RedLaser app, you can scan the bar code on a potential in-store purchase and see instantly if you could do better online!

[262] "Geolocation services have become an increasingly important marketing tool for small businesses, especially those that depend on customer traffic like restaurants, retailers and bars. The growing importance of the services, which exploit the ability of communication networks to pinpoint the location of smartphones and other mobile devices, is underscored by the recent introduction of Facebook Places, which allows users of the Facebook mobile application to check into locations and share their whereabouts with friends... Location-based services can play many roles. They offer customer-relationship tools, rewards programs, social networks, games, business directories, city guidebooks and review sites. They help businesses present coupons, reward loyal clientele and gather valuable data about customers." New York Times, October 6, 2010 Companies like FourSquare are building such geomarketing capacities, taking advantage of such consumer location data that can be mined from geographic information posted on Facebook or even from GPS capacities in mobile phones to offer incentive advertising to consumers (usually on cell phones) passing near the relevant retail outlet, restaurants. Their Website (foursquare.com) notes: "Foursquare on your phone gives you & your friends new ways of exploring your city. Earn points & unlock badges for discovering new things."

[263] "The announcement -- made by Belo, Cox Media Group, E.W. Scripps, Fox, Gannett Broadcasting, Hearst Television, ION Television, Media General Inc., Meredith Corp., NBC, Post-Newsweek Stations Inc. and Raycom Media -- comes a day after FCC chairman Julius Genachowski initiative...According to a release, the service 'will allow member companies to provide content to mobile devices, including live and on-demand video, local and national news from print and electronic sources, as well as sports and entertainment programming' using the 'existing broadcast spectrum.'...By aggregating existing broadcast spectrum, the new venture 'will have the capacity to offer a breadth of mobile video and print content to nearly 150 million U.S. residents.'" theWrap.com (April 14, 2010)

[264] The initiative began in 2009, but getting European Union permission consumed almost four years. The January 30, 2009 New York Times: "[England's] communications minister, Stephen Carter, is eager for the media, telecommunications and technology sectors to pick up part of the slack as other parts of the British economy, including financial services, decline. By 2012, the government said in a report, 20 percent of all commerce in Britain will occur online."

[265] "Nielsen, the ratings company, said that 96.7 percent of American households now own sets, down from 98.9 percent." New York Times, May 3, 2011.

[266] At the time of this survey, U.S. broadband penetration was approximately 65% of home Internet access. That number barely moved, according to the June 15, 2011 LATimes.com, even two years later, when number twitched up to 67%.

[267] Hollywood Reporter, January 8, 2008. By 2013, the ad spend numbers reflected the gradual shift from television to other media. "The current upfront [U.S. television ad sales] market is a telling indicator of the relationship. Expectations overall are for the market to be flat or slightly down from the $8.8 billion to $9.3 billion in advance ad commitments secured in each of [2011 and 2012], a signal that advertisers may still love TV, but not any more than they did in 2011 and 2012 (and maybe a little less)... Meantime, advertising on digital media is primed to explode, according to projections from Magna Global. The media research firm expects digital ad revenue, cobbled from a variety of areas, to rise 13.4% to $113.6 billion in 2013. Meanwhile, TV ad sales are projected to increase just 2% to $196.5 billion." Variety.com, June 21, 2013.

[268] CynposisDigital, April 29, 2013 citing an April survey.

[269] DuitchConsulting.com, Client Bulletin 13-22, May 28, 2013

[270] "Attracting those additional advertisers has been great for Google, which reported a 42 percent increase in paid clicks, year over year, for the second quarter of 2012. But the heightened competition has driven up the prices for keywords and made it harder for small companies... While about 96 percent of pay-per-click advertisers spend less than $10,000 a month, according to AdGooroo, a research firm that studies the pay-per-click market, big-budget advertisers spend hundreds of times more. In the first half of 2012, Amazon reportedly spent $54 million, and the University of Phoenix $37.9 million." New York Times, October 17, 2012. Planning around the raw need to buy key word priorities can drive traffic with clever content and appropriate connective communications in social media, a much more cost-effective approach, particularly for smaller businesses.

[271] "It appears as if the larger canvas can feature rich media content such as videos, photos, games, and more. Google says internal tests show that this "smart hover" feature eliminates nearly 100% of accidental expansions and increases engagement by 6-8X over standard click-to-expand display ads." CynopsisDigital.com, October 3, 2012.

[272] "[B]rand advertisers don't want to measure clicks. They want to measure 'reach'--who actually saw their ads. And while they can 'pre-buy' demographics, by choosing to place their ads on sites who their target customers tend to visit, they haven't been able to measure results to determine whether those were the people who actually saw the ad.... [Nielsen] Online Campaign Ratings [is a metrics subscription service not] just to advertisers but also to publishers, who may want to get a better handle on how well they're delivering specific audiences...Here's how it works: Advertisers tag their ads and then place them on their targeted sites around the web. When the ads are viewed, the ads make a call to Facebook, which then searches its own user database to identify the viewer of the ad. It then gathers up that person's demographic information (but not personally identifiable information) and sends it to Nielsen. Nielsen is then able to report back to advertisers who saw their ads in a particular campaign....Facebook isn't the whole solution for Nielsen, however. Only about half of Americans are on the social network which means that OCR can only provide accurate demographics on about 42%, on average, of a campaign's impressions... So Nielsen will still have to bring in more publishers to play the same role as Facebook and fill in the remaining gaps " FastCompany.com, August 3, 2011.

[273] NYTimes.com, July 14, 2013.

[274] Yet according to a March 20, 2012 BBC World Report radio program, *half* of all Africans have access to mobile phones.

[275] *What Works – Smart Soaps: The Population Media Center Mixes Science with Soap Operas to Protect Public Health,* Stanford University Graduate School of Business, Stanford Social Innovation Review, Winter 2008

[276] Entitled "U.S. Telecommunications and Cable & Satellite: The Poverty Problem" (May 31, 2011) by Craig Moffett, summarized in theDeal.com, June 24, 2011.

[277] Fred Guterl, *Can Children Teach Themselves?* ScientificAmerican.com, February 27, 2013. Dr, Mitra is a professor of educational technology at Newcastle University and noted TED lecturer.

[278] Raymond Kurzweil, *The Law of Accelerating Returns*, March 2001.

[279] As postulated Douglas Rushkoff in this book *Present Shock: When Everything Happens Now*, Penguin Group, 2013.

[280] Ibid.

[281] As analyzed in FastCompany.com, March 25, 2013.

[282] From age seven into adolescence, children begin to move away from a self-centered focus into looking at and questioning their environment: "They begin to question: How does Santa really get to all those houses in one night? They can now reason logically but only on a concrete level, not hypothetically or abstractly. When [an age seven to adolescence] child is shown a blue block and asked 'Is the block green or not green?' he or she will probably answer 'Neither, it's blue' That blue is not green is too abstract. They solve problems logically but haphazardly." *What is Critical Thinking?* by Elizabeth T. Tice, M.Ed., published in the Journal of Excellence in Higher Education, University of Phoenix, 1995-2000. Carl Obermiller, Albers School of Business, Seattle University, and Eric R. Spangenberg, Department of Marketing, Washington State University, have written two relevant articles on the subject: *On the Origin and Distinctness of Skepticism toward Advertising*, published in Marketing Letters, Springer Netherlands, Volume 11, Number 4 (November 2000) and, for a detailed presentation of the continuum of the development of skepticism, see also, *Development of a Scale to Measure Consumer Skepticism Toward Advertising* published in the. Journal, 1998, Vol. 7, No. 2, Pages 159-186.

[283] According to a January 11, 2008 report from the Tobacco-Control Resource Center and the International Union Against Cancer.

[284] See *Eureka! How Distractions Facilitate Creative Problem-Solving, ScienceDaily*.com, October 2, 2008.

[285] See the discussion in *Driven to distraction: How to help wired students learn to focus*, eSchoolNews.com, November 13, 2012.

[286] Stephen A Rains & Monique Mitchell Turner, *Psychological Reactance and Persuasive Health Communication: A Test and Extension of the Intertwined Model*, Human Communication Research (April 2007)

[287] Tanya L. Chartrand, an associate professor of marketing and psychology Duke University's Fuqua School of Business. Duke Ph.D. student Amy Dalton and Gavan Fitzsimons, professor of marketing and psychology at Duke, *Nonconscious relationship reactance: When significant others prime opposing goals*, Journal of Experimental Psychology (September 2007)

[288] NYTimes.com, September 3, 1967 (digital archive).

[289] "[In 2010], support for gay marriage was 44%. The current [May 2013] 53% level of support is essentially double the 27% in Gallup's initial measurement on gay marriage, in 1996." Gallup.com, May 13, 2013

[290] Marketing executive Rei Inamoto writing in the June 27, 2013 FastCompany.com.

[291] Douglas Van Praet writing in FastCompany.com July 16, 2013.

[292] Ibid.

[293] *Can't Buy Me Like: Why Companies Have To Romance The Same Consumers They Once Bought* By Bob Garfield and Doug Levy, FastCompany.com, March 7, 2013

[294] Biased reporting seems to generate an audience. As of April 2012, right-leaning Fox News was holding strong ratings and left-leaning MSNBC was growing, but more neutral CNN was witnessing the lowest ratings in a decade. NYTimes.com, May 5, 2012.

[295] According to Wikipedia, WikiLeaks "has described itself as having been founded by Chinese dissidents, as well as journalists, mathematicians, and start-up company technologists from the United States, Taiwan, Europe, Australia, and South Africa." It has disgorged countless documents, much embarrassing to the United States and its diplomatic and military counterparts, based on the release of classified documents, and appears to be headed by the elusive Julian Paul Assange, whom Wikipedia describes as "an Australian publisher and internet activist. He is best known as the spokesperson and editor-in-chief for WikiLeaks, a whistleblower website. Before working with the website, he was a physics and mathematics student as well as a computer programmer. He has lived in several countries and has told reporters he is constantly on the move. He makes irregular public appearances to speak about freedom of the press, censorship, and investigative reporting; he has also won several journalism awards for his work with WikiLeaks." With access to major Internet payment services cut off by government pressure, however, WikiLeaks effectively shut down in the fall of 2011 for lack of funding.

[296] FastCompany.com, June 29, 2010

[297] LATimes.com, March 29, 2009.

[298] Autos.aol.com, June 19th, 2013.

[299] New York Times, February 6, 2010

[300] For example, California-based ReputationDefender, Inc. (reputation.com) offers a litany of privacy and reputation-tracking software intended to "undo" some of the damage from the unwanted dissemination of unwanted personal or false information on the Web. For anxious parents, it also offers online tracking (through their MyChild software) as to Web-references where their specific child/children might be mentioned. For companies, they have specific reputation-directed solutions, such as the following capability noted on their Website: "MyEdge Pro combines cutting edge technology and live support from experienced Reputation Advisors. It is proven to increase positive content and actively combat false, misleading or irrelevant Google results for businesses and business owners including doctors, lawyers, executives, contractors, real estate agents -- anyone whose business depends on their reputation."

[301] LATimes.com, July 8, 2011.

[302] In mid-September of 2013, with 200 million active users, Twitter announced its was going public (valuation $15B+) with revenue growth from sponsored Tweets, advertising (including short videos) and consumer tracking data derived from Twitter usage.

[303] Based on Omnicom's research arm, Brodeur, which conducted an online survey of North American reporters and editors between December 18, 2007 and January 3, 2008, inviting a randomly selected 4,000 reporters to participate; a total of 178 completed responses. A summary of the results can be found in the January 9, 2008 edition of marketingcharts.com.

[304] Effective December 1, 2009, the Federal Trade Commission required bloggers who review products or services to disclose any affiliation with the provider of such product or service... even the receipt of free products! Celebrities on talk shows, Twitter, etc. are bound by the same disclosure requirement.

[305] The report is summarized on Bmighty.com, September 23, 2008.

[306] The September 2008 New York symposium was entitled, *The Future of Media*, covered by The Hollywood Reporter, September 23, 2008 (at page 9).

[307] According to Marketing Magazine, November 2, 2007.

[308] On December 2, 2009, he blogged: "I have let my family down and I regret those transgressions with all of my heart. I have not been true to my values and the behavior my family deserves. I am not without faults and I am far short of perfect. I am dealing with my behavior and personal failings behind closed doors with my family. Those feelings should be shared by us alone." Reports that his wife extracted huge financial concessions by reason of his behavior only added fuel to the fire.

[309] Woods December 11, 2009 Website also stated: "I am deeply aware of the disappointment and hurt that my infidelity has caused to so many people, most of all my wife and children... I want to say again to everyone that I am profoundly sorry and that I ask forgiveness. It may not be possible to repair the damage I've done, but I want to do my best to try." He added: "I need to focus my attention on being a better husband, father, and person." On April 8, 2010, Woods returned to professional golf with the Masters.

[310] "In the world of athlete celebrity endorsements, an article in *Promo Magazine* (Sept. '07) talked about the need for careful 360-degree research on athletes, ensuring their 'brand attributes' match those of the marketer to be endorsed and the need for an 'exit strategy' in case things head south. The marketing research firm, Marketing Evaluations, Inc. The Q Scores Company (Manhasset, New York) tracks 'Q scores' of roughly 1,800 celebrities. The scores are used to evaluate how positively or negatively the public feels about a celebrity and show how fast things can change after an incident. Two years after the rape charge, Kobe Bryant's unfavorable Q score was 53% (vs. 35% before the incident). Michael Phelps' unfavorable Q score went from 11 to 21 pre-post the bong photo." December 11, 2009 FastCompany.com

[311] With Verizon finally getting the right to sell iPhones in January of 2011. AT&T's $39 billion potential acquisition of T-Mobile USA in 2011, an effort to expand bandwidth and volume requirements, was pulled after both the U.S. Department of Justice and the Federal Communications Commission voiced strong opposition to the merger, which they hailed as anticompetitive.

[312] According to a study (*American Moviegoing 2007*) published in March of 2008 by Nielsen NRG

[313] A Harvard-trained social scientist, author and teacher.

[314] SRI International is an independent, nonprofit research institute founded after World War II, spun off from Stanford University, which works for clients, governmental agencies in fields ranging to hard technology, biochemistry to social research.

[315] Companies like Virginia-based YouEye and California-based Gazehawk offer such online consumer tracking and testing services. For those who wish to explore your deepest thoughts further (with willing participants), a California-based company wholly owned by Nielsen Research (NeuroFocus) offers "a product called Mynd, the world's first portable, wireless electroencephalogram (EEG) scanner. The skullcap-size device sports dozens of sensors that rest on a subject's head like a crown of thorns. It covers the entire area of the brain... so it can comprehensively capture synaptic waves; but unlike previous models, it doesn't require messy gel. What's more, users can capture, amplify, and instantaneously dispatch a subject's brain waves in real time, via Bluetooth, to another device--a remote laptop, say, an iPhone, or that much-beloved iPad... Neuro-Focus [has given] away Mynds to home panelists across the country. Consumers will be paid to wear them while they watch TV, head to movie theaters, or shop at the mall. The firm will collect the resulting streams of data and use them to analyze the participants' deep subconscious responses to the commercials, products, brands, and messages of its clients." FastCompany.com, August 8, 2011.

[316] NYTimes.com, April 13, 2009.

[317] Reproduced with permission from Claritas, Inc. ©

[318] If you would like to learn a bit more about segmentation analysis, visit Nielsen's mybestsegments.com site. If you would like to see the characteristics of your own zip code, enter your information at that site, add the code shown on the page, and learn a bit more about your neighbors.

[319] According to the May 22, 2009 Mediabuyerplanner.com, Google invaded the so-called up-front television advertising bonanza in the spring of 2009. They are now offering advertisers to ability to upload their television commercials (for example, through Echostar's satellite television service), slot them into specifically targeted homes on willing channels (e.g., the Hallmark Channel, MSNBC, etc.) and generate tracking information on the relevant consumer. Google literally handles the media placements and delivers the advertising to the targeted homes.

[320] The December 31, 2008 New York Times: "Advertising agencies have dabbled in side businesses for decades, but 'inventing their own brand, not dependent on clients' largess, is the big new thing,' said George Parlim, an ad agency consultant and writer of AdScam, a blog about the industry. As the economy worsens and ad budgets tighten, 'the creation of intellectual property and new products is something you're going to see a lot more of,' he said."

[321] For example, Buffer is a marketing service focused on social media. It allows "users of their service to schedule social media posts across popular social networks (most notably Facebook, Twitter and LinkedIn) reaching audiences at exactly the right times of day, at set intervals, without having to consistently login to their social media accounts to do so... This simple but effective social media monitoring tool also allows you to track the effectiveness of your social media blasts so you can further refine your post frequency, publication times, and content for a improved ROI." Jobstock.com, October 16, 2013

[322] This particularly noteworthy cross media technology, created by Los Angeles-based Americhip, provides the ability to create video-like imagery on a printed page. The August 20, 2009 Cynopsis: Digital notes CBS' use of this invention "to promote its new fall season this year in [the magazine] *Entertainment Weekly* with an ultra-thin embedded video ad co-sponsored by Pepsi Max that plays clips from the network's Monday night primetime lineup." According to their Website, Americhip's engineers create "products with circuit boards and voice chips, LEDs and fiber optics, electroluminescence and RFID. They create magic on paper using devices like paper-thin motors and wireless electronics. They can make paper talk, light up, move, whistle, sing and interact with your laptop... We even have scent and taste experts who develop custom scents and flavors that become vital elements in our very original books, magazine ads and direct mail."

[323] Wikipedia.

[324] "Layar Vision enables the mobile phone to recognize real world objects and show digital content on top of them. When holding their phone over posters, magazines and newspapers users are able to view and interact with these digital experiences... Layar Vision is an extension of the Layar platform, already used by over 10,000 developers worldwide to create Augmented Reality [AR] experiences for smartphones. With this extension the platform is now able to enhance existing media like print with augmented reality experiences. These experiences offer brands and publishers new ways to engage with customers. Layar is already installed on 10 million mobile devices ensuring an extensive reach across multiple platforms." Pitchengine.com, August 2, 2011.

[325] New York Times, March 4, 2009

[326] As of September 2020, "[f]ifty-four percent of small and midsize businesses are using social media to promote their businesses, double the number using these sites in December 2009, with 35% posting daily updates to sites such as LinkedIn, Facebook, and Twitter, a new study found...And, although only 17% of [small and mid-sized businesses – SMBs] surveyed used incentives to attract online followers, friends, and fans, 60% credit social media with positively impacting their businesses, according to the poll by Daryl Willcox Publishing. In addition, 46% said their company's brand awareness has increased and 36% have attracted new business as a result of their social media efforts, the British study of 269 SMBs found." Informationweek.com, September 7, 2010. As a result of the necessity of marketing through social networks, the value of such sites appear to be rising to meet or exceed values attributed to established companies like Microsoft. The huge potential inherent in a major public offering of Facebook has yet to be tapped, but the first major social network to breach the public marketplace, LinkedIn, performed way above expectations: "The IPO of LinkedIn, the first big social network to go public, didn't disappoint on Wall Street. Shares more than doubled out of the gate to open at $83/share on the New York Stock Exchange (up from its $45 offering price) and reached as high as $112 - a mark that values the company at more than $10 billion." Cynopsis: Digital, May 20, 2011. Facebook finally announced that inevitable public offering, seeking a mere $5 billion, on February 1, 2012.

[327] FastCompany.com, July 6, 2011.

[328] FastCompany.com, July 13, 2013.

[329] "In the 'passive' broadcast version, the app would automatically post to a user's newsfeed as they interacted with the product, such as declaring their favorite movie or writing a scathing movie review. In this version, new user adoption jumped 246%,

compared to a version in which broadcast messaging was disabled.. .For the 'active-personalized' version, which combined passive broadcasts with a prompt to send personalized direct messages to friends (such as, "Hey! check out my new favorite app"), overall adoption was 344% higher (or a 98% bump over the broadcast version). Thus, adding a personalized message feature substantially increases adoption (three times more effective per message), but because fewer users will bother to send the message, adding personalized messages produces less of a bump than passive alone... In the 'passive' broadcast version, the app would automatically post to a user's newsfeed as they interacted with the product, such as declaring their favorite movie or writing a scathing movie review. In this version, new user adoption jumped 246%, compared to a version in which broadcast messaging was disabled... For the 'active-personalized' version, which combined passive broadcasts with a prompt to send personalized direct messages to friends (such as, "Hey! check out my new favorite app"), overall adoption was 344% higher (or a 98% bump over the broadcast version). Thus, adding a personalized message feature substantially increases adoption (three times more effective per message), but because fewer users will bother to send the message, adding personalized messages produces less of a bump than passive alone." Ibid.

[330] LATimes.com, March 8, 2013.

[331] For example: "Crackle is partnering with comScore to provide advertisers with unduplicated audience size and demographics across all screens and platforms the streaming service is available on. This 'Video Everywhere' audience measurement initiative includes online, mobile/tablets, connected TVs, and game consoles, all together covering more than 20 Crackle apps. 'Before this new capability, there had been no audience measurement of connected TV and game consoles, so publishers and networks could not provide an unduplicated audience number,' said Eric Berger, GM of Crackle and EVP/Digital Networks for Sony Pictures Television. Using comScore's census-level measurement capabilities, Crackle hopes to change that." CynopsisDigital.com, March 19, 2013.

[332] An absolutely terrific book on this subject is *Wikinomics: How Mass Collaboration Changes Everything*, by Don Tapscott and Anthony D. Williams (Portfolio/Penguin Books 2006).

[333] From Google's own blog (July 8, 2009): "Google Chrome OS is an open source, lightweight operating system that will initially be targeted at netbooks. Later this year we will open-source its code, and netbooks running Google Chrome OS will be available for consumers in the second half of 2010. Because we're already talking to partners about the project, and we'll soon be working with the open source community, we wanted to share our vision now so everyone understands what we are trying to achieve." Netbooks are stripped-down, light-weight portable computers that rely heavily on Web-based applications (versus more sophisticated notebooks, laptops and desk stations, where processing speeds and hard drive capacity allow the user to choose between installed programs or Web-based applications). Microsoft somewhat countered Google's Chrome OS announcement days later saying that it would provide consumers free Web-based versions of its Office suite of programs (a word processor, spreadsheet, presentation software and a note-taking program).

[334] Wikipedia.

[335] WallStreetandTech.com, May 11, 2009.

[336] New York Times, July 31, 2010.

[337] Even figuring out the scope of the problem and how to present the issues to the problem-solvers gets online help. The August 31, 2008 New York Times describes a Website where people "can share more technical types of displays: graphs, charts and other visuals they create to help them analyze data buried in spreadsheets, tables or text... At an experimental Web site, Many Eyes, (www.many-eyes.com), users can upload the data they want to visualize, then try sophisticated tools to generate interactive displays... The site was created by scientists at the Watson Research Center of I.B.M. in Cambridge, Mass., to help people publish and discuss graphics in a group. Those who register at the site can comment on one another's work, perhaps visualizing the same information with different tools and discovering unexpected patterns in the data."

[338] BusinessWeek.com, February 15, 2007.

[339] The most recent updated version of this book was published in 2006 by Farrar, Straus and Giroux.

[340] So many outsourcing vendors market themselves on the Web: sites like www.HRXCEL.com is great for outsourcing your business benefit plans, Websites and applications outsourcing can be found all over the place (like www.thekreativeedge.com or www.sgdnetworks.com), and you can even cover a whole country with a single Website (try www.FondestAwake.com for China, by way of example).

[341] For example, Stamford, Connecticut-based Gartner, Inc., a large publicly-traded consulting firm, not only will manage major new outsourcing programs for larger clients, but frequently holds relevant "summits" – programs explaining how to create and manage outsourcing-vendor relationships.

[342] www.sourcingmag.com is just one such example.

[343] NYTimes.com, September 6, 2009.

[344] As lucrative as paying for placement high up on the search lists based on keywords (higher and featured costs more, particularly on the most sought-after key words) may be, there are very significant revenues from placing ads next to Web content. "The Internet search leader's [Google's] partners get 68 percent of the revenue from ads placed alongside articles and other content on Web pages. Websites keep 51 percent of the revenue from Google's ads shown next to their own search results... Ads shown next to Google's own services brought in $15.7 billion in revenue last year compared with $7.2 billion from marketing messages that Google distributed to other websites." Washington Post, May 24, 2010

[345] New York Times, March 13, 2009

[346] The April 20, 2009 Time Magazine (pages 43-44)

[347] But overcrowding even in this place as resulted in casualties. In mid-February, 2010, Veoh closed its doors.

[348] FastCompany.com, January 6, 2011.

[349] TruView from Seattle-based Visible Technologies, which helps companies track what's said about them on the Web, should do the trick (www.visibletechnologies.com). But wait, there's more. The company unveiled a major upgrade in late October of 2010: "Its new Google-inspired architecture better distinguishes the relevance and the sentiment of the mountains of social media

conversations... But the latest iteration of Visible's platform, called Visible Intelligence, has been built from the ground up. It has a scalable, Google-like architecture that can render tens of millions of blog posts, tweets, and forum entries within seconds... The platform also has some new bells and whistles. There's a sophisticated sentiment analysis algorithm, for instance. Teams of people from all over the country combed through blogs, forums, and tweets, scoring individual communications on a sentiment scale. Gradually, over a period of five years, these legions of social media scavengers nurtured a sentiment-detection algorithm--one that can distinguish between when someone says a product is 'sick' in the positive sense a snowboarder would use, and when someone says it in the negative sense an outpatient would use." October 28, 2010 FastCompany.com

[350] Ibid at pages 148-49

[351] *Wikinomics; How Mass Collaboration changes Everything*, cited above, at page 139

[352] Here what the starwars.com Website said: "Play in the *Star Wars* galaxy like never before with a major new feature added to StarWars.com that allows you to 'mash up' favorite moments from the saga, create your own *Star Wars* shorts, and interact with fellow fans around the world like never before... "There are more than 200 video clips to choose from that can be mixed and mashed using online video editing technology from Eyespot.com. Browse dozens of media sets that collect a wide assortment of *Star Wars* multimedia ingredients -- video clips, music, pictures -- and drag and drop them right into the mixer. Add your own user-generated video, stills and audio and you can mash it all together. Once you're happy with your mash up, you can post your videos for other fans to see, and they in turn can use it as a foundation of their own mash up. It's easy, addictive and absolutely free to all registered members to use."

[353] NYTimes.com, May 8, 2008.

[354] Renamed the Syfy Channel in July of 2009.

[355] WashingtonPost.com, August 11, 2008

[356] Such as the field leaders, www.technorati.com, www.visibletechnologies.com or Google's www.measuremap.com , or taking a look at various sites that provide information as to the effectiveness of search engine links (SEO – search engine optimization sites), such as www.seoquake.com, which tracks volume and usage, link by link, or www.bruceclay.com, which helps "promote a website or product not only in search engines, but also in other Internet marketing channels." If you blog, Mark Cuban's Icerocket.com can track your efforts through the blogosphere: "It is an invisible tracker that will count your blog visits and other blog statistics. This product is completely free! We will not put any ads on your blog." If you really want to get sophisticated in this arena, learning the vocabulary of what you are reading is a very good idea, and www.seo-theory.com/wordpress/seo-glossary/ is a great place to start. Understanding how this space is measured and analyzed is also valuable: see www.seo-theory.com/wordpress/category/seo-metrics/ and www.marketingcharts.com

[357] Such as www.searchenginewatch.com.

[358] According to the January 15, 2008 New York Times, San Francisco start-up, InsideView, is focusing on examining social networks to provide information that might be relevant to a corporate client's sales staff, even including searching for shared connections with potential customers' management, from colleges to favorite restaurants. "The company's primary product, SalesView, acts as a sort of [an] online divining rod. The service trawls through more than 20,000 public Web sites, social networks and public data sources like LinkedIn, Facebook, Reuters, Securities and Exchange Commission filings and even company blogs. With that information, SalesView can create company snapshots intended to help sales teams identify potential clients."

[359] There are so many companies in this field, many tailored to specific industries and needs. Some more general sites include www.clicktrack.com and www.netinsight.unica.com, and a useful tool to find even more material on tracking the interaction of Web communities on any number of topics can be found at www.teamxweb.com/doc/relatedWork.shtml. The search engines themselves provide useful information to their customers, but valence-tracking is often beyond their capacity. Part of the experimentation in solution-oriented consulting and applications comes literally from planting key words onto your search engine and seeing what pops up on the screen. Seattle-based Visible Technologies is considered one of the pioneers in this growing and complicated field of "impact" and "sentiment" analysis, where the emotional significance of consumers' reactions and statements can be tracked. Buffer (Bufferapp.com), which provides its marketing expertise in designing and placing messages and content into all forms of social media, analyzes consumer responses, including *when* they view the material, advertising that: "Buffer shares your content at the best possible times throughout the day so that your followers and fans see your updates more often."

[360] Boulder, Colorado-based Collective Intellect (www.collectiveintellect.com) advertises that they turn "social media into business intelligence" by providing three distinct services: (i) "digital intelligence" (real-time online topic tracking), (ii) "predictive marketing intelligence" (sentiment and impact analysis, vetting online authority, ascertaining activity levels) and (iii) "social media campaign management" (literally running your online interface with consumers at all levels). They'll compare your efforts to those of your competitors.

[361] Even Microsoft has challenged Google's search engine with a relatively new product called "Bing!," by addressing the consumer's priorities and enabling those choices to move to the top of the page. Initial consumer acceptance was reasonably positive. An alliance between Yahoo and Microsoft should help accelerate Bing's market penetration significantly. The July 29, 2009 FastCompany.com: "But Microsoft arguably gets the better half of the deal--its Bing search engine will now power Yahoo's search function, albeit largely behind the scenes, since Yahoo is insisting it will 'innovate and own' the user experience on Yahoo! properties, including search.'" Microsoft's August 2009 announcement that it was offering some of the sophisticated business, scientific and computational search capacities from Wolfram Alpha suggests powerful strategic values to Bing as well. Exactly what the long-term impact these search combinations will have on Google remains to be seen, however, although after Microsoft's heavy introductory advertising campaign for the service slowed in the fall of 2009, and the growth rate during 2010 was very small (but still positive), with additional growth expected by reason of a new (October 2010) strategic alliance with Facebook noted above. With Microsoft committing to a massive marketing campaign on the order of magnitude of $100 million, Bing!'s *growth rate* easily eclipsed Google's maturing annual growth rates, but Google still seems to be holding on to its overwhelming market share advantage: "According to reports, Bing's market share has been steadily growing. Experian Hitwise says Bing's searches increased 5%

[in December 2010], with Bing-powered searches now accounting for nearly 26% of the market (that's counting Yahoo, which uses Bing's tech; comScore has the two combined totals at 28%). Year-over-year growth rate in December [2010] was 49.4%, according to Barclays, compared with just 20.6% for Google... Experian's data indicates Google's market share dropped just 1% over the period, but still dominates the market at close to 70%." FastCompany, January 25, 2011. However, battle lines between search engine giants Google and Microsoft's Bing! drew particularly nasty as News Corporation, owner of such diverse assets such as MySpace [dwindling], Fox Broadcasting and Twentieth Century Fox, plotted an exclusive right to search News Corporation's media sites to Bing! – taking away its links currently displayed on Google. Sensing a behemoth grow too big to control, News Corporation's major shareholder and CEO, Rupert Murdoch, began these aggressive moves against Google in late November of 2009. If you define a search engine as one that answers inquiries electronically, you'd probably have to add Twitter: "Twitter now reaches some 800 million search queries per day. That's over 24 billion searches per month, more than Bing (4.1 billion) and Yahoo (9.4 billion) combined... While [Twitter] is still a long way off from Google, which supports around 88 billion search queries per month, Twitter is quickly catching up." FastCompany.com, July 8, 2010. That would make Twitter the second largest search engine on earth!

[362] "Instead of using an algorithm to produce results, as Google and Yahoo do, [search-by-texting firms] ChaCha and KGB rely on people to generate their answers. ChaCha provides a free service that allows users to send queries by text or voice message and then receive a text reply, often accompanied by an advertisement, from one of the company's approximately 50,000 part-time responders. Competitor KGB has a similar setup, although its users pay 99 cents per answer and are spared the outside advertising with each response... Both firms are banking on the premise that cellphone users want a single, direct answer to a question. Many people still don't have phone plans that allow for Web use, and those who do, the companies' executives contend, cannot be bothered with sifting through search results on a tiny screen." Washington Post, August 14, 2010

[363] Facebook already has a capacity that seems to portend this inevitability. "Much like the face-detection algorithms used on some modern digital cameras, a face is automatically spotted in an image once it's uploaded to Facebook, and a box pops up prompting you to enter the Facebook name of the person in the photo. It seems much simpler than manually having to click on each and every face you want to tag...But we suspect that face detection is merely the first step Facebook is making to simplify the process of cataloging your photos. The next step is likely to be automated face *recognition*. And that'll put the over-sharing cat among the privacy pigeons for sure. Because it's one thing to use, say, iPhoto's face recognition feature to group people together in your own private digital photo album at home, or even to self-tag your photo in a 1,300 megapixel photo of a 70,000-person crowd at Glastonbury music festival. But Facebook's recognition powers extend to 400 million [now over 500 million] active users with billions of photos. Soon, your name could pop up in photos you didn't even know existed (or, worse, photos you knew existed but believed were anonymous)." FastCompany.com, July 2, 2010. Even as to its regular search engine, Google has hardly been sitting on its hands. It is switching to an entirely new search algorithm that moves off of its single keyword paradigm to looking at word groupings instead: "[Their new] Hummingbird [algorithm] is the culmination of a shift to understanding the meaning of phrases in a query and displaying Web pages that more accurately match that meaning." NYTimes.com, September 26, 2013.

[364] FastCompany.com, January 14, 2011.

[365] Nova Spivack writing on twine.com, March 11, 2009. Note that Wolfram Alpha enables the iPhone-Siri (voice activated) search-response "personal assistant" capability. A new more elegant service – Wolfram Alpha Pro – made its debut on February 8, 2012, providing an amazing ability to transform the mathematically-based Web-questions into 3D graphs and visualizations at very high speeds. NYTimes.com, February 7, 2012

[366] While Wolfram Alpha works in the ether of the Internet as a "search engine," even more extraordinary breakthroughs will alter our capacity to react to change. The ability to analyze massive floods of data "on the fly" becomes an exceptionally powerful competitive tool. For example, I.B.M. has developed software to support what they call stream processing (or "System S") that analyzes data *as it is created*. It reacts to real-time information flow and provides instant visual and mathematical results. Versions of System S are currently being used by research scientists, but applications in the fields of finance, governmental planning and management and behavioral tracking are clearly on the table.

[367] TruCast from Seattle-based Visible Technologies (www.visibletechnologies.com) is an "enterprise level solution [that] enables [client companies] to complete the [interactive online] conversation by allowing them to track, analyze, and participate in blogs, forums, social networks, and online communities."

[368] Digg.com is a Website that allows its users to evaluate (rate) online content, and big winners move to the top of the list, generating RSS feeds and accelerating levels of traffic to the site (and hence to the relevant content). Delicious.com goes one step further with what they call "social bookmarking." If you like a video or a Webpage while on Delicious, your bookmark aggregates into bookmarks for all Delicious users (showing the descriptive "tags" that apply to each choice), organizing your video/online content/Webpage viewing choices automatically. YouTube itself will allow you to access "most popular" or "most viewed" videos. Digg.com is also evolving a new consumer-proactive advertising model where ads are interspersed within its content. As consumers create positive reviews of the ads, the price of placing an individual ad on the digg.com site will actually fall; less popular ads will cost more until they are literally pushed off the site.

[369] Forbes.com, May 6, 2013

[370] NYTimes.com, August 14, 2008.

[371] Technorati.com, May 8, 2012

[372] "Getting it right means gaining the trust and loyalty of women, the world's largest economic power making up to 85% of consumer purchases in the 'she-conomy'." FastCompany.com, July 8, 2011.

[373] "[S]oftware companies like SurveyGizmo and QuestionPro have made it possible [even] for small companies to create customer surveys at a fraction of the cost of traditional surveys done by established research companies. Businesses of all sizes, desperate to lock in customer loyalty, see surveys as a window into the emotional world of their customers and a database that will offer guidance on how to please them." NYTimes.com, March 16, 2012.

[374] Ibid.

[375] Ibid.

[376] Ibid

[377] The November 15, 2009 New York Times addresses this consumer "insecurity" based on a number of studies at various universities and private consumer research organizations: "'You give people a really good bargain on this bucket of minutes,' explained Roger Entner, a senior vice president for telecommunications research at Nielsen. 'People are risk averse, so you have a relatively high overage charge, which gets people to overbuy. You also get really predictable revenue out of it, which Wall Street loves.'" But consumers really hate being charged for every call they make or receive – the pay-per-use model has been dead in the U.S. cell phone industry for years.

[378] CNN.com, October 18, 2012

[379] NYTimes.com, October 10, 2009.

[380] Ibid.

[381] FastCompany.com, July 25, 2011.

[382] At $79/year, this subscription service was announced in early 2011 and generates an effective $6.58/month charge.

[383] Announced in December of 2012, pricing here created an electronic only price, $6/month, elevating to $8 if the consumer wants up to an additional 4 hard copy rentals per month. $0.99 per film creates a one-off rental.

[384] For example, Redbox Instant provided initial availability "online, on iOS and Android devices, the Xbox 360, and some Samsung connected TVs and Blu-ray players." CynopsisDigital.com, December 3, 2012.

[385] But when a film rises to the level of becoming a "classic" or a "collectible" – such as *Avatar* – even 2D versions of a 3D movie break DVD/BluRay records: on April 22, 2010, exclusive of sales to companies that will rent the units to consumers, first day sales of this film shattered the record book for the U.S. and Canada – 2 million DVDs and 1.2 million BluRay discs. The September 27 – October 3, 2010 Weekly Variety reported that the numbers for traditional DVD sales were continuing a downward slide in the first half of 2010, reflecting a 15% annualized decline, off-set slightly by Blu-Ray units, for an overall 3.3% fall in home video.

[386] The October 21, 2009 online Wall Street describes Disney's "Keychest" system: "The technology would allow consumers to pay a single price for permanent access to a movie or TV show across multiple digital platforms and devices—from the Web, to mobile gadgets like iPhones and cable services that allow on-demand viewing. It could also facilitate other services such as online movie subscriptions...Keychest uses the same "cloud computing" logic that underlies Web-based applications, such as Google Docs, permitting users to store files and photographs on remote Internet servers and access them from anywhere, rather than keeping them on their own computers... With Keychest, when a consumer buys a movie from a participating store, his accounts with other participating services—such as a mobile-phone provider or a video-on-demand cable service—would be updated to show the title as available for viewing. The movies wouldn't be downloaded; rather, they would reside with each particular delivery company, such as the Internet service provider, cable company or phone company." A musical equivalent – Palo Alto-based mSpot – provides a "locker" technology "that lets people upload their tunes onto mSpot's servers and stream their music on any Web browser or Android phone." Los Angeles Times, August 25, 2010.

[387] "Warner Brothers... which ... commands a 20 percent share of the DVD and Blu-ray market, has decided to center its buy-not-rent hopes on Flixster, a small social network for movie buffs that it bought in May [2011] for about $75 million...Warner [has] ... introduced technology that makes Flixster the home base for a new movie storage service called UltraViolet. The free service, backed by most of the big studios, allows people to buy a movie once and watch it anywhere — on a computer, mobile device or Web-ready television. The strategy is to make owning more compelling than renting by loading digital portability into purchases." NYTimes.com, November 11, 2011.

[388] A Sony-led consortium of five major studios, Comcast and Intel (markedly absent are Apple and Disney) pursuing a technology with similar goals under the label "UltraViolet."

[389] FastCompany.com, October 16, 2009

[390] Most likely not really a BlackBerry, but a comparable and vastly more secure device, the Sectera Edge, manufactured by General Dynamics.

[391] Cisco System Chairman & CEO, John Chambers in the August 2, 2009 New York Times: "Today's world requires a different leadership style — moving more into a collaboration and teamwork, including learning how to use Web 2.0 technologies. If you had told me I'd be video blogging and blogging, I would have said, no way. And yet our 20-somethings in the company really pushed me to use that more. [It's the way] the way we interface with customers, our employees. The top has to walk the talk."

INDEX

CPSIA information can be obtained
at www.ICGtesting.com
Printed in the USA
LVHW02s0646221217
560522LV00006B/121/P